Piecing It All Together

Piecing It All Together

A Collection of Memoirs

Kathleen D. Lindsey

ELM HILL

A Division of
HarperCollins Christian Publishing

www.elmhillbooks.com

Piecing It All Together

A Collection of Memoirs

Published in Nashville, Tennessee, by Elm Hill, an imprint of Thomas Nelson. Elm Hill and Thomas Nelson are registered trademarks of HarperCollins Christian Publishing, Inc.

Elm Hill titles may be purchased in bulk for educational, business, fund-raising, or sales promotional use. For information, please e-mail SpecialMarkets@ ThomasNelson.com.

All Scripture quotations, unless otherwise indicated, are taken from the Holy Bible, New International Version‘, NIV‘. Copyright © 1973, 1978, 1984, 2011 by Biblica, Inc.‘ Used by permission of Zondervan. All rights reserved worldwide. www.Zondervan. com. The "NIV" and "New International Version" are trademarks registered in the United States Patent and Trademark Office by Biblica, Inc.‘

Library of Congress Cataloging-in-Publication Data

Library of Congress Control Number: 2018963503

ISBN 978-1-595559630 (Paperback)
ISBN 978-1-595559692 (eBook)

Preface

B efore I, Kathleen Dorothy (Williams) Lindsey, was formed in my mother's womb, God chose me. He had set the course for my journey. I'm a person who loves to share the gifts and talents that God has given me. When I share my gifts of talents, testimonies, and my faith in God, I am shining for Him, because they all come from Him. But if I don't shine for Him and appreciate His greatness, I am not showing His light. For without Him I can do nothing. Through my testimonies of faith, I reach out to those who know or don't know the Lord, or to those who need their faith strengthened and restored.

Through years of perseverance, I share my life experiences intertwined with many other people's, who walked beside me on my journey. I share my years of spiritual growth and learning of God's great love and mercy. Through my trials, tribulations, and failures, He delivered me from those heavy burdens. Through heartache, grief, tears, and fears, He touched me and made me whole. And through those happy times, my goals, and my successes, I continue to manifest and glorify His Great name. What a Mighty God I serve!

DEDICATION

For many years, I pondered on what I could leave my children when I'm no longer here. I have no family heirlooms that have much meaning. But one thing I knew they would cherish would be my memories. I decided to write my life's story and dedicate it to my loving husband of fifty-two years, David Sr., and to all my children—David Jr., Darrell (deceased 1988), Donald, Dean, Natasha, Sade, and Jaquille. And to my beloved offspring who will learn that their great-great-grandmother lived to love the Lord.

Table Of Contents

Kat 2nd grade 1957

Kat age 15 - 1965

CHAPTER 1

In the Beginning

Mom and Dad's
13th Anniversary 1953

Our Mom approx. age 16

B eing a part of the "baby boomers, the Silent Generation," we were said to be seen and not heard. Not in the Williams household! I was born the seventh child out of nine, and you can bet there was always a bit of chaos and chatter, but never a dull moment in our household. Kids were seen and heard from every room!

On October 13, 1939, in a small town called Woodbury, NJ, William Henry Williams and Mae Williams (no relation) were joined together in holy matrimony. She was sixteen and he was twenty-three. Immediately they started a family. They lived on Cortland Avenue, in Woodbury, NJ, for a short period of time, then moved to Clayton, on North Street. Later they purchased a small, white bungalow with a white picket fence that surrounded the front yard, located on East Clayton Avenue.

William, better known as "Wiggy," was a railroad laborer at the age of twenty-four. Later he became a railroad mechanic. My father worked hard and would have many other jobs over the years to support his ever-growing family.

As a young boy, he worked before and after school for Doctor Greene, who owned a mansion in Clayton, which was located where the Clayton Acme now resides. He took care of the heating system in that house, putting coal on the fire, taking out the ashes, and keeping the huge mansion warm and cozy for the doctor and his family. He was paid ten cents a day. He often talked about working at this job from late fall to early spring and never missed a day. Our father dropped out of school in the fifth grade, and much education was necessary for him to achieve his goals and succeed in life. He often talked about his mother complaining of headaches and not feeling like getting her children off to school. After frequently missing too many days of school, he finally gave it up and started working at a very young age. He would always say that if he had had the encouragement of his parents, he would have stuck it out.

When he was about nineteen, he joined the Civilian Conservation Corps, otherwise known as the CC Camp. Nationwide, during the span of nine years, over three million young men built trails, roads, camp-grounds, and parks; planted trees, fought forest fires, and performed many other duties. Our dad happened to be a cook in his camp, and all this took place during the Great Depression. He was paid $30 a month and $25 was sent home to his family. Most colored boys took residence at the camp and our dad happened to be one of them. Most camps provided classes for those who needed to further their education. I guess my dad didn't feel he needed it.

Our mother would teach him how to read, to further his knowledge and vocabulary. Later, he would learn from listening to other ministers present their sermons, and he finally developed his own style of preaching. In 1949, he became an ordained minister; he had a fantastic memory when it came to the scriptures!

After his death in 1974, at the age of fifty-six, I inherited his first Bible, which was given to him by our mother when he became a Church of Christ minister. This leather-bound Bible has seen its days. The black leather jacket is completely worn down to brown suede. Many of the pages are falling apart and coming lose from its binding, mostly in the New Testament, which he loved to study. But all of his short notes and underlined scriptures remained intact. One of these days, I will restore it.

Our mother was a stay-at-home mom who worked hard at being a good mom, excellent wife, a dear sister, and close friend to those who knew and loved her. She had many talents, like singing, sewing, a little crafting, gardening, and of course cooking, because she had to. I wonder how she had time for anything else.

Although I never heard her listening to worldly music on the radio, which she forbade us to do, she mentioned a favorite singer called Frank Sinatra, who made his debut in the forties. I heard her singing one day and asked her to sing again that song "Dream" by Frank Sinatra. How did she know these songs? I was clueless.

Mom enjoyed listening to Liberace, as well, and she told me he was a famous piano player who was very rich and sparkly. She must had been exposed to this world of music when she was younger, having had fifteen siblings who sang and some even played the piano and drums. Her mother, Grand mom Elnora, was a very high-strung person and would curse you just to look at you. Rumor has it that she beat our cousin who was cripple from birth, because he, Martin, had a bowel movement on her fur coat; she beat him uncontrollably! Poor boy, never walked or talked, but he could laugh and cry his eyes out. I loved Martin.

Mom's father was a mean good for nothing who made bootleg whiskey from a still and sold it to anyone who wanted a snort full. He lost his leg one night crossing the railroad track. He was so drunk and paid no attention to the oncoming train. It struck him and cut off his leg. He received a prosthesis wooden leg from the accident as a payoff. Later, they say he poisoned himself with his own bad batch of liquor. Some say his relatives killed him. Nevertheless, neither one of Mom's parents knew the Lord or served Him.

I don't know much about our mother's childhood, but my father often talked about coming to blows with several of her older brothers who happened to be ignorant and bad-to-the-bone bullies. Before she married my father, my mom had the responsibility of preparing meals for her siblings when her mother was working or away from home during the day. When she and my father started courting, he would visit her during the late afternoon. One day two of her older brothers came home from work hungry and asked her why their dinner wasn't ready. She told them she had been busy all day cleaning and taking care of the younger kids, and she didn't have time to start cooking, so dinner was going to be late.

All of a sudden, one of her older brothers slapped Mom across the face and told her to start cooking immediately. At first Dad said nothing to him. He didn't need to. Dad said, "I just lit into him like a bull in a china shop and I almost broke his doggone neck! I told him, 'Handy, as long as you live, you better not ever lift your hand to her again, or I'll kill you, you no-good, rotten skunk!'" Needless to say Handy never did it again. I'm sure my Mom had to fight off several of her brothers because some had a heavy appetite for incest. My father realized he had to take her away from this dysfunctional bunch of heathens.

Mom and Dad around 1942

Grand pop James and grand mom
Elnora Williams
My Mother's Parents - Around 1920

CHAPTER 2

The Silver Tones

The Silver Tones Dad is 2nd from left - around 1945

O ur parents had beautiful singing voices, and Dad was part of a sing-ing quartet called the Silver Tones, known today as the Swan Silver Tones. He loved singing and would practice much during the week, and spent most of his weekends on singing engagements. This left Mom to hold down the fort, so to speak. At this time they had three children. Finally, she gave him an ultimatum: leave the quartet or they were done! And all this took place before I was born.

Mom and Dad made a record called "The Garden of Prayer." We played it so much that every other word would skip, or as we called it, stutter. I included one verse of this song in my story.

THE GARDEN OF PRAYER

There's a garden where Jesus is waiting,
There's a place that is wondrously fair:
For it glows with the light of His presence,
'Tis that beautiful garden of prayer.

Oh, the beautiful garden, the garden of prayer,
Oh, the beautiful garden of prayer;
There my Savior awaits, and He opens the gates
To the beautiful garden of prayer.

CHAPTER 3

Time to Start a Family

The first child was a boy, of whom Mom and Dad were truly proud. William Henry Williams Jr. They nicknamed him Junie. Six months after his birth, our brother became ill and was diagnosed as having pneumonia; he passed away in his sleep. Dad and Mom would grieve the loss of their precious baby boy for many years to come. They buried him in Cedar Green Cemetery, in Clayton, but I don't know exactly where. Our mother was only seventeen years old when she gave birth to Junie. They say he was a beautiful baby.

From time to time, as youngsters, we would mention his name and ask Mom questions about him. Her eyes would fill up with sorrow and she would walk away in despair, trying to busy herself with something else that needed her prompt attention.

Mom had a special way of hiding her feelings. Later on in my life, I would come to know how difficult it was for her, and her painful experience of such a great loss. At the age of thirty-nine, I would experience the same pain, sorrow, and grief as my mother did. Only then would I learn what her grieving was about.

After the death of our brother Junie, Mom immediately got pregnant again and gave birth to a baby girl. Her name was Elnora Lucille. In years to come she would be known as El or Miss Elly. She was bright eyed, high yellow, and full of life, which brought my father and mother back to reality, and brightened some of their gloomy days. Although Dad missed his son William Jr., Elnora had become his little princess. Elnora was named after our grand mom Elnora, our mother's mom. More about my big sister Elly later.

Loretta Mae, or Ret as she was called, was my second sister. She was born with a black membrane or veil over her face; old wives' tale referred to this as a superstition, meaning born for good luck, and thought to have special talents and amazing powers. It is also called a "caul." This strange and rare occurrence appears in one out of every 80,000 births. Strange as it seems, Loretta was gifted but had little or no luck at all.

Ret was the child who often suffered from untimely blackouts and continuously had nervous breakdowns when she became troubled. And there were times when she faked her seizures to get her way. She often thought as herself as being the black sheep. But that's the way she was sometimes made to feel. Dad was very hard on her and just didn't know exactly how to deal with her emotional behavior. He would use harsh discipline on her continually, but nothing helped Loretta. If anything, she would get worse. Ret was talented in many ways and had such a sense of humor. But if anyone crossed her, she was always ready to rumble. Later during her adult life, Loretta was diagnosed as bipolar and schizophrenic.

Ret loved to read to us and would borrow books from the Clayton Library, but she never returned them. Finally, they told her she could only read books on the premises. No more borrowing. Shortly after, she stopped going. We loved hearing her read stories about "Little Orphan Annie" and "The Raggedy Man." She read with such feeling! She changed her voice with every character in the story. Now that was a gift!

At the age of sixteen, she married a guy named Rudolph, who was in the US Army, so they traveled a lot wherever he was stationed, and lived overseas where he met his untimely death.

Phyllis Amanda, or Phil as we call her, is like a little mother hen. She was born during the big WWII. My Dad was drafted and somehow managed to break free of this unfavorable task of war to stay home with his wife and three children. Phyllis was the crafting sister. She liked to fiddle with throwaway stuff and turn it into something likeable. And she was a saver of everything. No, not a hoarder! Just a "save it for a rainy day" kind of kid.

Phil would come up with some fun entertainment for us little kids from time to time, but we always had to finish our chores first. "No work, no play" was her motto. Phil was the apple who didn't fall far from the tree. Everyone agreed that Phil was a reflection of Dad. Mirror, mirror on the wall, I am my father after all. She always had work for us to do and tried to keep us on task. There were no idle hands when Phil was around. It seemed she always kept us little kids busy and out of trouble. I think she liked trying to play the role of the "mother hen." She was and still is today a skillful, little workaholic. When I see that pink Energizer Bunny, I think of my sister Phyllis—or Mandy, which was another nickname given to her by the Jackson girls who lived down the street.

Ida Elizabeth, or Ike as we called her, later became known as Miss Iddie. She was number five in line who was somewhat quiet and shy. "Ida is a good ole girl. But sometimes she can turn on you," as Loretta would say in later years. Don't cross her or she'll come right back at you. Ida could stand up to anybody. No matter how large. She once picked up a full-grown man weighing over 200 pounds. The man made a bet with her that she couldn't pick him up, but with a bit of struggle she did. And for a lousy nickel. Ida was just about seven years old when this happened, and weighed a mere sixty pounds. Mom and Dad were furious when they found out. Dad paid that man an unpleasant visit. He sure did!

Ida had reddish hair with a complexion to match. She could make you laugh even if you didn't feel like laughing. Later in my adult years, she became my pillar of strength.

Poor Ida hated school with a passion. Mom, who was always pregnant, had to walk Ida to school nearly every day and pray she wouldn't leave the schoolyard when Mom turned her back for that long journey homeward. The walk was approximately two miles each way. I can remember holding on tightly and riding on the side of the big, gray baby coach, and baby Billy rode inside, while my sister Bert road on the other side, and was dropped off at the youth center. Ida went to the elementary school on Academy Street. This went on for a while, then the older kids started taking Ida and Bert to school after Ida got used to it.

Bertha—Bertha Adelaide Billy Williams—was the sixth child born. She was nicknamed Bert. Heck was another nickname given to her by Mom's brothers because Bert, out of curiosity, got into so much trouble when she was a baby. They say she got into everything! She ate a deadly chemical called lye, which made her mouth swell so bad that they thought she might be a goner. She was forced to drink lots of milk, then they induced vomiting.

My parents named her after Daddy because they thought she would be their last child and Dad wanted to have a namesake, even if she was a girl, or "Bloody Hussy," as he often called his girls. How tacky! Bertha Adelaide Billy Williams. She was the shortest of the girls but had a lot of guts and a devious attitude to go with it. No one could get away with messing with her. If you crossed her, she would wait you out, and just when you think she had forgotten what you did to her earlier, she would be on you like white on rice. Clinging to you like a mad pit bull. Sometimes, if she could get a good grip, she'd find somewhere to sink her teeth. I was never bitten by her but was often given a thrashing with her teasing tongue.

As I mentioned earlier, our sister Ret used to read to us kids a lot. She read with such feeling and drama. There was a children's poem called "Little Orphan Annie." Part of the lines was "the goblins will get you if you don't watch out!" That poem always reminds me of my sis Bert, because she loved to tease everybody. I will recite what I can remember.

The Scary Things

Long ago a little girl used to always laugh and grin.
She poked fun of everything, her family and her friends.
One time they had some company and old people were there,
She mocked them, then she shocked them, and she didn't
even care.
Suddenly, she turned her heels up, and tried to run and hide,
There were two huge scary things waiting by her side.
They thrust her through the ceiling in the cubbyholes, no less
And threw her up the chimney flew and everywhere else, I guess.
All that they could find was her dress and shoes about,
And the scary things will get you, so you better watch out.

~ by Kat Lindsey ~

Yep! That was my sister, Miss Bert, and we were sure enough bosom buddies (Frick and Frack), as we are called today. We were inseparable and she had come to prepare the way for me.

In 1949, I was born, Kathleen Dorothy, or Kat as most people call me today. As a youngster, I was skinny, sick looking, and somewhat spoiled, so they say. One might describe me as looking like a refugee. I stayed the baby for nearly four years. Most of the time, usually when I was hungry, I could get my way for an early morning snack. A piece of bread and butter would suffice. My sister Ret nicknamed me Bucky Butter, because I loved butter sandwiches and I had big buckteeth to boot.

"I want this. I want that. Give me this. Give me that," I would beg. I ate snacks all day long and never gained an ounce. Mom was inclined to believe that something was wrong with me, and there was. I had a tapeworm nearly fourteen inches long that took residence in my frail body. Okay readers, I was given another name. Are you ready for this one? They called me Tapes! And that was downright cruel!

The three youngest kids were often referred to as Tapes, Tubes, and Tootles. Or better known as Kat, nicknamed Tapes; Ida was called Tubs, because she was a little chubby; and Bert was referred to as Tootels, only because it sounded right. Most of the time we were just called the "Little Kids."

A few of our mom's younger brothers lived with us after their mother died in 1951, shortly after I was born. Our uncle Dave, who lived with us the longest, loved to make up silly songs and composed a little jingle that annoyed me to no end.

Little Kat Meet, Little Kat Meet, she's the leader of the house.
She can holler for her cake… "I want C-A-K-E!"

Yep! I was the baby girl and that was that. As they say, "A Kat is a Kat and that is that!"

CHAPTER 4

Should I Say Elephants?

My first encounter with the "birds and the bees" was a strange one. I was still the only preschool child at home until the afternoon when Bert came home. Mom would give me lots of little chores to do so I would not be so lonely. I fed the chickens, emptied the trash, took out the garbage, and ran little errands for her, like going to the corner store. Her sister, Aunt Rose, lived across the street and sometimes we would go and visit her or she would come to our house.

One day after peeling potatoes, she sent me out to feed the potato skins to the rabbits. "Be careful, and don't forget to lock the cage door," she would always tell me.

The cage was in the backyard and I had to walk past the chickens to get to the rabbits. Before I opened the cage door, I saw something scary and strange. A pile of hairless things with long strings hanging were moving very slowly, in the corner of the cage. "ELEPHANTS!" I screamed. "MOM!"

Mom came running out to see what the problem was.

"Little elephants are in the cage, Mom! See?" I shouted.

She looked in the cage and busted out laughing. "Kat, they're baby rabbits." She explained to me, as best as a 4-year-old could understand, that the mommy had babies and the daddy had to be separated because he might hurt them. She took the father out from the other section of the cage and put him in a bushel basket with a lid.

"Why?" I asked her. I was always asking why.

Time to call Aunt Rose and tell her what Kat had done today! They kept that party line hot!

Another event that I was curious about was the day mom was hanging clothes. She dropped some clothespins on the ground and asked me to pick them up.

"Why?" I asked.

"Because I said so," she said in a frustrated tone.

"Why?" I asked her again.

She said nothing.

"Mom, are you afraid you might bend the baby in half?"

"Girl, you better pick up that clothespin," Mom scolded. And this time she wasn't playing. Need I say more?

Back to the party line. Mom and her sister Rose were very close and both were very beautiful women who talked nearly every day. One day after I came home from school, Aunt Rose came over to take me to the store with her. We had many little mom-and-pop grocery stores in Clayton in the fifties, before the Acme was built. There was one right across the street called Millers, and one right around the block called Cheeseman's. This particular day we walked to Cheeseman's store.

On the way, Aunt Rose gave me a nickel and told me numerous times to buy a brown toe. When we got there, I looked at all the candy that I wanted, but Aunt Rose told me what to buy. Hum... Finally, after much thought, I blurted it out. "Well, I'll guess I'll take a brown toe!"

The storekeeper looked at Aunt Rose, who was about to burst with laughter, and said, "We don't sell them!"

I ended up buying five pieces of penny candy, which I wanted in the first place.

Aunt Rose couldn't wait to tell Mom. And boy, did they laugh!

The owners were very prejudiced, and most colored people wouldn't shop in their store, but I guess Aunt Rose needed a good laugh that day. They say she spoiled me rotten!

And what was a brown toe? A slang word for a Brazil nut.

Mom and Aunt Rose loved the daytime radio serials and tuned in most days. These were their favorites: *Search for Tomorrow*, *The Guiding Light*, *As the World Turns*, and *The Secret Storm*. After the shows were over they would hit the telephone and discuss the day's episodes.

Another incident during my childhood years was when Mom sent me out to feed the chickens, and this was not my favorite chore. We had a nasty rooster that would chase you and attack you from behind. He was as mean as the devil! One day while feeding the baby chicks, the rooster took me by surprise and began chasing me all around the fenced-in chicken yard. I began to scream, "Mom! Mom, help! He's after me!"

Mom yelled from the back door, "Stop running, Kat, and he'll stop chasing you!"

I had a pan in my hand, and when he got close, I hit him hard and ran out as fast as I could.

Sometime later, I was glad when they killed that ole bird. Mom said he was even too tough to eat. Later in life, I added this memory to my first children's storybook called *Sweet Potato Pie*.

CHAPTER 5

It's a Boy!

Bert, Kat, and Billy - 1953

Now birth control was unheard of back in the day. You see, Dad being a preacher man believed that married couples should be fruitful and multiply at will. Poor Mom, all she could do was yield.

Mom started thinking that this was it. *Six kids are enough for any household.* But Dad just wouldn't let up. He had to have himself a boy or else, to carry on the family's name. When Mom became pregnant again I felt frightened that I would lose her attention. I felt very uneasy when she talked about the new baby coming soon. I didn't want to share Mom and Dad with no ole lousy baby; I wasn't ready to give up my throne.

"It's a boy!" Dad shouted late one night.

Yep! It's a boy all right. I could hear lots of commotion coming from my mom's bedroom. Now hospitals were unheard of in our household—and who could afford one, anyway? Just call the doctor, time the labor pains, get some clean towels, and boil some water. And oh yah, wait!

The next morning, I could hear Mom calling me from her bedroom. "Kat! Kat! Kathleen, come in here."

Normally, I would be in her room at sunrise, wanting some bread and butter to nibble on before she fixed our breakfast, but something was holding me back this time. Usually, I would lay in bed and wait until Dad left for work, then I'd get up before my sisters would stir, to get ready for school. This morning was too quiet. I slowly walked into the ever-so-small bedroom and Mom pulled back the blanket.

"Come here, Kat," she said. All I could see was a little fat face with black, curly hair, sleeping peacefully in my mom's arms. "This is your baby brother, Edward Lee."

I flew out of the bedroom and buried my face in the covers, where many of my siblings were still sleeping. I felt betrayed and cried. I would be thrown away like cast-off old rags. *They can't do this to me*, I thought as only a four-year-old could.

It seemed like everyone was out to tease and point their finger at me, reminding me that I was no longer the baby in the family. I was teased about this daily, which made things worse. But as time went on, I began to love my little brother Edward Lee, after I discovered that he wasn't going back. So I might as well try to accept him and get over it.

After a couple of months or so, my parents changed his name again to William H. Williams Jr. I was told they had to be sure that he was healthy because they had lost their first son.

Mom knew I was having a hard time giving up my throne, so she made a decree that I would be called A-Baby. Sister Bert would be called, B-Baby, and my baby brother Billy was The-Baby. Mom sure knew how to compromise. That boy was spoiled rotten by everybody. Why of course, he was the only boy out of six girls.

Billy was about twelve months old when this happened. Mom gave him and me some Saltine crackers for a snack. I took them out of the package and gave him a large one, which had to be broken into four perforated sections. Billy had a huge appetite for a baby and, in his own babbling vocabulary of words, demanded a whole cracker. He threw a hissy fit and began brutally banging his head on the hard linoleum floor. I mean hard! He had the worst temper in a baby that I have ever seen as a child or in my adult life. He would get on his knees and start banging. Mom would just say, "When he gets tired he will stop." She couldn't control him when he started, just had to wait him out. I even tried giving him another cracker. That didn't help, either. He was a stubborn little knucklehead! I'm pretty sure, at that time, mom was pregnant again because Billy and Anna were eleven months apart. And I wasn't in school yet.

I often tease my now sixty-four-year-old brother that he shook something loose in his head, back then.

I recall the stream of water that flowed from our back porch to the side yard, and drained off to the middle of the backyard. This stream of contaminated water came from the old well and Lord only knows from where else. The kitchen sink, laundry water, bath water, and whatever was dumped down the drain. Mom had to wash a lot so the well was always overflowing and forming a wide stream of filthy water. During that time, we didn't have a bathroom yet. It was nasty! The water was green and slimy, which was very unhealthy, to say the least.

A big, green bullfrog lived under the thick wooden boards that covered the well. Early in the spring it would make an appearance and would scare the daylights out of us. I think that toxic water caused that big frog to grow very large.

Every so often, I still had an urge to get back at Billy for snatching me from my royal throne. One summer day when no one was looking, I pushed him in that filthy, disgusting water. After realizing what I had done and watching him roll around in it for a while, I ran in the house screaming for mom. "Mom, Billy fell in the tweem," I yelled over and over again. "He just fell in the tweem!"

"Weren't you watching him?" Mom asked, with her eyes directly focused on me. Now, our mom was smart and she knew that I would never allow Billy to even get near that nasty, disgusting stream. So she figured it out quickly and came to the conclusion that I had done it. Mom also knew I was very protective of my little brother, but this time I had done the unthinkable and pushed him in. He smelled and looked like green doo-doo! And I was reprimanded for that little incident. I was definitely a little hussy that day. Ouch!

CHAPTER 6

The Fly Chasers

During the warmer days, we always had a problem with flies. They were always buzzing around the water well outside. We kids ran in and out of the house all day long and the flies poured in behinds us.

"Close that door," Mom would yell. "You're letting the flies in!"

If she cooked cabbage or any kind of greens, the flies would dance their way into her kitchen. Mom used a pump sprayer with a metal can filled with insecticide. That was fun watching her zap those flies.

When there were just too many flies, she gave us girls tea towels or white diapers to shoo them from each room, then out the front door. Believe it or not, this was fun because we got to run around in the house, knocking into one another and laughing. When we emptied one room, Mom closed that door, or put up a blanket over the doorway. Then we ran around chasing flies in the next room. After the chasing was done she put cotton balls on the screens. I still don't know exactly why. Some people used sticky fly paper that hung from the ceilings. But Mom used us, the fly chasers.

CHAPTER 7

The Last of the Litter!

Mom and her girls, Easter 1955

About 11 months after Mom had Billy, Anna was born. I remember the night Mom and Dad brought her home from the hospital. She was the last child Mom would conceive and deliver, and Dad was okay with that, because he had finally gotten his boy.

Anna was the only child Dad could afford to have Mom give birth to in a fancy hospital. "Your mom really needed the rest," he said.

No! They both decided to have her tubes tied before she came home. Smart!

Dressed in pink and pretty as a baby doll, she looked like a little Caucasian child. Is she really our baby sister or did Mom and Dad bring home the wrong baby? It's funny, we all came from the same parents but we all had different complexions.

"What color are her eyes?" we kids kept asking Mom.

Mom sat for a long time holding little Anna in her lap. She let each one of us take turns holding Anna's tiny hand. And boy, did she have a tight grip, as most infants do. Anna was always crying and sometimes it got on my nerves. Mom would always check her diaper to see if a pin popped loose, or if she had a pain in her stomach. One night she cried so much that Dad took her and started singing silly songs to her. This one I remember.

Bye baby bunting
Papa's going hunting
Catch himself a rabbit skin
To wrap that baby bunting in.

After singing this song over and over and gently bouncing Anna across his knees, she stopped crying. Mom said, "She must have had a little stomach gas."

Humm… Did they put gasoline in her bottle? I thought.

In 1954, Mom had an accident in our moving wood-grain paneled station wagon. We had just left Aunt Dobb's house for Thanksgiving dinner. The door wasn't shut tight and Mom was thrown out of the car. As she whirled out of the car, she pushed lil Anna, who was sitting on her lap, away from her. We all saw her fall out and began to scream at our father. "Dad, stop the car, Mom fell out!" Everybody was screaming and crying.

When the accident happened, Dad had just driven over some railroad tracks and was picking up speed. Good thing he wasn't going any faster.

He slammed on his brakes, got out, and ran to Mom, who was lying by the side of the road. Mom was badly bruised from head to foot but didn't suffer any broken bones. No hospital! She said, "I'll be okay." Thank goodness, the Good Lord was with her.

Our mom was known to all the neighborhood kids as Aunt Mae. Everyone loved and respected her. In the summer, Mom would freeze Kool-Aid cubes in ice cube trays for all to enjoy. We didn't have much but she shared whatever she could. We played until way after dark, long after the streetlights came on. This was so much fun! And a lot cooler. We played games like red light; lemonade; tag; dodge ball; kickball; baseball; stickball; what time is it, Mr. Fox?; statue; jump rope; hopscotch; red rover; old mommy witch fell in the ditch, picked up a penny and thought she was rich; high water low; and zoo-dee-ack (walking down the alley all night long). Not to mention riding bikes, hula hoops, jacks, skates, Old Maid, marbles, Little Sally Ann, and much more. No one stayed in the house after the sun went down. Those were the "good ole days," or the "good times."

During the day, we captured Japanese beetles or June bugs, as we called them. Wrap some thread around their legs and let them fly! Sometimes if it was really hot, Mom would bring out the water hose and squirt us. After the hose was cut off, we played leap frog and had Kool-Aide ice cubes.

When hula hoops became popular, all the kids on our street owned one, except us. But we enjoyed sitting on the curb and watching them walking up and down the street twisting those hoops around their waists, necks, hands, and legs. It was like a parade! Sometimes the kids would take pity on us and lend us their hoops for a little while. Or we might find old bike tires, but they didn't work too well. Too heavy and floppy!

CHAPTER 8

Flags on Parade

S peaking of parades, there was the Memorial Day Parade, when all the kids rode their decorated bikes and pulled wagons with the red, white, and blue streamers blowing in the wind. Some kids put balloons on the wheel spokes to give a sound like a motorcycle, or fastened playing cards between the spokes, fastened with clothespins. That was really cool!

The Clayton High School band played the same song every year as they marched to the Cedar Green Cemetery, for the Memorial Day ceremony. "Abide with Me." One year they asked my dad to give the benediction. He was all dressed up, wearing a priest collar. He looked very sleek and he knew he did. He started out with a few words of encouragement in prayer that blossomed into a full-blown sermon. Dad started preaching! After that year, they never asked him again.

After the parade was over, the fun frolic began. We kids had so much fun; we never had money to spend, but it was free to get into the Haupt Football Field. Lots of vendors lined the field, selling their wares or giving away great stuff or junk they no longer wanted. There were pony rides, a small area for petting farm animals, games for kids, clothing for sale, lots of food to eat (if you had money to buy it), cake sales, and much more. This fun-frolic day was equivalent to a small county fair. If you stayed until it was over, you would come home with lots of goodies that the vendors would give you, or else throw them away.

Then there was the Halloween parade. It seemed like the entire parade consisted of raggedy bums with big butts and boobs, and beautiful high school floats. My sister Phyllis was the first black girl to be nominated "Queen in Clayton." "Madam Butterfly" was the theme and her float, which won first place. She was so beautiful! I have to laugh! Because all the little colored bums followed her float to the football field. Someone said it looked disgraceful! A few would have been okay, but it was herds of them holding on to the sides of that beautiful float and making all kinds of racket. "She's gonna win!" they yelled.

Then everyone in the parade and those watching it would get a free hot dog and soda. Someone would stamp your hand with ink before you got your refreshment. The kids would lick it off and get in line again. Some folks would come from other towns just for the freebees and load up the trunk of their cars with hotdogs and soda.

CHAPTER 9

The Twin Kiss

On trick-or-treat night, the Twin Kiss gave out a free small ice cream twist or small root beer soda. A small ice cream twist was only ten cents back then, but we never had the luxury of going. It was too expensive for Dad to fork out eighty cents for his eight kids. This ice cream polar is a famous landmark in Clayton, opened in 1955, the year our mom died. During that time it was owned by the Casper family. Today it's owned and operated by our dear friends, John and Stacy Chamberlin. They expanded their inventory; they serve all kinds of delicious sandwiches and whatever your taste buds are craving. They play all the oldies songs over the PA system, with lots of picnic tables, and they even had a playground for children installed on the premises. If you've never been to the Twin Kiss (TK), you don't know what you're missing!

Yep! Those were the good ole days!

In the summer, some of my pastime pleasures was playing in mud. Making mud pies and cakes was fun! We decorated them with tiny stones, seeds, and flowers. Then let them dry, smash them, and start again. Ida was the greatest mud pie maker, which eventually, in her adult years, landed her a job as head baker at Glassboro (Rowan) State College. Who would have thought it?

Our winter fun consisted of playing in the snow, sledding on an old beat-up sled or trash can lid, making snow men and snow angels, and waiting for Mom to make hot chocolate for us to warm up after we got inside. Those who didn't have gloves would use socks on their hands and extra socks on their feet. Usually by the second or third snow, Mom would make her famous snow ice cream. She always said the air had to be clean and always use the new fallen snow at top of the old. That way we wouldn't get germs from the old snow, and sore throats. She'd get a big bowl or pot, go outside, and gently scrap off the top of the new fallen snow. Then she'd add sugar, a can of milk, and vanilla. This mother-made ice cream was so good, but you had to eat it slowly or you might experience brain freeze. Yikes!

On rainy, cold, or inclement weather days, we played inside. Whether it be listening to our long-playing, vinyl classical records on our little, brown record player or playing church, we had fun!

When I started kindergarten, some days were very cold or rainy. Mom would call a cab service from down town. The proprietor's last name was Lacy, so he called his company Lacy's Cab Service. How unique! He was a roly-poly, short, fat face white man who took up most of the front seat. No one was allowed to sit up front with the driver, he said, but Mom told him, "Its okay. They will be good." And of course she trusted him. With a fat round cigar stuffed in his face, he loaded us up in his car and off to school we went. If it was still raining after school, there was no curbside pickup. You walked!

It was ten cents a head, but the following year the price went up sky high. Sometimes we had extra kids, but Mom paid for them, as well. The older kids held the younger kids on their laps. One time there were ten kids in that cab. Way too many! Mr. Lacy thought he was gonna make a killing that day by making two trips, but we squeezed everybody in, like sardines. Seatbelts were unheard of!

We had two back rooms off from the kitchen where the star boarders or sojourners lived until they found a place of their own. Later as teens, these rooms would become our bedrooms. Many, many families lived with us from time to time and all eight of us kids were flung into one small room. Our father felt because he was a preacher, he had an obligation to be a "good Samaritan." I don't think any of them offered him a dime for rent or helped with food. Most of the time they purchased their own, and Mom reserved one shelf in our small refrigerator for the "star boarders." Dad had a kind heart toward other people. But always at the expense of his family.

Mom loved hearing us play church and would often supply us with crackers and water for communion. Everybody had a part to play. Elnora did the preaching, Ret and Phil led the singing and communion, Ida took up the penny collection, and Bert and I sang and made fun of the sermons. One day somebody wanted to be baptized and that's when mom had to draw the line and said, "You'll done gone too far with playing church." No baptizing! I honestly believe that we were our mother's only entertainment. But some things were just not going to happen. Not on her watch!

We would sing with harmony and melody in our hearts to the Lord and Mom loved hearing that. When the communion plate came around, sis Phil would always say, "Don't take too much." Especially when she was serving Ida. Mom would give us each a penny to put in the collection. I still don't know who the money holder was but somebody definitely was!

We organized our services the same way we learned in a real church on Sundays. Someone who could read did the Bible verses and someone prayed. Often we imitated people from our Sunday congregation. Mom laughed at first as she ironed or folded clothes in the kitchen. Until we started to get carried away and began making fun of people. This was not acceptable. "That's enough you kids," she'd call from the kitchen.

Somehow Dad found out how much fun we were having and forbade Mom from letting us play church anymore.

On Sunday mornings, Mom would give us girls a clean handkerchief for church. The older girls helped dress the young ones then we had to sit down and wait for Mom and Dad to get ready. Sometimes Mom would let us blot our lips with her lipstick tissue that she used to blot hers. She always looked so beautiful when she wore her make up. But for sure, she was just as pretty without it. Dad always bought her very nice clothing to wear. She even had a fur coat. Dad thought it was important for the preacher's wife to look her best. And that made him look good, too.

Because I was so squirmy, Mom would give me a pencil, crayons, and some old junk mail to keep me quiet in church. She knew how to recycle junk mail long before the word was ever invented. I would pretend to write or scribble down stories and illustrate pictures to go with each story, and I never spent one day in school. Not yet! Then I would read very fluently to anyone who would listen. This had to be the beginning of my writing career.

In 2003, I became an author of a children's book.

Yeah, Mom!

CHAPTER 10

Lost at Parvin State Park

The first summer that I can remember was when I was four and a half years old. We went on a picnic and swimming at Parvin State Park. We rarely went anywhere but this time Dad packed us up and took us to have some fun in the sun. While Mom prepared lunch at the picnic site, we all went to the lake to play. I wanted to go back to our table so I asked Bertha to take me, but she refused. So I went by myself.

I walked through the stone building entrance and crossed the main highway, to the parking lot. I was lost! I walked down the street until I got to a golf course where men were playing. I wondered around until a man walked over toward me and asked me, "Where's your mommy, Little Girl? And what are you doing here all by yourself?"

I told him I couldn't find her.

Another man said, "I think she's lost."

The man took me by the hand and we walked all over the park. He hoisted me up on his strong shoulders so that I could see well. And he said, "Tell me when you see your mommy."

"Whose little girl is this?" he kept saying over and over again.

"Not mine," the people would say, and motion him away.

Lots of people said to him, "We'll see if anybody is looking for a little girl."

Finally, I spotted my mom. "Mom!" I screamed, and the man took me down from his shoulders and I ran to her. The nice man told Mom where he found me, way over at the golf course, and mom was so grateful.

"Thank you so much," she said over and over again.

I could have been hit by a car on that busy street, or worse.

Mom peeled a hard-boiled egg for me to eat, and I wouldn't go back to the lake to swim, but stayed by her side for the rest of the duration. God had sent someone to watch over me and he was my guardian angel.

CHAPTER 11

The Party Line

O ur old black phone, Tulip 1-4602, would be changed to GL4-4602, and that was our telephone number. Everyone back in the day had a party line. A party line is when three to four families would share the same phone line, but had different rings for the different numbers. Two long rings were for us; one long, two short for someone else; and so on.

When the phone rang the older kids listened to see if this ring was for us. Sometimes it wasn't but they would pick up the receiver anyway and listen to neighbors' conversations. It only took one person to start then the others would join in. They listened to the neighbors' gossiping. Then my sisters would join in their conversations. Laughing and acting silly. They drove the people nuts! Then somebody reported them to Mom.

When Mom found out about this, she was livid and banned them from ever answering the phone. "Don't you touch this phone again!" she said.

We were all little devils!

To this day, over sixty-three years later, that phone number is still in use. Wow!

CHAPTER 12

The Church in Construction

The Church of Christ 2018   Front of Church 2018

In 1953, Mom and Dad's dream came true. I was about for years old when the church construction began. Dad was a full-fledged minister by then and it was time to start building, to expand God's Kingdom. I heard them talking from time to time about bricks, windows and doors, and pews, but I couldn't quite understand the concept.

Daddy came home from work early one day to take Mom to see how the construction was coming along. We had to wait for Bert, who was now in kindergarten, to come home so we could leave. Dad piled us into the car and drove to the site of the new church building. As Mom stepped out of the car, Dad extended his hand to take his son to show off to the construction workers. "Here's my boy!" he called out. Mom smiled and looked around at the site, while Bert and I stayed close by her side.

Piles of orange dirt, sand, and tiny pebbles surrounded the gigantic hole in the ground. Long boards, cinderblocks, cement with the mixer were off to the side. Shovels, rakes, and wheelbarrows were spread out here and there, covered in cement. This was so exciting to me because I could see that Mom and Dad were truly grateful and happy that the Lord had blessed them with a new building. They would work together witnessing to many people, sharing God's Word, and bringing them close to Christ.

I remember seeing a few of Mom's brothers there, as well. Uncle Sam and Uncle Paul. Both were expert bricklayers by trade. Dad's brothers, Uncle Dave and Uncle Johnny, were there, too, but I don't know exactly what their jobs were.

As I noted in the beginning of my story, my mother's maiden name was Williams. Dad and his brother David Williams married two sisters, Mae and Rosetta Williams. No relation!

The name of the church is the Church of Christ, which is still active today. For many years we worshipped in this little church, and four of us girls—Elnora, Loretta, Ida, and myself—got get married here. In this church, Dad would marry two more times after mom passed away. This church has a lot of history, of which some were happy times or very painful.

Usually three times a year the church would have an "All Day Meeting." These meetings fueled the soul with good singing and preaching. But mostly to build up the building fund. We had about twenty giving members on a good Sunday, and the rest were children, a total of about thirty-five who worshipped there. Having these meetings was also a good time to fill your gut with good food and take a plate home to eat the next day.

My sisters would help our mother, who would start her cooking on a Saturday, before the All Day Meeting the next day.

There were other families that would pitch in and do their part. Someone might cook all the greens and ham, another person made the mac and cheese, and so on. Mom always had the hard part—roasted turkey and gravy—and nearly everyone would whip up a pound cake or sweet potato pie, and don't forget the famous banana-and-wafer pudding. The Kool-Aide or fruit punch was made in a big ceramic crock, half filled with ice. The older girls had to set the long tables using real dishes, glasses and flatware. Whoever came to eat first was served the finest. But it didn't help if they packed several plates to go. That meant slim pickings for others who came later.

After everyone got their fill of free food, most would go to their cars and fall asleep until afternoon service. Some took their nap on the pews, then at 3:00, everybody was back in church.

The singing started and the feet began to pat. Louder and louder. They were singing and making melody in their hearts to the Lord. The cleanup people in the basement could hardly hear each other speak for all that joyful noise upstairs just banging away. This was the way black folks got the spirit and the rhythm. In the feet or with their hands. When it was time to take up the collection, folks pretended to be asleep or throw a quarter in the money plate.

The churches traveled from Darby, Chester, Ursellton, Philadelphia, and Bridgeton, NJ, to worship and eat at the Church of Christ in Clayton NJ. I would hear people (most of which were connoisseurs, and had the body weight to prove it) say, "This church got the best food."

One late Sunday evening, the church was still tarrying when a big rainstorm came rolling in. My father thought this would be the perfect opportunity to put the fear of God into some of them heathen folks. Now, our dad was a HELL, FIRE, AND BRIMSTONE PREACHER, and he loved to give a good performance when preaching!

Suddenly, the Lord cracked the sky. BOOM! POW! ZIP! The thunder roared and the lightening crackled and flashed across the night sky. And the rain did fall that night! Dad stood up and started to preach, again! We thought he was going to dismiss the congregation. Not! "This is the work of the Lord and he's telling you to come, come, while the blood is still rushing warm in your veins. Come, come and be saved."

The louder the storm got the more Daddy preached. Suddenly, a bolt of lightning flashed and the church lights went out. Folks started screaming! "Oh, my Lord! Save us, Lord! Amen, Brother Williams!"

Then Daddy really started dramatizing, walking up and down in the pulpit while the storm continued to roar. It was so dark in the church; between the flashes of lightning, all I could see were their eyeballs.

"Come, come!" he yelled over and over. "The time is now! Don't wait until tomorrow because tomorrow might be too late. On that great day of judgement, the stars will fall from the sky, and the moon will drip away like blood. You will run to the rocks and say, 'Rocks, fall on me, and hide me from the face of Him who sits upon the throne!' You'll run to the rivers and the rivers will be boiling! AND WHO WILL BE ABLE TO STAND? Repent and be baptized! He's waiting for you! Harden not your hearts! Believe in Him and be baptized for the remission of your sins!"

Folks were scared sure enough!

Then somebody would start singing "I'll Fly Away" by Albert E. Brumley.

Then before you could catch your breath, another song started. This was the invitational hymn to come and be baptized.

O WHY NOT TONIGHT?

O, do not let the world depart and
close thine eyes against the light;
Poor sinner harden not your heart: Be saved, O tonight.
O why not tonight? O why not tonight?
Wilt thou be saved? Then why not tonight?

After the storm passed, the lights came back on and it was time for dismissal. We sang another song called "God Be with You Till We Meet Again." Everyone bowed their heads for closing prayer, praying that all would get safely home. Then folks hugged, kissed, or shook hands. Daddy was proud because he had stirred them to think about their soul's salvation.

Our dad loved preaching a good fire-and-brimstone, shakedown sermon.

CHAPTER 13

Victor

There was a young boy in our neighborhood named Victor. He was brutal! He always played the part of a bully, and that's what he was. Even though he had the trait of brutality, he was a very generous kid with a kind heart. To my knowledge, he never physically hurt anyone too badly. When we played games, Victor would capture the little kids and put them in a headlock, squeezing their little heads like a melon and screaming out, "I AM THE BRAIN CRUSHER!"

We were all afraid of him because he was so much bigger than everyone else. He always knew where to find the weak kids and applied heavy pressure on them. Most of the time, when Victor was present, I'd stay on the front porch and watch. When I would see him running hot on someone's trail, I would duck under the porch wall and hope and pray he didn't see me. *He's not gonna crush my brain*, I thought.

Victor always did well for the first few minutes, but after that he became a pain in the neck. He cursed at us, hit us upside our heads, belched in our faces, and made farts under his armpits. "Daaag" was his famous drawn-out words.

It was a lazy summer evening, just before dusk dark, and Victor came over to play. Mom only let him come when she could keep somewhat of a watchful eye on all of us. If she heard him swearing she would come out and reprimand him or send him home.

We were having a good time singing hymns and telling jokes, teasing, and having a good time, when all of sudden a big black cloud appeared in the sky. And it got really dark and still. Mom came out and told all the kids to go home quickly because she heard thunder and it was about to rain. It started to thunder, then it got louder and louder! All the kids scrambled and headed for home, except for Victor. Even his cousin Sandra, whom he taunted daily, went home. She was a really good friend of Rets. Both were like "double trouble!"

Victor was a big-mouth tough guy who wasn't afraid of anything. So he stayed longer, laughing and acting foolish. All of a sudden, the sky opened up and the rain came down in buckets. Lightning crackled across the sky and the loud thunder boomed and roared as it shook our little house. Being afraid, I eased my way over to my sister El for her protection. I remembered folks talking about our cousin Carl, who was struck and killed by lightning when he was nine years old. He was on his way home, pulling a wagon with kitty cats, when he was struck.

Mom always told us to be quiet during a storm, and that this was God doing his work, so be still and listen. She always had the candles or oil lamps ready just in case the electricity went out, which always frightened her children.

We witnessed that the tall, wild cherry trees across the street, which our grandfather had planted, were now bending over. We all started singing "Didn't It Rain."

Victor's bravery turned into fear and he became more frightened with every song we sung. Now Victor was also a hard-nosed cursing heathen, who swore constantly, using the Good Lord's name in vain, and that's the one thing our mother didn't like anybody to do. Mom came outside and said to him, "Victor, didn't I tell you to go home?"

"Yes, Aunt Mae, I know you did, but I'm scared. I might get struck by that thunder and lightnin'."

Mom knew that Victor wasn't going to budge, and that he was trying to manipulate her into staying longer, by talking sweetly to her and everybody around him. Mom wasn't falling for that little scheme. She went in the house and got her umbrella, came out, and took him by the hand to walk him home. Needless to say, she had to coerce him.

On the way home, which was only a few doors down, Victor promised her that he would start going to church and would be a good kid from now on. "I love God, Aunt Mae. He been good to me."

Humm…

When mom came back home she said, "That little stinker is full of the devil." But she really cared about him, and where life would lead him.

Well, the next day Victor was back to cursing, using God's name in vain, terrorizing our neighborhood, and raising the devil. And that was the only time we ever saw Victor afraid and crying. He was a bully and he was proud of it! Took pride and pleasure in farting and spitting on anyone he could intimidate.

Was it really the thunder and lightning or the Williams kids' singing songs about hell, fire, and brimstone? Here is the song that got Victor trembling and put some temporary fear into him.

Oh tell me where should I go
When the first trumpet sounds
It's going to sound… So loud!
That it will wake up the Dead
Oh tell me where should I go

Why don't you…. (Bass)

(Chorus)
Run to the rocks and the rocks will be falling
Run to the trees and the trees will be bending
Run to the water and the water will be boiling

Tell me where should I be, Oh Lord, I'm gonna be down on
my knees
Just praying, when my Lord sounds that Trumpet Loud!

Verse II
The rich man lived, he lived so well and when he died, he
had a home in Hell.
I'm so glad my Lordy fixed it so, the rich and the poor
together must go!
Sinner… Hear him pray…get right, get right with God.
Oh tell me where shall I be, Oh Lord I'm gonna be down
on my knees, just praying when my Lord sounds that
trumpet loud.

CHAPTER 14

Our New Bathroom

The year before mom died, Dad had a bathroom installed. Everyone in our neighborhood had an outhouse for years but they were finally fading out fast. All the kids were excited and came over to see the diggers and the heavy machinery dig the cesspool. The men told us not to come close, but when they were finished we could see how deep the hole was. We gathered on the back porch and watched in anticipation.

Without fail, Victor started terrorizing several of the younger kids, including myself, to tears. He made a solemn promise that he would throw me down that hole and nobody would ever find me. And I would live with the rats forever. I was so frightened. I think he was jealous because our family was getting something new, or maybe he just wanted Mom to come out and talk to him. He craved her attention, at any cost.

And may I add? After all the construction, purchase of the fixtures, and decorations, we had the newest and prettiest bathroom in the neighborhood, and our mother was proud to have it.

Every night before bedtime we would line up to use it. Phil would be last in line, so she could flush the toilet. Dad was not a wasteful man when it came to saving water, so one flush was all we needed to do. And most of us had to use the same bath water. Yuck! Just add a little more hot water, hurry up, and get out. He never let us use the shower, either. No shower curtain would ever be put up for that little luxury. No siree!

Mom enjoyed her beautiful pink bathroom for nearly a year before she passed away.

CHAPTER 15

The Old, Rusty Swings

We had a set of rusty old swings on the side of the house that we enjoyed and swung to our hearts content. One day we decided to start swinging high enough to try and reach the sky. All of a sudden Ret struck up a tune, "Shake, Rattle and Roll." And to our regret, we all joined in. "Get out in the kitchen and rattle those pots and pans. We gonna shake, rattle, and roll!"

Well, Mom heard us singing at the top of our lungs and came out with some switches. Tore our little butts up! No child of hers would start singing that devil's music. No, no, not in this family! And that was one of her strong beliefs!

Those old swings seem to get everybody in trouble at one time or another.

One day after I got home from school, I ate my lunch and went to swing on the swings. Bad idea! My sisters would often twist themselves up on the swing and spin around. That was so much fun, even if it made them dizzy. I wanted to try this by myself and began twisting with the back of my dress over my head. What was I thinking? I twisted until my feet left the ground and I was then ready to spin. Not!

"Hey, nothing is happening and I'm feeling tight around my neck," I thought to myself. My dress had gotten caught in the chains and I couldn't move an inch. "Mom! Mom!" I tried calling her but my head was in a down position and nothing but a whisper could be heard. I waved my hands back and forth and this caught our neighbor's eye.

Miss Sadler was always at her kitchen window, watching the Williams kids at play. This time she saw danger. She came running out and tried her best to unwind me. But to no avail. She resorted to something else. "Don't move," she said in a calming voice, and ran back to her house, got a large pair of scissors, and proceeded to cut my dress off me. Eventually she slid my little body through the opening. "Don't tell your mom. We don't want to upset her, do we?" she said with a smile. She took the mangled dress and went back home.

God was with me and He saw my distress.

Another time I was sitting on her front porch, petting her cats. I love to hear the sound they made, like a purring in their stomachs. "Miss Sadler, why do you have so many cats, and who's the mommy and daddy?" I asked her.

"I don't know," she replied. "I guess they all like living together."

I looked up at her rocking in her chair and said to her, "Well, if the cats get married, then they can be a family."

Several days later, Miss Sadler came over to our house and told Mom what I had said. She gave me a little, black ceramic kitty cat that I still cherish to this day.

CHAPTER 16

The Tapeworm

When I was about four years old, I got terrified one day. I had gone to the outhouse to do number two. When I started to wipe, I felt something moved. I tried wiping over and over, and it still kept moving. "MOM!" I yelled. She was in the house and came running out to see why I was screaming so loudly for her. I pointed to my bottom and said, "Something is moving down there!"

She lifted me and flipped me over between her legs to see what the problem was. A look of horror came over her face. "Oh, my Lord," she said. She had to think quickly. "Okay, sit still, Kat. Don't move." She ran back to the house and got a Mason jar with a lid. Flipping me over again, she told me to be extra still. Good thing she didn't tell me what it was or I would have freaked out. With my head between her legs she began pulling, then she would stop, then pull some more. I heard her give a sigh of relief and say, "Okay, okay, you're all right."

Whatever it was, she quickly grabbed the Mason jar and put it in.

When Dad came home and my uncles were present, she showed it to them.

"Wow, it's about fourteen inches long," Dad said.

"A tapeworm," someone else said. "Holy moly!"

Mom said she had to be very careful not to break it because it was full of eggs. Dad put together some kind of tea called bitter herbs, and I had to drink some for a few days and sit on the potty after every meal, just in case another one should slide out. No doctor! No, siree!

Oh yeah, for a little while my name was changed to "Tapes."

Now, some people say this incident happened in the kitchen, while I was sitting on the pot, but it didn't. It was in the outhouse (outside toilet). You see, we never used the pot during the day, only at night, and everyone on that particular day was still in school. I often asked them if they saw Mom pull it out.

No comment!

Mom probably put me on the pot, in the kitchen, later that day for observation. She was one smart cookie!

CHAPTER 17

Little Uncle Dave—"Onk"— and Aunt Natalie

In 1951, when I was about two years old, our grand mom Elnora died. Uncle Dave, Mom's younger brother, or "Onk," as we called him, came to live with us. I think they said he was a senior in high school. He was in the Clayton marching band, and he could wail on the drums. Several years ago, I borrowed a 1952 yearbook from my quilting friend. She went to Clayton High School and knew my uncle very well, because of his popularity in the marching band. She told me she had a big crush on him. Wow! And she was a white girl, too. That was unheard of back in the day.

I was so excited to see how handsome Onk looked like back in the day. Onk was a real hunk! No wonder Natalie Scott fell for him! I copied that picture and sent it to his daughter Libby Jean and his son David Jr.

My fondest memory of Uncle David was when Mom and Dad went to see the older kids in a school play. The four little kids stayed home with Uncle Dave. Yep, my parents had a live-in babysitter.

When I woke up from my mid-evening nap, he took us to Miller's store across the street and bought us twin popsicles. He loaded us up in the big, gray, hooded baby carriage and ripped through the streets as fast as he could run. "Okay, ya'll, hang on tight!" he said.

Bert and Ida rode on both sides of the carriage while Billy and I rode inside. Up and down Clayton Avenue he went, singing and waving to everybody in sight. Fun! Fun! Fun!

After he graduated from high school, he would wake up my sisters and tease them with a little song he made up. "Little Chillin' gotta go to school this morning. Dee-ta-dee-ta-dee-ta dee."

He was the best uncle any kid could have! And he had a beautiful tenor voice, too. His son David Jr. has an excellent voice, as well. Like father, like son.

Natalie Scott, or "Scotty," as most folks called her, was short, under four feet high, and the sweetheart of Uncle David. She was as round as she was tall and had a smile that made you feel loved. Before they were married, she would come and visit us. When we knew she was coming, we would gather on the front sidewalk and wait to see her walking from the downtown bus stop to our house. She would travel from Philadelphia to 311 East Clayton Avenue to entertain her soon-to-be nieces and nephew. She knew how to warm her way into our hearts and into Uncle Dave's, as well. "Here she comes, I see her," one of the older kids would say.

This was pure joy! We knew we were in for a treat that day. Whenever she came to visit, she would come a-packin'. Goodies, goodies, and more goodies!

Tootsie Rolls, Mary Janes, Candy Buttons strips, peanuts, Life Savers, jawbreakers, mints, pretzels and Cracker Jacks, and any other penny candy she could afford to buy.

We would all gather around her, wringing our hands but trying to be patient. Usually she had to have small talk with Mom before the fun began. She always wore bright-red lipstick and kissed everybody as soon as she arrived, and left her lip print on our little faces. When she got to the little kids, she would reload and apply more of her Avon lipstick on us. We would run to the mirror to see her lip prints.

Aunt Natalie loved to sing and she taught us a lot of Christian camp songs. We all sat at her feet on the living room floor and listened to her every word. Here are a few songs that I remember: These songs I sung to our children, and now to our grandchildren.

LITTLE FEET BE CAREFUL

I wash my hands this morning, O very nice and clean,
And gave them both to Jesus, 'cause He's our
Heavenly King,
So Little feet be careful, little feet be clean,
So Little feet be careful, 'cause He's our Heavenly King.

We also sang "Just Fall in Love with Jesus" by Zac and Shelley. After we had a little devotion and Aunt Natalie was just getting warmed up, she started singing everything she could think of.

Take me out to the ball game Take me out to the crowd,
Buy me some peanuts and Cracker Jack, I don't care if I
never get back,
Let me root, root, root, for the home team,
If they don't win it's a shame.
For its one, two, three strikes you're out,
At the old ball game

THE WATERMELON SONG

O' plant a watermelon upon my brain, and let the juice
(slurp) run through,
I had a dream thee other night, I dream that Billy was in
the icebox,

So plant a watermelon upon my brain and let the juice
(slurp) run through.

This song was sung until every child's name was used in
the lyrics.

WALKING THROUGH THE DINING ROOM

Walking through the dining room, walking through the parlor,
My foot slipped and I fell down, and I began to holler,
Pick out the one with the rolling pin,
Pick out the one with the money,
Pick out the one that you love best and kiss and call him
honey!

At that, she would give us another kiss.

The other songs were:

That's what I learned in the school.
(I point to myself right here, right here)
O soldier, soldier, would you marry me?
How much is that Doggy in the Window?

We sang until we were tired and worn out. I still sing these songs today to my grandkids, and hopefully they'll pass them down to another generation.

Dad had a special name for Aunt Natalie: "Ole Dusty Butt." Come to think of it, she did have a fat, round butt, and she was almost dwarf size.

After Mom died, Aunt Natalie and Uncle Dave didn't come around much. When their two children Libby and David Jr. were very young, the couple divorced. Aunt Natalie passed away in 1992, right after teaching a Bible class. Uncle Dave died in 2008. Both left an everlasting impact on me and my family.

CHAPTER 18

The Sears Catalog

It was Christmas, but not for the Williams kids. No, siree! Our parents didn't believe in it. No toys, no hard candy, Christmas tree, decorations, clothes, or anything related to that pagan holiday. It was just another day. And how would you miss something you never had?

Every year Dad would order the Sears and Roebuck catalog for him and Mom to order different things that they needed throughout the year. Bert, Ida, and I would wait diligently for its arrival to play a game called "That's Mine." We would sit on the sofa, and usually Ida was sitting between me and Bert. She would open the catalog and turn the pages slowly. If you liked what you saw, you had to slap the page fast and say, "That's mine." The first hand to go down was allowed to lick that page. This was fun and we would crack up laughing. Most of the pages that we loved were in the Christmas candy section.

Brach's chocolates of every shape and size, candy canes, hard candy, glass candy, fudge, bonbons, cookies, fruit cakes, all kinds of nuts, smoked hams and turkeys, and so much more. We even licked the toys! Occasionally Ida would turn to the ladies' bras and men's underwear, which was considered taboo for us. You had to be on your guard not to slap those pages or you would be forced to lick them. How sick was that?

Mom never knew just what this game was all about. She just saw that we were entertaining ourselves and having a blast.

This game could go on for hours, until we got tired. Well, that catalog was starting to look pretty torn up after a few days. After the Christmas season was over, Dad asked to see his catalog so he could place an order. Nobody knew where it was. After much searching, high and low, he found it stuffed under the sofa, all matted and crumbled up. He yelled, "Who did this to this catalog? Doggone kids! Little hussies! Who did this?"

But of course, no one knew who would have done such a thing. With his eyes bulging out and his lips pressed tightly, he tried his best to press out the wrinkled pages, but some were torn from the binding. That made him even madder. "Where's that order sheet? Look, Mae. The whole tool section is gone! Stinking kids!"

When he mentioned the order sheet, I started to tremble. I tore it out because it didn't look important to me. I was always afraid of getting a whipping from Dad because he would always say, "Tell me the truth! Don't you lie to me! Or I'll bust you wide open!" Then the beating would begin. Usually, he used a switch, his belt, or the fearsome cat-o'-nine-tails. This was a wide leather strap used to sharpen straight-edged razors, then it was cut in nine long strips.

When he finished beating you, he would throw you in the nearest chair. You prayed that he would have a perfect aim and not miss the chair, or else you might hit the wall or roll around on the floor. He always had a great aim! He had lots of practice!

Lord, have mercy! The whelps would rise!

Most people knew Daddy as being a great father who loved his children, and I'm sure he did. But he was hard on some of us, and never ever spared the rod.

CHAPTER 19

Hurricane Hazel

Hurricane Hazel was one of the deadliest and costliest hurricanes in 1954. Many people lost their lives in this massive storm. The storm killed at least 400 people in Haiti before striking Canada. It made its way to the borders of North and South Carolina. Traveling up the Atlantic coast, it affected Virginia, Washington D.C., West Virginia, Maryland, Delaware, Pennsylvania, New York, and New Jersey.

I was five years old when this devastating hurricane hit our home and the entire east coast. It brought down the gigantic mulberry tree in our front yard, which barely missed Dad's car. We were so scared of the loud winds, let alone the destruction she made. Mom got out the candles and lanterns because she knew the lights would go out. Dad said he didn't want anybody going outside because it was so bad.

The next morning, after the storm, our yard was a big mess. The tree had knocked over our white picket fence. Mom and we kids watched out the front window as Dad and a few of Mom's brother's cut our beautiful mulberry tree and hulled it away, along with the white picket fence.

CHAPTER 20

Kindergarten Baby

Time to start kindergarten! After my fifth birthday, it was time to be vaccinated for school. Mom kept reminding me, "Kat, you'll be going to the doctors soon to get a shot. But it won't hurt. And if you don't cry, Doctor Davis will give you a lollipop, okay?"

I thought that day would never come. Because I loved sweets so much.

Dad came home one day and asked Mom if she was ready to go. She got my little brother ready and off we went to the doctors. I didn't know where we were going until we got there. Oh no! It was ole Doctor Davis's office! Ouch!

I was somewhat of a shy and timid child and would often allow my playmates to take advantage of me. I didn't know any better. When I started school at the youth center, I had very few friends. There was Shirley, Pale Face Mary, and Karen who was a chubby little white girl who looked just like Shirley Temple. She loved to hold my hand when we were in the singing circle or marching with our toy instruments. Every morning we sang this song:

Good morning, good morning, good morning to you
Good morning bright sunshine, and how do you do
Good morning, good morning, we're glad you are here
You make us really happy, and bring us good cheer.

I liked Karen so much that I asked my aunt Rose, who was pregnant at the time, to name her baby Karen, if it was a girl. And she did. Her nickname was Toby.

It was a student's birthday and her mother brought beautiful pink cupcakes in to celebrate. I never saw icing piled so high and I couldn't wait to sink my teeth into one. This little girl always wore the prettiest clothes and gave the correct answers to whatever the teacher asked. She was smart, she was cute, but very spoiled.

As the little miss cutie passed out her birthday cupcakes to each table, the kids would gasp. Wow! Finally, she came to my table and gave each child one. When she came to me, she paused, then turned away, wrapping her lips around my cupcake. The beautiful icing was gone!

"Here," she said with icing covering her lips.

Her mother said nothing. I knew she saw what her daughter did, because she was carrying the tray. After everyone was served and got our milk, we sang happy birthday to her. I was crushed but sang and ate the cupcake anyway. That's the way it was!

Shortly after I had started kindergarten, our class went outside to play. I chose to play in the sandbox. The sand was so white and clean, and it resembled sugar. I was in awe of it all. It was a little windy that day and I didn't know that the wind would blow this super fine sand every-where. When our teacher blew the whistle for us to come in, I stood up and shook the sand from my dress. The wind did the rest! Sand went in the kid's hair and eyes, and I was in big trouble. Again!

"I didn't mean it," I tried to explain. "It was the wind."

When we got inside the teacher made me hide my face. I never played in that sandbox again.

CHAPTER 21

It's Picture Day!

It was Picture Day in kindergarten, and I wanted to look my best. Mom combed my hair and dressed me up really nicely. "Don't forget to smile Kat," she told me.

My sister El would walk me to school and it happened to be a different route than the other siblings would take. Sometimes her friend Esther Jackson would walk with us.

I went to the youth center. Years later, it was named Dr. Pals Day Care.

My class boarded the big yellow school bus to go to the Academy Street school to have our pictures taken. I remember seeing my sister Ret walking into the big, green gymnasium, but she was too far away to hear me call her name.

The pictures were taken on the stage in the auditorium. We all lined up from the shortest to the tallest. I was midway. The photographer used little black combs to freshen up hair that was somewhat out of place. Then he'd throw the combs in a big box. I didn't need freshening up because mom had just combed my hair that morning. Mom had put a few bobby pins in my hair to hold down my braids. And this so-called wannabe, stand-up comedian of a photographer decided to mess with my hair.

It was finally my turn and the photographer sat me down and placed my scrawny hands in my lap and tilted my head toward the camera. "Oops, don't move," he said with a smile on his face. That's when I really began to smile and giggle. He took one of my bobby pins and used it to prop up my front braid. He laughed out loud and his female assistant laughed, too, and said it was cute. "Smile for the camera," he said.

And I did!

My teacher and the students were behind the curtain and didn't see what happened.

When the pictures came back, our teacher let us open our packet to show each other. Well, everybody screamed laughing when I showed mine.

"Buck Wheat!" somebody yelled.

"No, she looks like Alfalfa!

I didn't know who Buck Wheat or Alfalfa was because we had no TV. I didn't like what that man did to me. Why didn't my parents let their voices be heard? As I said before, "that's the way it was."

CHAPTER 22

Junie

Now Victor had a nephew named Junie, who was twice as ornery as him. Junie would fight anybody. We went to kindergarten together, but only for a short time. He would fight the teacher, throw chairs, and cry nearly every day. He definitely had some issues.

One day, as we rode the school bus heading for home, Junie sat next to me. He had his school papers in his hand, sat down, and laid them between us. When the bus turned the corner to let us off on the corner of his house, he got up first. And snatched his papers that I happened to be partially sitting on. He started screaming and yelling at me. "Look what you did! You tore up my picture that was for my mom!" The bus driver immediately ran to where we were sitting. She tried to reason with him but he refused to listen. She pushed him back in the seat and told me to run home as fast as I could. I took off like lightning, hoping and praying that Mom would have the door unlocked.

When the bus driver finally let him off, or he got away from her, he tore after me like a runaway locomotive. As I passed Mrs. Sadler's house I looked back, and there he was gaining on me. When I turned onto the sidewalk I started screaming, "Mom! Mom!" The door was unlocked and I bellowed into the living room. "Junie's after me!" I cried. Mom tried to shut the door after I got in, but Junie tried to overpower her, to force his way through the front door.

"What did you do?" she asked me.

"Nothing, Mom," I said while trembling with fear.

He banged and kicked our door while screaming, "She tore my paper and I'm gonna beat her up!"

"Oh no, you're not," Mom told him. "If you calm down, I'll let you in." For a little while it got quiet and I thought he was gone, but Mom wasn't buying it. She ran to check the back door. He was trying to get in through that door, too. Nothing doing!

Well, he finally calmed down and Mom let him in, but held my hand and I stayed behind her because you never knew if or when he would charge like a bull. I remembered him pushing kids around, and crying all the time in school.

Mom told him that I would never do this on purpose. But Junie insisted that I tore it and that he drew this picture for his mother. Mom looked at the picture, which was nothing other than a bunch of scribble, and got the scotch tape to fix it. "Okay, Junie, is that better?" she asked.

"No," he said, "are you going to beat her? I want you to beat her!"

"No, Junie," Mom replied. "It was an accident." My mom was very smart. She told him that if it was the other way around, Kat wouldn't want him to get a beating.

Junie thought about this situation long and hard and decided to let bygones be bygones. When we walked him home, Mom told Miss Alice, his mother, what happened. His mom said, "I was wondering why it took him so long to get home, because I heard the school bus go by.

The next day Junie was not on the bus. He was kicked off! He wasn't in my class but possibly went to the afternoon session.

One day he came up to our house to play, and my sister Loretta said something that ticked him off. All of a sudden he shot across the porch and rammed her in her stomach area. He hit her so hard that she doubled over in pain and began to cry. He laughed and said his father taught him how to use his head to hurt people.

"The cocoa butt," he said.

Loretta stayed like this for a few days and complained that her lower stomach was hurting. Dad did nothing! She should had been taken to the ER. I'm not implying that it was his fault, but it's a logical coincidence. When she had the miscarriage, the doctors said she had one ovary left and that it was scarred. Her chances were fifty-fifty on having children. Loretta had no children, and when she did get pregnant it was a tubal pregnancy, which nearly killed her. The doctors said they had to beat the angels away from the operating table. She and I were pregnant at the same time.

On another time, our dad was playing with him and picked him up. Junie went ballistic on Dad and started screaming for Dad to put him down. He was crying something awful.

Junie had a lot of emotional problems later on in his adult life. He would pass away while incarcerated and I was asked to write a memorial for his funeral. He had a lot of good in him. He taught me how to fish, play marbles, baseball, how to read the stats on baseball cards, and how to be the neighborhood tomboy.

Needless to say, we became good friends from that day on until my father said I couldn't play with him any longer. I was around thirteen years old and starting to blossom, and Dad had enough problems to worry about. No more afternoons of playing Jacks, flying June bugs (Japanese beetles), or eating Baby Ruth candy bars, which he always shared with me. "Time to grow up, Kat," Dad said.

I missed playing with Junie. I taught him how to play Jacks and jump rope, and he taught me how to play baseball and sometimes ran all the bases and tagged himself out. He'd generously give up any unwanted, wrinkled, and torn baseball cards to me.

Junie was a great fisherman…caught lots of fish, eels, turtles, frogs, and anything that came out of Silver Lake.

Babe Ruth was my favorite candy bar, but not necessarily his. That didn't matter; if Junie had a nickel, he'd run to Dick Gordon's (Miller's) store to buy one and give me half. "Half-eze," he called it.

My stepmother gave him a nickname: "Money Man." I never had money, but Junie did. Mom would give me sugar cookies or day old biscuits with strawberry jam made from the strawberries we picked, from a field down on Clayton Avenue.

One day I got my foot caught in a crack of his grandfather Kurt's big oak tree. My father had to cut my shoe off to get me out. Junie had dared me to climb that tree. Yes, he taught me how to be a genuine Clayton Avenue tomboy.

After Dad got me out the tree, he took off his belt and beat me in front of all the kids in the neighborhood who were watching us. I was so hurt and embarrassed. I thought Junie would never stop laughing while Daddy was beating me. I laid low for weeks. Couldn't face anyone. I never climbed another tree again.

Green Japanese beetles or "June bugs." Junie thought God made them just for him! He even tried selling them for a nickel each, to the kids on the block who couldn't find or catch their own. I remember my sisters and I would tie a thread on one of their hind legs, attached a little note on the string, and hope they would fly over to Junie's house. We wrote bad things about him because everyone was so sick of his antics. Just string 'em up and let 'em go sailing through the air! This was fun. We didn't need toys!

Junie was one of the first kids on the block to get a transistor radio. He let me borrow it one night and I fell asleep and left it playing all night, thus running down the batteries.

"That's okay," he said. "I needed some new batt-trees anyway."

When we became teenagers, he would often talk about what was going on in the neighborhood. And the people who were noisy and got on his nerves. Usually it was the old folks who believed in raising everybody's kids. Most of them felt that it took a whole neighborhood to raise a child. And he was one of them.

One summer evening, when I was about fifteen years old, I was waiting on the front porch, dressed and beautified up for my date to arrive. I spied Junie walking up the street, all dressed up in a powder-blue two-piece suit. He looked so sharp, he could have cut himself.

"Hey, Junie! Where're you going all dressed up?" I asked him.

He gave me a big grin, showing all his pearly whites, and replied, "I'm coming to see you. Your simple boyfriend called me and asked me to take his place." Then he busted out laughing. And I did the same. He could be so humorous sometimes.

Two years later, we both got married and started families of our own. He was a proud papa of a little girl named Sylvia, (AKA, Sibby) and I had a boy, Davey Jr. He was so proud of his daughter and repeatedly showed me how he taught her to wave bye-bye when I visited his house behind Dick Gordon's Grocery Store.

His wife Sarah is a great person who loves the Lord. Immediately I saw the beauty of Jesus in her, and after fifty years, we met again at a fabric store.

"Excuse me, Ma'am, have we met before?" I asked her. We'll, we got on the subject of Clayton, and the rest is history.

CHAPTER 23

Dad Was a Yeller!

O ur dad was a yeller. I believe he spent most of his time looking for anything or anybody to yell at. Many times he would come home from work in a terrible mood. He would start in on Mom, who was always in the kitchen cooking dinner. If dinner wasn't on time he would get angry and take it out on her. If some of us were in the kitchen helping her, he would yell and say, "Get out of the kitchen!"

Mom would try to explain to him that she needed help, which made him even madder. Then he would yell again and say, "If you're not helping your mother, get out."

Till this day, I hate to hear my husband speak too loudly!

My dad was a little man who stood about five feet six inches. But he was fit as a fiddle with a six pack to match. I think he suffered from little man syndrome because he was always saying how nobody would mess with him or how strong he was. Poor Mom, she married a conceited, pompous, want-to-be tall Jack*** Preacher. And I don't mean jackleg.

As young as I was, I had great empathy for Mom. She didn't deserve this from him.

Before she married Dad, there were a few other men who were in love with her, including her own brother-in-law's, who were very tall and handsome. Dad was the runt of the litter but knew how to work his way into her heart.

There was another man she dated when she was fifteen years old, in the eighth grade, whom Dad told us about when we were teenagers. He told us he stole her from him. Why did she choose our dad? They say Dad was a charmer and knew how to impress the ladies. But if she hadn't chosen him, we wouldn't be here. Thanks, Mom.

Mom's health began to fail. Lil Anna would never have remembered our mother. You see, Mom died when little Anna was only eighteen months old and Elnora was thirteen. The rest of us fell in between. Our lives would be changed forever. And at the tender age of six I knew my mother was not well. Not knowing anything about death, I watched her slowly slip away, getting thinner and sicker day after day.

Mom was feeling rundown and tired all the time. She didn't smile the way she used to. Her teeth were going bad, as well. Eating vanilla ice cream and Tastykake Chocolate Cupcakes were agony. She held it in her mouth for a long period of time; because of the coldness and sweetness against her teeth, it would cause her much pain. There were times when she wouldn't eat the frosting because the grease bothered her ulcerated stomach.

She was the most unselfish person I have ever known. She would send someone to the store to get a large vanilla Dixie Cup (with the little wooden spoon), and a pack of cupcakes. We would gather around her, and with eight spoons, she would divide her treat with all eight kids. You just don't find too many young mothers these days who would do that. She was teaching her eight children how to share.

She always reached out to people who were in need. These are the values she would passed down to her children.

Mom, with all the children she had, always kept a tidy house, but now cleaning was always done on a good day when she had the energy. Dad started taking her to the doctor more frequently, to find out what the problem was. The doctor kept saying that she was anemic and needed to build up her blood, but it was more serious, that.

I was in my last few months of kindergarten when Mom's health began to fail. I would come home from school and she would still be in bed. She would tell me to run and get Aunt Rose so she could help her get on the pot. Even though we had a bathroom, she was too weak to walk that far. Away I ran to get Aunt Rose, who was usually on her way to our house to check on Mom, anyway. She would come in and help Mom out of bed. Almost immediately Mom would begin to regurgitate and Aunt Rose had to send me out and close the door. This went on for some time; the days and weeks went by. Mom wasn't getting any better.

Sometimes Dad would cook dinner when he got home or Aunt Rose would fix something and bring it over. I don't remember if others helped us, but I guess they did, even if it was a few dollars.

Aunt Dobb, Mom's sister who lived in Woodbury, NJ, kept Billy and Anna when Mom wasn't feeling that great. I missed them so much.

CHAPTER 24

Mom Passes Away

Early one morning, the ambulance came and took our mother away. I was asleep then, but when I woke up a little later, I discovered that she wasn't there. They say she was in a coma when she left. I remember my sisters asking our father that night when Mom would be coming home. Dad would reply, "I don't know, Kids. I just don't know."

A day after she was admitted to West Jersey Hospital, she passed away. At the age of thirty-one, she was diagnosed with leukemia, a disease that consumed her body and took her life, and our lives would never be the same.

The morning of her death, we were all sitting around in the living room with Aunt Rose and the telephone rang. El answered the phone. It was the nurse from the hospital. She wanted to know if there was an adult with us she could talk to. Elnora handed the phone to Aunt Rose. We watched Auntie and heard her saying, "Hello. Yes, I'm their Aunt." Then she said the unthinkable. "Oh no! Not my sister."

We all knew that something bad had happened to her. Something happened to Mom!

Aunt Rose continued. "Is he there yet? Oh, okay, I will." And she hung up. We all looked at her and she said, "Girls, your mom is gone."

September 14, 1955, our mom went home to be with the Lord and be with her baby boy. *Gone where?* I thought to myself. I didn't understand what death meant. But everyone began to cry. So I started crying, too. No one attended school that day, but Phyllis went in the morning session. When she came home she had been told by some of the kids down the street that Mom had died. She refused to believe it because Dad had come to school dressed up to tell her that Mom was going to be all right. As she walked home alone, Elnora met her on the corner and told her that Mom had died. Phyllis nearly fainted.

When Dad came home from the hospital with a heavy heart and weeping eyes, he told us that when he got to the hospital he didn't know she had died and a lady was in the same room and bed that Mom was in. He thought the lady was Mom. Then they told him, "Mr. Williams, your wife is gone." And hearing those words, he broke down in despair.

I don't recall how many days went by before the funeral took place, but this was one gloomy, sad, and painful day that would last forever.

Sometime during the week, our aunts and uncles got together and decided who was going to take what kid or kids to raise. They never even considered asking our father. Aunt Dobb was taking Elnora and Anna, the oldest and youngest and happened to be high yellow. Mrs. Culbreath wanted Ida because she was her godchild. Aunt Rose was taking me and Bert. Aunt Julia was taking Ret. Phyllis didn't have anyone yet, and Billy, well, they would have to fight Dad to get him, because he was Dad's pride and joy.

When Dad got wind of this, he nipped it all in the bud right away and said, "In other words, I made a promise to Mae that I would keep our children together if anything should happen to her. And I am!"

CHAPTER 25

The Funeral

T he day of the funeral was damp and rainy. The older kids dressed the younger kids and we waited for the limousine or family car to arrive and take us to the church. I sat up front with a heavyset, fair-skinned lady who kept smiling at me. She appeared to be a nurse of some sort and was there for us kids. Elnora told them the way because they got turned around and needed better directions. The lady asked if we wanted to listen to the radio because it was so quiet. By the time she tuned in to a decent station, we were there. The church was only three and a half miles away. The cars were double parked on the narrow road and some parked on every little side street. Even across the railroad tracks! Mom had a lot of people who loved her

When we walked into the church, we saw that there were people everywhere. Our little church was packed with standing room only. We never knew how many friends our parents had until that day. The flowers gave off an aroma that permeated the church. Almost a sickening smell. We sat on the front pew with our dad, who slept off and on during the whole funeral service. Poor Dad, he was so tired from running around trying to make arrangements for his wife's final internment. He looked so sad and bewildered. Most of the time he rubbed his forehead. He always did this to comfort or calm himself, or if he had a headache. That's where I get it from. Our dad fell asleep during the eulogy.

They sang lots of songs, some of which Mom loved. They talked, preached, and preached some more. Every minister who was there had to get up and give a few words. I was about to fall asleep when a tall, handsome man dressed in a service uniform picked me up from the pew and sat me on his lap. It was my mother's brother, Uncle Lester, who at that time was in active duty in the armed forces and had arrived late to attend his sister's funeral. He pulled out his white handkerchief and wiped his eyes in silence.

It was time for us to say good-bye to our mom before closing her casket. My father stood up and gathered all of us in front of the casket. I looked up at him, and watched as he tried to hold back his tears. Mom looked like she was asleep, all dressed in blue. I wanted to shake her and wake her up, but no one else was even talking to her, just crying over her. Later on, one of my sister's told me, "Dead people don't hear, breathe, talk, or do anything. They just lay still." Now, I was more confused!

Aunt Dobb, who was carrying baby Anna, fainted, and a Puerto Rican lady named Miss Katie grabbed the baby before Aunt Dobb could hit the floor. The undertakers revived her with smelling salts.

As the people walked by the casket to pay their respects, they would turn around and touch us and say things like, "She's in Heaven," "She loved you kids," "She's not suffering anymore," and "Take care of each other and be good." At six years old, how could I comprehend what they were saying or what was going on? I wanted to tell them, "This is a dream, everybody, and Mom will wake up soon. You'll see."

After the funeral service was over, we got back in the big black car and headed for the Cedar Green Cemetery, in Clayton. When we arrived, there was a big, long hole in the ground and a partially covered pile of dirt nearby. *What's going on?* I thought. Some of the women, most of which were the older Jackson girls, were carrying flowers. They gave each of us flowers and I didn't know why.

"These flowers are for your mom," they said.

When should I give them to her? I thought to myself. *When?*

It started to rain again and I felt like I had to pee. I squirmed, folding my skinny little legs, trying to hold it in, but my weak bladder just wouldn't let me. The pee found its way to the insides of my new shoes. All I could think of was, *I'm in big trouble!* But nobody even noticed, or cared.

After the people talked, prayed, and sang a song, Dad laid some flowers on top of the casket that held his beautiful wife Mae. We followed him and put our flowers there, as well.

I don't remember going to a repass, or if they had one. Perhaps we all came home because it was such a long, dreary day for us kids.

This is a song that she and Dad recorded on a vinyl record when they were younger. They both had beautiful voices, and sometimes when I close my eyes, I can hear them singing a hymn. It's called "The Garden of Prayer."

A young man by the name of Author Anderson, who became a funeral director, wanted to marry Mom when she was very young, but she refused. Years later after she passed away, Dad would hire his company to bury her. His establishment was all the way in Trenton, NJ. Mom's family knew about this past love affair and knew that this man loved our mom dearly. They said that dad gave her back to him in a box. Now that was cold and calloused!

Her funeral cost $375. I wonder if Dad got a reduction.

CHAPTER 26

Daddy's Grief Comes Down

One night as we all sat around the dinner table, eating whatever mess that my sisters El, Phil, and maybe Ret were able to conjure up, someone asked if Mom would come back soon and if she was in Heaven.

All at once everyone looked up at Dad for a positive answer. Dad, who was eating, stopped chewing, raised his head, and stared like he was confused at the question that was asked. He paused for a moment, dropped his fork, and replied, "She's gone forever! She's never coming back!" Suddenly he broke down crying and ran to his bedroom. My big sisters Elnora and Phyllis followed him and tried to comfort him. Poor Dad was broken. That was the first time I saw and heard my daddy actually cry.

At the age of sixty-eight, I think of my mother every day and sometimes find myself talking to her picture that's displayed in my bedroom, on my dresser. I do look a lot like her, especially in my younger years.

CHAPTER 27

Miss Sadler Comes to the Rescue!

I was a bit of a cry baby and would sometimes have temper tantrums when I knew no one was paying attention or bothered to care what was troubling me. One day shortly after Mom passed, I was so hungry. Elnora at the age of thirteen was trying to hustle up some grub for her siblings. Time passed into the late afternoon, and El wasn't making any headway with her endeavors. That's when I began to scream and cry at the top of my lungs for some nourishment. At six years old, I couldn't take it any longer. My little tummy was on fire for something to eat. I began to cry and carry on like a baby. "I want my mommy! When is she coming back? I'm hungry!" Blah, blah, blah!

Then Elnora started screaming louder than I was. "Stop crying, Kat," she begged me. I wish I was dead instead of Mom. I hate this!" she yelled.

All of a sudden I stopped crying to listen to why she had started crying.

Mrs. Sadler, a short busybody of a Negro woman in her late sixties, had come to see what all the fuss was about, and what she could report to our dad when he arrived home from work. She always watched us play through her kitchen window and would sometimes come outside to reprimand us, or sometimes ask somebody to go to the grocery store for her. I would grow to love, respect, and appreciate her as I matured. As the old African proverb goes, "It takes a whole village to raise a child." She was our village for sure.

She hugged and tried to comfort El, who was crying and wiping the tears from her bloodshot eyes. As we sat on the back porch steps talking, Mrs. Sadler asked El, "Honey, are you pregnant."

"No!" El said. Poor El, she just needed someone to understand what she was going through while trying to take care of her seven siblings. We would all have our trials and grief of losing our mom at such young ages.

When Dad came home, Mrs. Sadler called him over to tell him what had happened that day. They talked for a while and Dad came home with a big smile on his face. He never mentioned a word to us about what they had talked about or even the event that took place on the back porch with me and El. Humm....

Another time, when El, Ret, and Phil had to cook dinner, Ret decided she wasn't going to help them. She was extremely lazy! El begged and pleaded but Ret was so stubborn and was not giving in. She became enraged and threw a one pound can of peas at El, who ducked. I caught the edge of the can against my forehead and blood shot out everywhere. El and I started crying, and once again El said, "I wish I had died instead of Mom."

Ret yelled back, "Well, go ahead and die, Dummy!"

These words were becoming the norm with El. I really don't think she wanted to die. She just wanted us to take pity on her, and try to be more cooperative and obedient. Poor El, she was only thirteen years old and forced to be in charge of everyone, including herself.

When Dad came home from work, everything had quieted down and I was my old self again. No one told Dad, so nothing was acted upon. He did see the big bandage across my forehead, but said nothing about it. Once again Ret went scot-free. And my scar remains to this day.

CHAPTER 28

First-Grade Baby!

It was 1955 and I was in the first grade. My teacher was Mrs. Andrews. Even though our school was integrated, as most schools in the North were, there were still people who hid their prejudices well. My teacher didn't teach me a whole lot. And it was for certain that she always held back most of her black students. I was one of them. When she visited each child's desk to make sure they were staying on task, she always, without fail, bypassed me. I guess she felt I wasn't worth the trouble.

Before Mom died, she taught me how to write all the names of my siblings. But for some reason I couldn't remember how to write my own name. I knew it began with the letter K, but that was all I could remember. I would write all the names on the top of my school papers. This infuriated my teacher and she scolded me for this. "Go stand in the corner," she told me. What had I done wrong? I was proud just knowing how to write their names, because Mom taught me. I wanted to impress my teacher so badly with what I had learned.

I continued to put the names on my papers. She said she was going to write a note to my mother. I wanted to tell her that I didn't have one, but she was feisty and didn't want to hear it. Children were not permitted

to speak their minds, and if they did, they were sent to the corner immediately for talking back.

She gave me a piece of yellow lined paper with my name on it and
said, "Write!"

My name is Kathleen Williams. Now I remember and I would never
forget it. I had to fill up both sides of the paper.

I think I had shut down after Mom died because I did nothing in
school that whole year but daydream; this was my form of grieving. I
don't think my teacher even knew Mom had died or even cared to ask
questions about why I was so unresponsive. That year, she held me back.
I would repeat the first grade again. That's the way it was!

CHAPTER 29

It's TV Time

We never had a TV, but when we lost our mother an appliance store in town, called Doughty's, donated a TV to our family. This is what I was told. I would often hear Dad say, "Your mother never wanted a TV," but I'm not sure if it were the real truth. I think he was too cheap to buy one. Once we got one, he watched it more than we did. We were only aloud to watch TV in the evening after he got home, but we snuck and looked at it, anyway.

CHAPTER 30

Stranger in Our Midst

Sometime after we had lost our mother, a strange man came knocking on our door. He was a tall, fair-skinned fella, probably in his early thirties. He looked like a homeless person, totally ungroomed. Scruffy beard and long, dirty fingernails; he carried a watermelon under his arm like a football. He said he had come to see Brother Williams and he didn't mind waiting for him. This was in the early afternoon and Dad wouldn't get home until 4:30.

El, being only thirteen years old, was a little reluctant about this character and kept a sharp eye on him. He asked her for a big knife and El brought him the dullest one from the kitchen drawer. He looked at it and said, "It's dull. Don't you have anything sharper than this?"

El went back and got a sharper one. He took it from her and began cutting his melon open. Staring at us with his deep-set gray eyes, he began eating, all by himself. He didn't offer us any and he even ate the seeds. We watched him guzzle down piece after piece. Was he going to kill us after he was done eating?

El, Ret, and Phil huddled all the little kids in Dad's bedroom, opened the window, and hoisted us out one by one, lowering us to the ground.

Some fell on grassy ground and some fell upside down. El told us to run over to Aunt Rose's and tell her what was going on. Aunt Rose came over right away and told that man, "Leave now! These kids don't know you. You're a stranger! You better leave or else." And with that, the man got up, left his mess, and flew out the door.

El locked the door behind him and we stayed in the house until Dad got home. After telling Dad what happened, he said he knew him. "Aw, he's a lonely, harmless man, looking for a wife."

Dad had sent him to our house, but didn't give him any specific time that he would be home to receive him. Dad was not a cautious man and trusted strangers around his kids. Later, the man told Dad that we didn't respect him and kicked him out of the house. This particular incident would come back to haunt our dad many years later. Never trust strangers. To this day, I believe Dad was trying to set up his daughter El with that unsavory old character.

He told El that "it was better to be an old man's darling than a young man's slave."

When Loretta was fourteen, Dad allowed her to date a Puerto Rican man, who was twice her age. He seemed to be a nice guy, but deep inside he was a child molester. Was Dad trying to marry his girls off to anyone who looked like they had money? This man worked in the peach orchard, down the street, and had a wife in Puerto Rico. One day he found a little stray puppy and gave it to Loretta. He named the puppy Blackie, which he pronounced Blocky. The puppy was brown and white. Ha! Ha! Ha! He would always say that he sends his money to his Mama Mia. Loretta soon got tired of his empty pockets. When they met he gave her everything she wanted. Except cigarettes! One day he cried like a baby as Ret displayed one of her emotional temper tantrums. After dating a few months, they parted.

Dad always looked at the outward appearance rather than the heart of a person.

CHAPTER 31

The Old Glass Factory

U sually when Dad left the house for work, early in the morning, I was awake and listening to the sound from the glass-blowing factory called Clevenger Brothers, which was just around the corner. It was loud but very soothing. Almost like a hum! Sometimes my little brother and I would sneak around the corner and watch them through the fence as they worked blowing the glass to make bottles and such. It was very hot where they worked and the furnace was always a blazing fire. The men had bands or scarves around their heads to keep the sweat from trickling down into their eyes. If they weren't too busy, they'd give us a wave and a holler, "Hey, Kids." Sometime we'd ask for their empty soda bottles and cash them in for two cents each.

There was crates and crates of finished bottles in the storage yard, ready to be shipped out to various parts of the country. This factory was owned and operated for over 100 years and changed ownership many times. It still exists but not operating. Today, I have one of the bottles that I highly regard as a keeper.

There were certain smells and sounds in Clayton that I would never forget. The smell of the peach orchard in July, and that meant we could get free peaches. The drugstore smelled like rubbing alcohol and per-fume, and the Clayton Bank smelled like old paper money.

The sound of the Presbyterian Church bells that rang every Sunday morning at nine o'clock, chiming the melodious sound of "Abide with Me." That meant it was time for us to get up and get ready to go to our church, which started at eleven.

The sounds of the roaring, fiery furnace in the old glass factory. The train whistled as they blew from crossing to crossing, from Franklinville to Glassboro, and of course, the twelve o'clock whistle that lets you know it was time for lunch. Some of these memories still exist today. A few childhood memories of my earthly home in Clayton, New Jersey.

CHAPTER 32

Koo-Koo-Ka-Choo, Mrs. Robinson

S everal weeks after Mom passed, Dad decided to have a live-in family come and take care of our home and his children. Or should I
say take over his home, seduce our father, and neglect his children. And
that's just what she did. As young as I was I still remember the cruelty
she displayed each and every day to me and a few other of my siblings.
She had her favorites and made no apologies for it. She had her un-favor-
ites and I happened to be one of them. I was a bed wetter and she never
knew how to handle my problem. I was forced to go to bed at seven
o'clock with no water to drink after dinner. Even on those hot nights,
when all the neighborhood kids were still outside playing by the light of
the moon or the corner streetlight, I was in bed.

The heat was so unbearable! We had no fan or air conditioning,
which was not popular during that time, anyway. There was one window
in our bedroom that didn't go all the way up, and if it did, the mosquitoes
would pour in and eat you alive. You just sweated until you fell asleep.

I missed much of the early summer when she moved in with us back in October of 1955. During the day, I had to sit in her bedroom, on a hard-back chair, until my frail back ached from sitting so long. I would have been happy just to walk around the floor for exercise.

All the neighborhood kids would play together after dark, while I had to sit waiting for this so-called housekeeper to come and check to see if I was asleep. My tongue stayed parched from thirst, but I learned how to go without water so I would stay dry all night. "I'll teach you not to wet the bed," she'd always say. "No more water after dinner."

Today, this form of punishment would be considered child abuse, and somebody might just go to jail!

Time out for me was time in!

I have to laugh when I see little kids in Time-Out for four minutes. What a Joke. I had to stay in the house for weeks at a time, while my siblings played in the sunshine. But I have to admit that sometimes she would let me get up and sweep and dust her two-room living quarters while her kids did nothing!

Desserts were not allowed for me. As I laid in bed, I could hear the sound of clanging spoons hitting against the sides of everyone's dessert bowls. Sometimes they popped corn, which I loved. And boy did it smell good! It seemed that some waited until my bedtime to remind Dad or Miss Emily that I had wet the bed maybe two days prior and was still on punishment. "Go to bed!" Dad would yell.

Thinking on it, I guess it was more dessert for everyone else if I was excluded from those delectable goodies. Because of what this unkind woman had done to me, I made a solemn promise to myself to never treat my children this way.

Her children were given the best of everything. The fried chicken breast went to her son. Legs and thighs were given to her and her two girls or Dad, because he was a thigh man. Whatever was left from two chickens, like the backs, necks, feet, was split among the eight of us kids, even when she cooked extra meat on Sundays. That's the way it was!

It took me eleven years to eat oatmeal again, because that's all we had for breakfast—lumpy, bumpy, cold, and sometimes milk or sugarless oatmeal. Sometimes if we were lucky, she would cook cornmeal mush or Farina instead. I don't mean to sound ungrateful but how do you justify giving eggs and bacon to your kids?

Where was our dad and what would he say or do about this situation? The sad part about this was that you couldn't tell Dad or anyone else what was going on. I guess you could say it was fear of getting into trouble. One of her famous phrases was, "Stop your tattletale!" I miss eating my mom's fried chicken, scrambled eggs, and hot buttered toast.

I remember so well one night when that woman, in plain white slip, paid a visit to our dad's bedroom. Dad was in there, too, and they stayed a long time. *What is she going in there for?* I thought to myself as I watched the TV in the living room that was adjacent to Dad's bedroom.

She looked wild when she came out and said, "Thank you, Brother Williams."

Humm…

After a while she dumped all the bed-wetter's in one bed. It was horrible! The flies were so thick, they crawled all over our bodies. One morning, I was looking for my shoes under the bed and found that I was sleeping on a bed filled with maggots. These little creatures had eaten a big hole through our cotton mattress. The smell in our room was a profound stench that stung your eyes and made your throat feel raw. I shall never forget. Nothing was done! You just changed your sleeping position and packed the hole with rags. Oh, my God!

Miss Emily was really out of control one morning. Loretta had wet the bed and blamed it on Ida. So she beat both of them. After bringing the sheets in the living room for all to witness her cruel punishment, she made them get down on their knees to suck and smell on the dirty sheets. Poor Ida, she cried so pitifully. I knew she was innocent. She beat them until she was satisfied.

"The more you cry, the less you'll piss," she'd say.

She took most of her frustrations out on some of us because of Dad. She thought Dad was going to marry her. When she found out he was seeing other women, she was a woman scorned.

There was a young girl around our age named Kathy Wilson. She was the half-sister of Junie Wilson, whom I mentioned earlier in my story. One day when Dad was away, some of us kids sneaked down the street to play with this little girl. Miss Em's son happened to be with us. He told Kathy that we were her cousins and that her father that she lived with wasn't really her dad. Why did he do that for? We were never told about this story, and didn't know she was our cousin, but just loved playing with her. Her mother Alice came and told Mrs. Em, and she beat Ida and Ret. We all had to stay in the house for several days. We never knew how this boy found out, but Dad must have told his mother. As a teenager we discovered that she, too, had a beautiful singing voice. She loved to sing with us just like her father. Today, our cousin Kathy is seventy-one and looks just like her father, Uncle Harry, my mother's brother.

Too beat or not too beat! That is the question! Why did black folks like to beat on kids so much? Here's why! This form of punishment goes way back during the time of slavery. The master would beat his slaves into submission. This trickled down through the years. It didn't matter if the punishment did or didn't fit the crime. Everyone watch while the victim was brutally stripped naked, beaten, and humiliated. He would have his own slave children beaten and sold away. The slave beatings were performed on anyone, at any age, to show an example for other slaves who might dare to disobey. It became a sport!

PROVERBS 13:24 (NIV)
One who spares the rod hates his child but the one who loves his child is careful to discipline him.

PROVERBS 22:6 (NIV)
Train a child in the way they should go, and when he is old, he will not turn from it.

Ret became very bitter with everyone. She would steal from her teacher, smoke cigarettes, and Dad would beat her unmercifully. One night he tied her up, locked her in the basement, and turned off the light. We could hear her screaming because she was so afraid of the dark. Dad believed in never sparing the rod, but she was just a kid. And there was nothing we could do to help her. This form of punishment made her worse; this was the beginning of her journey to having emotional breakdowns.

One night she was taken to the emergency room. Some years later, when I was about twelve, our father took us girls to visit her. I had nothing to say to her, but out of respect I spoke. "Hello, Miss Em."

She looked at me and said, "Little Kat, you sure did grow. Look at you!" She must have known how I felt about her. Because she said nothing else to me for the rest of the time we were there. And I said nothing to her because as a little child, she had broken and crushed my spirit.

CHAPTER 33

The Big Brown Box

It was Christmas Eve 1955. We were all sitting in the living room, watching some Christmas specials, when there came a knock on the front door. Two, maybe three, men came in and said they were from the Kiwanis Club and they had a box of stuff for us. El greeted them in and they explained that the club had put together gifts and goodies for us. They went outside and came back in with a huge box filled with small, triangular boxes filled with hard candy, gifts, oranges, apples, and nuts. Each gift had a tag with a name on it. I got a sewing kit with fabric, needles, thread, scissors, and tiny patterns to make doll clothes. We were so happy! No one had ever given us anything for Christmas before.

Miss Em emerged from her bedroom and started picking out what she wanted for her and her kids. Dad wasn't home, but I'm sure that would not have made any difference. After gathering what she wanted, she said, "Now you'll can have the rest." And with that she turned and walked away with so much stuff, she could hardly carry them.

When Dad came home and saw what was left, he said nothing, because he didn't celebrate that holiday anyway and charity was not his thing. This was just one Christmas blessing I shall never forget.

CHAPTER 34

Ida, Is there a Real Santa?

A few weeks before Christmas, my sister Ida came up with a great idea. She would write a letter to Santa Clause and mail it in the special green-and-red Santa mailbox near the one patrol car in the Clayton police station. The next day, on the way home from school, we stopped to mail this letter. She opened her textbook to get the letter out but couldn't find it. She looked through her other books, but no letter.

Then she remembered. "It's in my sock! Hey, guys, listen. Don't tell Daddy, or I'll get a beating for writing to Santa Claus."

Then I asked her, "Ida, do you believe there is really a Santa Claus?"

"Oh, I don't know. He never came to our house," she said.

She opened the envelope and read it to us. This is what Ida wrote in her letter (what I can remember):

Dear Santa,

My name is Ida. I am in the third grade. I have a little brother. He is four years old. His name is Billy. He wants a toy for Christmas because he never gets any toys. Please bring him something nice or a toy for Christmas.

My address is 311 East Clayton Avenue.

Thank you,
Ida Elizabeth Williams

A couple of days later, during the night, there came a knock on our door. We always stood on Daddy's green chair that was in the corner by the front door, so that we could see who was knocking on the door.

Bert climbed up this time, peeked out of the half-moon window, and yelled, "It's a big fat, white man dressed in red."

Well, Ida kept her mouth shut! We let the big fat man in, who looked like he was drunk, and he asked to see Billy, because he had something special for him. Well, this was at around 8:00 p.m. and Billy was already asleep, but they woke him up, anyway. He rolled out of Daddy's bedroom still half asleep, wearing his yellow cowboy pajamas, and came into the living room where everyone was sitting. The big fat man said hello to Billy. Then Billy looked at him with his big, sleepy brown eyes and said nothing.

"I have something for you, young man." He motioned for Billy to come near.

Billy toddled over to the fat man and the man reached in his red suit jacket, pulled out a little candy cane, and handed it to him. Then he said good night and left.

Bert, Ida, and I were shocked! *Is that all? A stinking, little candy cane!?* And he didn't even say, "Ho! Ho! Ho!" I often wondered if the fat man kept what he was supposed to give our brother for someone else. Humm... I bet he did!

Well, Ida, I guess this means there's no real Santa! Huh, Ida?

CHAPTER 35

The Great Ice Storm

S hortly after we lost our mom, there was a great snowstorm in 1958
that turned into thick ice everywhere. Trees were down, electric and
telephone wires were lying across the streets, and very few people could
go to work because the roads were a sheet of ice. Everything in sight was
glistening with thick, heavy ice.

Bert, Ida, I decided to brave the freezing cold and go to school that
day. We never heard the fire siren sound that let Clayton residents know
that school was cancelled. Our older sisters had gone earlier and was on
their way back home. We went to the Clinton Street School, so we didn't
see them walking home.

Now, back in the day, girls couldn't wear pants to school. It was
bare legs, leotards, or bobby sox. We would still be freezing but leotards
helped a little. No pants and our little legs were freezing! By the time I
got to the seventh grade we wore pants but had to take them off before
school started. We didn't have gloves so we wore socks on our hands,
then took them off before we got to school, so we weren't laughed at by
those smart-aleck kids. It was better than nothing at all. Once my sister
Ida took her bologna sandwich in an empty sugar bag because we didn't

have wax paper. The bread dried up so she was satisfied eating the cold bologna. Yes, we were poor, having to use our wax paper and brown paper bags over and over again. Most of this took place when our step-mom left us.

As we were about to turn on Clinton Street, the school bus stopped and told us to go back home because school was closed. We started crying because we were nearly frozen.

Ida said, "Let's run and maybe we'll get warm."

I don't know how we made it back home, but we did, slipping and sliding all the way!

It was bitter cold that day and everything looked like it was covered with thick glass. The trees, houses, roads, telephone poles, and cars were covered in ice. There was no electricity in all of Clayton. No TV, radio, or phones, and the people who used natural gas or electric heat had no heat at all. Many were freezing, except us. There were very few homes in Clayton that were still burning coal. I guess you could say the Williamses were behind the times. Good thing! Many families had to go out and purchase kerosene heaters to survive the cold from this incredible ice storm.

At around 2:00 p.m., we heard the one and only police car coming down our street, and over a loudspeaker they said, "Take your bedroll and your food to the Academy Street School. You will have lodging, shelter, and a warm place to stay. Come before the temperature drops lower."

We never knew how cold it was until we went outside.

This was a town in crisis for about a week! We never knew how many of the town's people left their homes and went to the school for shelter. But we were warm and cozy. Thank you, God.

CHAPTER 36

Hiking with Ret

I was an explorer by nature, thanks to my sister Ret. She took us hiking and had the best time. One day we all got walking sticks and went hiking in the woods that bordered the railroad tracks with a dirt road between the tracks and the woods. "Come on fools," she'd say. Us little kids would run all the way to keep up with her.

The woods became a haven for teenagers who would cut class, smoke cigarettes, and fool around. Saturdays were their days off, so the whole woods belonged to the Williams kids.

Loretta had such an imagination. She was a great navigator and a super tour guide. We found an old, rusty railroad car that instantly became a log cabin. "Abraham Lincoln's cabin! Abraham Lincoln freed the slaves!" she kept saying.

Ret took us to play in these woods and this happened to be our first time. We packed Saltine crackers, surplus cheese, and a jug of warm, sour lemonade.

"We'll eat off the fat of the land, just like Abe Lincoln did," Ret said.

We sang songs, and looked for black berries that didn't grow there.

Finally, it was time for lunch and we ate the crackers and cheese and drank the weak lemonade. Ret kept yelling, "Lemonade, said Abe! Ade, said Abe!" Over and over again.

You didn't need TV when Loretta was around. She was the entertainment. She loved to read stories to us, and boy could she read with feeling. She used different voices, which made her stories come to life, stories like "The Raggedy Man," "Little Orphan Annie," and her all-time favorite, "Abe Lincoln who freed the slaves."

You would never have known that she had mental issues. She was so much fun.

CHAPTER 37

A Truck Filled with Ponies

The merry-go-round man would come on Friday nights. If I wasn't on punishment maybe us kids could sneaked down the street and get a free ride from our neighbors who always had extra money. The Jackson family would pay for us kids to ride because we never ever had money for pleasure. Dad never thought it was important for his kids to have entertainment, especially at a cost. Five cents per child. Just get in line and we will pay. Sometimes they would pay for the kids on the whole block to ride.

When we heard the sound of music that was played through a loud-speaker from his truck, we knew it was the merry-go-round man coming around the corner. We would drop what we were doing and down the street we'd run, hoping that Dad would not come home until after the fun was over. The merry-go-round man would play our favorite records over the loudspeaker. Yes, we did have records that our aunt Rose would purchase for us. My two favorite songs were "Two Little Magic Words (Please and Thank You)" by Tex Ritter and "Open up Your Heart (And Let the Sun Shine In)" by Stuart Humblen.

We played lots of games whenever the neighborhood kids came up the street to play with us. Dad never let us go anywhere. "Stay in the yard," he'd always tell us. It was his way of protecting us. But to others, we were considered uppity Negros. As we got older he became more lenient with us, only because he was too busy looking for another available woman to date. And of course we were older.

CHAPTER 38

It's Party Time!

Sometimes we begged Dad to let us go to someone kid's birthday party down the street. We would tell him that their parents invited us and they would be there to watch everybody. He would think long and hard and had to know all the details like who, what, when, and where, and sometimes why. "And you better not be dancing. If I catch you dancing, I'll bet the devil out of you'll," he would always say.

"Okay, Daddy, we won't dance," was always our reply. We never had a gift to take to the parties. He didn't believe in birthday or parties, either. It was just another day to him.

Well, what he didn't know never hurt him, or should I say, never hurt us. But when the music started kicking out, our feet commenced on moving. We watched the other kids dance first then we started to dance with everybody.

We did the cha-cha with Sam Cooke and rocked it with "Rockin' Robin"; did the stroll to the sound of "So Fine." We heard new songs like "Poison Ivy," "I'm a Searchin'," "Blueberry Hill," and "Splish Splash." Of course there was our old favorite, "Shake, Rattle and Roll." Ha-ha-ha! We all loved music and danced to anything that made our feet move.

After the party was over, we would come home with sad looks on our faces like we were so bored. Huh! Far from the truth!

It didn't take long for us to learn all the new dance steps. You see, we would watch *Band Stand* every day until Daddy came home from work. There was always a lookout person at the window for Dad's car to pull in the driveway.

"Hey, you'll! Dad's home! Quick! Turn off the TV," someone would shout. Then we would all scramble and run to the kitchen, pretending to look busy starting diner. Wow! That was a close call! Sometimes we would dance and do the twist behind his back and crack up laughing. We were a little nutty!

Our granny, who lived with us at the time, would threaten to tell Dad on us, then we convinced her to join in from time to time. And she did. Just standing in place, swinging her arms from side to side and bouncing up and down to the beat. That was "getting down dancing" for granny. We would grab her by the hand and try to teach her how to do the bop. "Get outta here, Gal!" she'd say.

Sometimes Dad would come home and feel the back of the TV to see if it was hot. He knew! But he never asked what we were looking at.

After we got a little older, Loretta stop caring about Daddy's wrath and started to do her own thing. She loved holding on to the door frame and dancing by herself. If you happened to walk near her or cross her path, she'd grab you and say, "Come on, Fool, dance." Poor Ida always seemed to be her victim.

Loretta started smoking and hanging out at the "Kool Kat," which was a combination of what you'd call a sandwich shop, ice cream parlor, juke box dancing, and high school hooky player's sneak away. This little whole in the wall was a stone's throw from the school, and the wild kids would cut class and hang out there all the time, smoking, dancing, and trying to look popular among their peers. The girls showing off their poodle skirts, black-and-white saddle shoes, and Bobby socks. And don't forget the long ponytails and colored neck scarves. The boys wore penny loafers, khaki pants, plaid shirts, and white socks. Cool!

Loretta, being fourteen years old, loved this place and would get her little sister Ida, who was eleven or twelve at that time, to skip lunch or recess to join her. Ret and Ida were dancers, for sure. The white kids loved to see them cut the rug. They would give Ret cigarettes and she thought she was hot stuff with her fake, matted ponytail. She had hardly enough hair of her own to keep the ponytail in place. The Jacksons gave her another nickname: "Wig" She looked so funny at the end of the day with loose bobby pins dangling around her head. We knew better not to laugh at her or we would catch her wrath for sure.

She danced the cha-cha, bop, the stroll, and any dance that could make her move her feet. She knew all the popular doo-wop songs that played on the jukebox; those songs were never played on her dime 'cause she never had money to spend, anyway.

Loretta didn't own a crinoline, so she made herself a wired-up news-paper crinoline slip that needed adjusting from time to time. Ret didn't care 'cause she knew she was hot! And nobody could tell any differently.

Readers, are you getting the picture? Yes, we were picture-perfect poor!

One day Ida slipped and told another sister about their secret rendez-vous. Ret got in big trouble. Dad slapped the mess out of Loretta. Not so much for cutting class but for dancing, smoking, and taking Ida with her. He said she was setting a bad example for the rest of us kids. Yeah, and Dad was a smoker himself but he cared more about his kids ruining his reputation and would threaten to put us in a home.

"Do as I say and not as I do," he'd tell us

One day, the high school principal got fed up and went to the Kool Kat, rounded up all the hooky players and class-cutters, and marched them back to the school. At one time, the school wanted to shut down this juke joint, but they came up with another solution: they stationed a few teachers near the property to send the kids back to the classroom. That little store still stands today, but not as the famous Kool Kat.

CHAPTER 39

Dad Marries Lavinia

O h boy! Dad got married again, six months after Mom died, to a
lady he barely knew. Lavinia Jane Brown. She was a Southern gal
who ruled with an iron fist. She stood about five feet nine inches and
walked straight and tall like she was carrying a glass of nitroglycerin on
her head. She was about four inches taller than Dad and weighed nearly
seventy-five pounds more.

The first time I saw her I thought she was a white lady. She was very
fair-skinned with long, black wavy hair, or good hair, as it was often
referred to. There wasn't much courtship involved; everything went
so fast!

One particular day she came to the house when my siblings were at
school. I stayed home that day, but I don't know why exactly. Dad must
have taken a day off because she lived in Avondale, PA, about one and a
half hours away. When Dad came in the house, he went to the back room
to talk to Miss Em. She left the house in a hurry, by the side door, and
never said good-bye. Then Dad brought Lavinia into the house, and both
of them were smiling.

115

Dad was so sneaky. He took Anna and Billy to Aunt Dobb's house that morning, for her to babysit. Little did he know that Miss Em would keep me home from school that day because I wasn't sick.

SURPRISE!

Dad and Miss Em played games a lot. She was in love with him but he didn't want her. So she used anything to keep him at bay. And though Dad knew how she felt, still he brought this pleasantly large lady to spend a few romantic hours with him. Bad idea!

Dad sat down on the sofa and said to me, "Go over Aunt Rose's and see if she is home."

Now Dad never like his kids to visit anyone for any length of time. But I guessed this time was an exception to his rules, and I did as I was told. Skipping across the street, I hoped that Auntie would have time to spend with me. I knocked on the door, and to my surprise she opened the door and told me to come in. I told her, "Dad wanted me to see if you were home and sent me to come and get you, I think."

"What does he want?" she asked me.

"I don't know, I replied. "He just said go see if you are home."

Aunt Rose said, "Oh, okay," and reached for the telephone to call him, then she changed her mind. "Come on, let's go see what he wants."

She took my hand and we walked back across the street. Aunt Rose knocked on the door, and waited, but no answer. She knocked again, then rang the doorbell several times. No answer.

"Is anybody home?" Aunt Rose asked me. "His car is here."

Suddenly, the doorknob turned, the door opened, and there stood Dad in his bathrobe.

"Oh, hi, Wiggy," Aunt Rose said. "Did you want to see me?"

"No," he said with an angry look on his face. "I didn't want to see you."

"Why did you send Kat to get me then?'

"I didn't. I told her to go see if you were home, that's all."

I think Aunt Rose knew what Dad was up to. "Is she sleeping in my sister's bed?"

That's when Dad blew up and tried to weasel his way out of a lie. He looked at me with such anger and I got scared.

What did I do wrong? I thought. All I could think of was "the belt."

He started hollering at me. "I didn't tell you to get her! I told you to see if she was home."

Which made no sense to a six-year-old child.

Aunt Rose said to Dad, "Oh, I see." Then she took me back with her. She told me not to worry because I did nothing wrong.

Dad was busted!

I think my stepmother held this against me for a while, for revealing their little premarital sexual encounter that she and Dad thought they were getting away with. The laugh was on them and the moral of this memoir is: never tell a child something that you don't really mean.

CHAPTER 40

The Wedding

In the early spring of 1956, Dad and Lavinia were joined together in marriage. It was a simple wedding, with us kids and about forty or so others. Some would not attend because it was too shameful seeing him marry someone he hardly knew. And to marry so soon after losing his first wife. They both married for all the wrong reasons.

It was on a warm night and we all gathered at the church for the ceremony. It was a real circus! Dad was looking the best I had ever seen him look, and she looked...well, okay. Her long, black curly hair flowed down her back and she wore a hat to match her dress. She wore blood-red lipstick, but no other makeup. She wasn't a glamor girl, and despite her size, she had natural beauty. She was a plain Jane. And that was her middle name, Lavinia Jane.

The old folks sang a song that sounded like "Ole Black Joe," an old Negro song that dated back to slavery.

When the preacher said, "If anyone feels that this couple should not be joined together, let them speak now or forever hold their peace," Dad got scared and looked around at the invited guests. I guess he thought there would be some objections.

Miss Emily was there and said, "This is the damnedest wedding I ever seen." She was jealous because Dad had dumped her.

I don't remember seeing a wedding cake, but maybe there was one.

After the wedding was over, our new mother, her sister Aunt Lee, and several of us kids went to see Uncle Johnny and his family. I don't know why we went, but Uncle Johnny and Aunt Maggie were happy to see us. And Aunt Maggie welcomed Mom into the family.

Our new mother and Dad didn't stay with us that night, and they didn't tell us where they spent their wedding night. Probably at her little house in Avondale, Pennsylvania.

My older sisters were very reluctant to accept a new mother, and warming up to her was difficult. As for me, I just needed someone to love me, not beat me, and be there for all of us. Well, for a while nothing changed; I was still the whipping post. Until she realized that I would love her unconditionally.

CHAPTER 41

Christmas with Our New Mother

It was Christmas in 1956. Our stepmom knew that Dad didn't celebrate Christmas, but she wanted to give each one of us something to make us happy. Dad wasn't about to celebrate a pagan holiday with his money, but he certainly didn't mind being on the receiving end. One Tuesday evening, Mom and Daddy went to Cowtown and Mom bought gifts for everybody. "They need to have something, Wiggy," she always told him.

"It's your money," he'd say.

Nothing was wrapped in pretty Christmas paper, and she wasn't allowed to call them Christmas presents. There was no tree, no decorations, and no goodies. The older kids got clothes, the younger kids got stuff that I can't remember, but I got a picture book. I still have it today.

She thought she had chosen each gift carefully. Mom knew I needed to improve my reading skills, so a book would be perfect for me. Only thing, it was on a fourth-grade reading level and I was still in the first grade. She didn't know that I wasn't able to read it yet. I loved looking at the colorful pictures over and over again. I would ask my sisters to read to me, and we all enjoyed this book called *Eight Nursey Tales*. My treasured story was "Little Black Sambo." Others were "The Three

Little Pigs," "The Little Red Hen," "The Gingerbread Boy," "The First Circus," "Chicken Little," "The Rooster, the Mouse and the Little Red Hen," and the classic tale of "Peter Rabbit." Who would have thought that in years to come, I would be reading these stories to my grand and great-grandchildren, from the same book?

One morning before I went to school, I asked Mom if she could read me a story. She took the book from me and looked at it. Then handed it back and said she would read it some other time.

For many years I didn't know that she only had a fourth-grade education. How sad!

CHAPTER 42

The Old Singer Sewing Machine

Mom liked to sew. She had an old Singer sewing machine that she brought with her when she married Dad. For hours I would watch Mom sew on that machine. Little did I know that my curiosity was preparing me for future sewing projects.

I loved guiding the fabric through the back of the machine, listening to the hum of the machine's motor. This was more fun than watching my favorite shows on TV.

At the age of seven, I asked her, "What makes the sewing machine go?"

She replied, "When I say go, it will sew, and when I say stop, it will stop."

Well, I tried it, and nothing happened. Did those magic words work only at her command?

One day while picking up scraps that were scattered on the floor, I accidently touched something that started the machine running. "Eureka! I found it!" Wow! Mom was pressing against this metal bar. She told me that when I was a little older, she would teach me how to use it. Unfortunately, she left.

When I was eight years old, it was important for me to have my own sewing supplies. An old cigar box would be perfect to hold my meager but necessary tools for sewing. My sewing box contained dual scissors, some stick pins, a needle, a spool of plain white thread, and an over-stuffed, handmade pincushion. I could hardly wait to get colored thread. My dad gave me his old carpenter's ruler and I was quite pleased with my sewing supplies; I started making doll clothes from small pieces of fabric, that otherwise would be thrown away. During my earlier childhood years, I learned how to make doll clothes and sewed items for many of my classmates. I would trade doll clothes for toys they no longer wanted, like Old Maid, puzzles, Jacks, dolls, or anything they were willing to part with.

CHAPTER 43

Big Rat! Big Bite!

Yes, we had rats and mice and anything else that crawled on all fours or eights!

We had a visitor one night. Bert, Ida, I slept together in one big bed before we got twin beds. If the roof was leaking, we positioned ourselves around the big wash tub that was in the middle of our bed. Because I slept on the edge of the bed, I was the rat's first victim. I was in a deep sleep when it happened. I felt something tugging at my shoulder. It felt like electrical currents, but I never woke up. When I got up to use the bathroom, the upper part of my nightgown was wet and my pillow felt wet, but I couldn't tell what it was. At first I thought I was sweating, until I turned on the light. It was sticky blood and a lot of it. I started shaking my sisters. "I'm bleeding, guys! Something is wrong! My shoulder hurts!

They finally woke up and one of them ran to tell Mom and Dad.

Mom came in and looked at me and she knew right away. "It was a RAT!" She cleaned me up and put pink salve on a gauze and wrapped it with white sheeting. For the pain, she gave me Aspirin, and told me to go back to sleep.

This really frightened me because when I was about four years old, I watched our real mother kill a huge rat with a broom handle and a hammer. This fat rat walked across our kitchen floor, just as bold as you please, in broad daylight.

I could see Mom now and imagine what she might have said. "Oh no, you don't, Mr. Rat, not in my house!" Mom battled with it for a long time before she killed it. She put on a bucket of water to boil. If all else failed, I think she was ready to drown it. All of us kids watched her from the doorway in the dining room. As soon as Mom thought she had knocked it out, that rat would get up again and try to get away. She was yelling, and these were some of the words I remember her saying as she hit it: "You… *bam!* Stay…. *bam!* Away…. *bam!* From… *bam!* My…. *bam!* Babies!"

Finally, the rat was defeated and Mom had won the battle. The victory was hers! We all cheered her on!

I never saw my mom as mad as she was that day. Don't mess with her kids!

Oh, yes, the fat rat was pregnant!

CHAPTER 44

Trouble in Paradise!

A fter the first year of marriage, something happened. Stepmom and Dad were growing apart. Dad was back to his old self, snappy and yelling his head off. He would embarrass her and call her names. She would put him down and belittle him in front of his children and church members. They were losing respect for one another. They had become very dysfunctional! Mom stopped going to church and he made excuses for her, to protect his reputation.

They were having serious marital problems; she left him for about six weeks and went back to Pennsylvania, to be with her sister. We were forced to fend for ourselves. This was the first time she left us.

The older kids didn't accept her. I think she tried too hard to take our mother's place, and Dad took up for some, when he shouldn't have.

She had a twenty-four-year-old son, out of wedlock, whom she didn't raise herself, but she saw him on weekends. Her son lived with an elderly couple who fostered other children. She didn't talk too much about the situation, but you just knew she loved her son. Every now and then he would come to visit us, riding his motorcycle. My first motorcycle ride was with our stepbrother, Donald Johnson.

Dad sometimes made it difficult for her to bond with us. He didn't make her feel that she could ever be what he had with Mom. I often heard them talking about intimacy, but I didn't know what sex was all about.

"Wiggy, all you want is my body! You don't love me!" she'd say.

I recall Ret having a breakdown. Or should I say, "fake down." One morning, Mom woke up all the kids to get them ready for school. Ret was giving Mom a hard time about going. She wasn't sick and didn't have a test to take that she wouldn't have studied for anyway. She was simply too lazy to get up and go.

Mom continued to call and begged her, but she paid no attention and pretended to be asleep. She finally got tired of Mom nagging her, so she rolled out of bed.

There were times when Mom would physically fight with my older sisters. One day she had her hand around my sister's necks. I got so fed up and scared that I screamed at her to leave my sister alone! She glared at me, then let her go. She knew that at that moment, she had lost it. My sister went away for a few hours, ending up at the schoolyard. That night Mom left us again, for the second time.

CHAPTER 45

I saw Mom!

O ne night as I laid in bed, I called my sister Bert to turn on the light so I could go to the bedroom. She said, "Do it yourself!" Then she went back to sleep. I continued begging but she didn't respond.

I hated to walk in the dark because of all the black and white slugs (snails) that would invade our bedroom floor at night. This always happened during the summer and early fall, due to the cracks under the door frame that led outside. Yuck! The bedroom door was so crooked that it couldn't close or lock properly.

I laid there for a while longer, thinking about my real Mom and how much I missed her. Suddenly without thinking, I jumped out of bed and made a dash to the kitchen.

Before turning on the light, I saw a faint light in the living room. I didn't think about fear anymore and peace came over me. I paused for a moment and looked again, trying to focus my eyes and collect my thoughts as to what I was seeing.

It was my beautiful mother, and she was smiling at me in a faint glow. Her arms were crossed, just as I remembered her, and that was her usual pose. The living room light was never on at night, so it would have been total darkness. I wasn't afraid anymore. When I turned on the kitchen light, she was gone. God had sent me a comforter.

The next morning, I couldn't wait to tell everyone that I had seen Mom. Some of my siblings asked me questions about my vision and others just left it alone.

When Daddy came home from work, somebody told him what I had seen last night. He questioned me over and over again, and each time I told him the same story. "You were sleepwalking, or maybe you were dreaming. And what was she wearing?" he said anxiously, while trying to convince me to change my mind.

"I didn't see what she was wearing because of the glow," I recalled. But I wasn't sleepwalking and I stuck to my story! I saw what I saw! And it was Mom!

Well, Dad started using a bed lamp after that. He used it so much that it started melting on one side, and because Stepmom had left him, he invited my little brother to sleep with him every night.

Oh, why was I cursed with having the fear of darkness? Here's why. After Mom died, I became a bit of a cry baby. One night I cried so much that they put me outside at night and locked the door. It was a full moon and very earie clouds moved across the dark sky. I screamed and hollered louder and louder, and banged on the door, but to no avail; they still wouldn't let me in. They yelled, "Boo, the bogeyman is out there and he's coming to get you!"

I guess that was their way of having fun. I remember thinking, *If Mom were here, they wouldn't have done this to me.* If they had turned on the porch light, maybe I wouldn't have been so frightened. Kids play!

Mom would always say this when any of us were afraid of the dark: "There is no such thing as a bogeyman."

We weren't convinced at all that the bogeyman wasn't real, so she had to change her thinking to end this terrible term of horror. She told us, "When you turn on the light, the light will eat the bogeyman up! And he will go away!"

Now this was believable! No more bogeyman! He's all gone!

Come to think of it, no one had ever seen this creature. Our uncles told us this lie as a scare tactic, and that it would frighten the living day-lights out of us and force us into good behavior.

If Dad had only kept a little light burning at night, it would have made my childhood fears a little bearable. He had a light! What was he afraid of, the bogeyman?

CHAPTER 46

Granny Annie Comes to Live with Us

Our Grandmom, Annie Williams -1963   Grandpop John Williams
Around 1939

S hortly after Dad married our stepmom, his mother moved in. She
was old as long as I could remember. Granny didn't have a birth
certificate, so there was no record of her age. Her insurance man figured
her to be roughly seventy-five years old, give or take a few years, when

she came to live with us. She was almost ninety-five when she died. My granny never went to school, so she never learned to spell her name, Annie Elizabeth Williams. Several of us tried to teach her, but she would always say, "I'm too old to learn. It doesn't matter none."

When I was in the fourth grade, I tried to teach her the alphabet. But the next day she would forget what she had learned. So all her life she signed her name with an X. That's how most people signed their name when they couldn't read or write. However, she did know how to count her money.

Years later, Granny's life would inspire me to write a children's story called *Wake up Granny, It's Time to Go to School*.

When I was in the first grade, I invited Granny to go to school with me. I could hardly wait to show her off to all my classmates. Because she walked slowly, with a cane, we left earlier than my usual time. She never went to school, and had no idea what it would be like to be in a classroom filled with little kids. She was so funny!

She laughed at the kids and made silly faces at them. She went to the restroom and blew it up. One kid went in after her and ran out holding his nose and yelling, "It stinks in there." Granny just laughed it off.

My teacher Mrs. Sutton was so nice to her and called her Mrs. Williams. Granny liked that and felt really special and respected. Granny kept asking me, "When is lunchtime! I'm hungry." She decided to leave before lunch and my teacher asked her if she wanted me to walk her back home. But Granny insisted she'd be all right and that she knew the way home.

By the time I left school at 3:30, she had not gotten home yet. I spied her sitting in someone's yard. She stopped to have lunch with an old white man she hardly knew. But he knew our father and that was okay with her. Granny enjoyed herself that day.

For some time, I tried walking with her to keep her from stiffening up, but sometimes she just flat-out refused to go. As young as I was, I would clip her toenails, wash her hair, empty her slop bucket, and other chores that she wasn't able to do for herself.

Even though our house was tiny, Granny was given her own bedroom that she shared with me. I loved sleeping with Granny. It was quiet and she always woke me up before she retired to her chamber.

She didn't have much money. She got her husband's pension check, which was only $37 a month, and she gave Dad half of that, leaving her with hardly enough to live on. After she paid her monthly insurance premium of about $2, she had very little left. She bought hair grease, Pall Mall cigarettes, liverwurst, potato chips, cream cheese, Anacin for her heart, a few spools of thread, and Helps, which was a throat lozenge. Oh, and she always saved money for Pepsi. Once in a while her grandsons, Uncle Johnny's boys, would stop by and give her a few dollars, and that made her feel very special.

Granny loved to smoke and her brand was Pall Mall, twenty-seven cents a pack. Every first of the month, Dad went to her bedroom to collect the rent.

Every morning before I went to school, I would make Granny a cup of hot coffee and a piece of buttered toast. That was her breakfast. She always sipped her coffee from the saucer to cool it down. Then she would comb my hair and put it in a ponytail with a rubber band, which broke my hair off terribly. Because of the arthritis in her fingers, she wasn't able to braid my hair. But she did the best she could. Every day she'd ask me, "Kat, how do you want your hair fixed today?" But every day it was the same! Ponytail time!

Our stepmom had left Dad again and this time for over six months. When she returned, she had to nurse my hair back to its original state. It took a long time!

Granny was a quilter and she sewed every quilt by hand. Because there wasn't a lot of room to work in her bedroom, she made little lap quilts. She'd cut up old cotton calico and solid cloths and cut out patches and sew them together. Before I left for school, I would thread about ten needles for her, because she couldn't see that well. Sometimes I would tease her and say, "Granny, stop faking." But now I know!

Granny could have had glasses if Dad had enough compassion to take the time to help her get some. Sometimes I feel so bad when I remember what she had to go through. She could barely focus looking at the television. But she had good ears!

My two sisters were carrying her one day and dropped her. She hurt her hip and was in so much pain that Mom insisted that Dad call old Doc Davis. He examined her and said that she fractured her hip, and for a very long time she walked with a slight limp. But Granny was resilient and bounced back. When I was twelve years old, I could carry her all by myself. I'd bring her in the living room and put her on the sofa to get some sunshine. She liked that. Granny and I had something in common. We both had a black mole on our left leg in the same, exact place.

It just seems that more could have been done for our grandmother.

Granny had a lot of visitors who would come and congregate in her living quarters. Needless to say, they brought some un-favored little insects with them. Bedbugs or chinches, as they were called back in the day. Our bed was infested with these bloodsucking creatures.

Every night I woke up covered with nasty, itchy welts. I would tell Mom and Dad the next day, but by then the itching and welts had disappeared. They were invisible during the day. But as soon as the lights were out at night, they started munching on me again. Granny put cold, wet washcloths on me to stop the burning and itching, but that didn't help. And no one would believe me! But Granny did.

Late one night I woke up crying and went to Mom and Dad's bedroom for some rubbing alcohol. One look at me and Daddy jumped out of bed. "Oh, my Lord," he kept saying. Mom ran to the bathroom for the Witch Hazel. Dad had a nearly empty bottle of rubbing alcohol in their bedroom, which he doused all over me. I looked at myself in the dresser mirror while they rubbed me down. I wanted to scream. I looked like a monster from outer space. I had welts on top of welts and my face was swollen beyond recognition. I didn't even look like myself. The welts had covered my entire body. Come to think of it, the bed bugs never bothered Granny. They wanted young, sweet blood. They fed on me at night, and by morning there was no evidence.

After the burning and itching stopped, Mom put me on the living room couch to sleep.

The next morning, which was a Saturday, Dad appeared to be angry at his mother for not telling him how bad the bugs were. He hauled the mattress outside to the backyard and sprayed it down with insect spray to kill the bugs. He was angry seeing his child's bloodstains all over the mattress, where Granny had smashed the bugs with her fingers.

After airing it out for a day or so, he brought the mattress back in. That night I fell asleep comfortably.

I wasn't asleep too long before these bugs came back with a vengeance and a furious appetite. I got a blanket and slept on the couch. The next day after work, Dad got another mattress and burned the infested one. Stepmom vacuumed and scrubbed everything down with Pine-Sol.

After El and Ret got married, I moved to the back bedroom and had my own bed. Yeah!

Dad thought he was a doctor and he performed many operations on anybody who trusted him to operate. Granny had a bizarre cyst behind both of her ears that were growing bigger. Daddy decided that it was unsightly and wanted them gone. He sat her in the chair in the middle of the living room, where we all gathered around to see the surgery take place. With a straight-edged razor, cotton balls, and alcohol, he began his operation. Granny kept screaming, "Ow! Wiggy! That hurts!"

"Hold still, Mama!" Dad told her. Then he cut some more with his straight-edged razor, which he sharpened on his leather razor strap. No sterilizing!

Oh, my gosh! When he took it out, the cyst looked like raw hamburger. It was absolutely the grossest thing I ever saw. She bled for a while, then Dad stitched her up with needle and thread. She had another smaller cyst on the other side of her ear, but she said, "Don't touch that one. Wiggy, please don't!"

So Dad took pity and left it alone, saying, "It's too small anyway."

Poor Granny, she had had enough of his bogus doctoring. Dad always loved an audience, whatever the cost to his victims.

My uncle was stabbed once, and Dad sewed him up with black thread and a needle. Probably what saved my uncle from going berserk was the fact that he was drunk.

Another incident with Dr. Daddy Williams was when I stepped on a rusty nail. Dad had a pink salve or ointment that he used for everything like cuts, burns, bee stings, mosquito bites, and any and all types of sores. Sometimes we kids would indulge on its sweet flavor.

We had an old junk and woodpile in our backyard. We didn't realize what a hazard it was, but dad forbade us to go near it. There were boards with rusty nails sticking out, old rusty items with sharp edges, and whatever else was thrown away would end up on the woodpile. Oh yes! He was also a junk man for a while.

One day I was playing near the woodpile and got a little bit too close to it. So close that I was jumping up and down on the rusty-nail-riddled wooden planks.

Billy and I were just singing "I'll Fly Away Oh Glory" when all of a sudden I felt something go through my shoe and I felt a crunch.

"A nail!" I screamed. "I stepped on a nail!"

My little brother Billy ran to the house to get Dad, who had just got home from work. Even though my foot and shoe were soaked with blood, I was more scared of Dad's anger. I knew that I had disobeyed him.

He picked me up and took me into the house and Mom washed it in warm water and Epsom salts. *Dum-dee-dum-dum!* The operation proceeded!

When Dad started probing around the nail puncture to pick out the fragments of rust, I cried and carried on something awful, until he brought out the pink salve. That's when my face lit up. As he applied this delicious-tasting ointment on my foot, I started to feel much better. I couldn't let him know that I liked the taste; he never knew that his kids were eating it. He'd just go to the drugstore and buy more.

"Okay, does it hurt now?" he asked me.

"No, Dad, it feels much better," I said.

I stepped down and started to limp across the kitchen floor, and with one big smack of his enormous hand across my butt, he said, "Stay away from that woodpile! Do I make myself clear?"

A tetanus shot was out of the question. Dad relied on his highly qualified medical skills and his pink salve. No tasting it this time!

Getting back to Granny, she would receive letters from her only daughter Helen, who lived to be 100 years old, passing away in 2016.

Years ago, Aunt Helen lived in Baltimore and her daughters would write letters to Granny. In return, my sisters would write back. This helped Granny to stay in touch with her daughter and her family.

When she was little, her mother died and Granny went to live with her aunt, who was very cruel to her. Her father left her with her aunt and took her little brother Amos with him, and she never saw them again. When she was old enough, she left Washington D.C. and moved to Philadelphia, where she met and married Grandpop John Williams. They had six children, two of which were stillborn, John Jr. being the eldest, Helen, William (our father), and David.

We loved listening to her tell stories about her childhood and growing-up years. Some were funny and some were sad. One of her sad stories was not being allowed to go to school. During those days, many black children and few whites ever attended school. If their parents needed help with finances or the farm work, school would be out of the question. She often talked about how she was once chased by a white man who tore her clothes off, but thank God she got away. She would tell us girls, "Always be careful out there."

We loved to kid around with her. We would tell her, "Hey, Granny, guess what? Abraham Lincoln just died."

Then Granny would say, "Oh yeah? I guess I'm next!" We would crack up laughing at her because Lincoln had died over 100 years ago. Our Granny was dead serious, too!

She shared stories about the Great Depression, and how everything was saved, things that we would throw away like old cast-off clothing, which she knew how to recycle.

"Give me that dress, Gal. I'll use that in my quilt!" she'd say, and she would.

I learned a lot from Granny Annie and would take heed to her stories.

Granny loved to play dominoes and checkers, and she was good at it. Her favorite TV programs were *The Tonight Show Starring Johnny Carson*, *Sally Star*, *The Beverly Hillbillies*, and *General Hospital*. And of course, the five o'clock news with Walter Cronkite. He must had been her secret TV lover, and Johnny Carson made her smile, too.

Shortly before the show was canceled, I wished that our grandmother could have been on that show called *Queen for a Day*. As a contestant, she would have won, hands down.

Granny sent me to the store one day to get a head of cabbage. Dick, the store owner, picked out the prettiest head of cabbage he could find and said, "Your granny will love this. It's only twelve cents a pound." And it was huge!

I bought the cabbage and ran home to tell Granny what he said. She was so pleased.

"I'm gonna make some ham and cabbage for dinner tonight!" she told me. It was hard for her to cut that big cabbage, so I held it while she cut off chunks.

After I got home from school, dinner was ready. It was so good! Everybody liked it. Ham and cabbage with cornbread. When Dad found out that she cooked it, he forbade her to cook anymore. "All right, Wiggy, I won't," Granny said. She went to her room and cried. And she never cooked again.

"Dad! Why are you so mean to your mother?" I wanted to say out loud. "She was only trying to help cook us a good dinner." There was no reasoning with that man!

Sometimes I think he had mental issues!

CHAPTER 47

Stormy Weather!

I was in the first grade again; I went to school half day because the two schools were so overcrowded. It was so crowded that they had to use several churches in town to accommodate all the children. I attended the Clinton Elementary School. I went from 12:00 p.m. to 4:00 p.m.

And my granny would make sure I got there on time, always leaving the house by 11:30. I remember running back and forth in the kitchen to see where the hands on the clock where, then I'd run back and tell her.

"It's not time yet," she'd always say.

It happened to be very windy and rainy that day and our teacher said that they were calling our parents to come and pick us up early. I watched the students leave one by one as they hugged our teacher good-bye. I kept looking outside, wondering when she would let me go, because I knew no one would come to pick me up. My stepmother had left us for a short time.

There was a little boy who lived right next door to us, and his friend's mother gave him a ride home. So I waited and waited some more. There were a couple of kids still waiting for their parents to arrive. But at least they had a ride.

Finally my teacher said to me, "I guess no one is coming for you, Kathleen. I'm going to let you go home, but you'll have to hurry home. The weather is bad!"

If only she had let me go earlier.

I put on my bandana (head scarf), buttoned my coat, and headed for home.

Before I could get a few blocks away from the school, it started pouring. The gusty winds turned into practically a tornado. It seemed like every step I took the wind would push me back two more steps. The sky was getting darker and I could hardly see in front of me. I turned onto New Street, where the side of the Cedar Green Cemetery is, and it got worse. My head scarf got blown off my head and the rain was stinging my face. I passed Mom's gravesite and prayed for her to protect me. It seemed like it took forever to walk past the Cemetery to get to the football field. But I kept going. Before I passed the ball field I tried to run, but my bony little legs wouldn't move. I noticed a few cars slowing down, but no one had time or wanted to stop to help me. I was virtually all alone.

When I turned the corner of Vine Street, the wind seemed to change direction again, so I walked backward for a little while. I was too scared to cry. All I wanted was to get home. When I finally got home, it was nearly dark and everyone was sitting and watching the snowy-screened television, as usual. Dad came in a little while after I did, and I heard him ask, "Did Kat get home yet?"

I was cold and soaked through and through, but happy to be home. I laid down and fell asleep on my sister Ida's bed.

I will never forget that scary day when I walked alone and the Good Lord watched over me and got me safely home.

CHAPTER 48

The School Dentists Return

The Mobile Unit Dentist Program would visit our school every other year. It was a big, long truck that most kids weren't anxious to see. This program provided dental services for the less-fortunate children whose parents couldn't afford the regular office visits.

First, you were given a consent form by the school nurse to take home to be signed and returned. A few weeks later the mobile truck would arrive. All the kids would get free dental work done. It seemed like all the black or poor white children were recipients of this service. After your examination you would come back for cleaning or fillings. Then you got a toothbrush, toothpaste, and a pretty cheesy ring that fell apart almost immediately.

All of my fillings lasted for many years until they needed to be replaced. I guess I had a lot of cavities back then.

CHAPTER 49

The Lovely Chicken Coop

We didn't have very many toys. Only what people would give us like hand-me-downs, or sometimes we'd pick trash. Dad didn't believe in frivolous things like toys. But we did have a playhouse, better known as the "Chicken Coop," that our stepmom had brought with her when she moved in. She wanted to raise chickens like she did before marrying Dad.

It was a heavy-duty little house that was pitched with black tar to waterproof the outside. It had a large window and two steps in front of the broken door. We took out the hen boxes and turned it into a chicken palace. Mom gave us curtains, some old beat-up pots and pans, a few cinder blocks for little stools, or whatever we could use to set up housekeeping.

Bert, Ida, and I spent hours of fun decorating, cleaning it daily, and making mud pies for each other or for our playmates who lived down the street. Some of those kids were envious of the playhouse and tried to wreck it.

Ida would make the biggest and prettiest mud cakes and pies you ever seen. She taught us how to grind red brick for frosting and use flowers and seeds to garnish them. We spent hours pretending to bake and buy from each other. Ida would pretend to send us to a fake store to buy eggs, milk, and sugar. Then she'd holler and tell us to go back and get some vanilla because she couldn't make her cakes without it. "Go back," she'd say. Then she'd give us little pebbles for money.

We enjoyed planting wild flowers without the roots. Just dig a hole and put them in the ground. Next morning they were all shriveled up and bent over. Then we'd do it again. Our stepmom saw that we were serious about these flowers growing, so she gave us zinnias that we planted along the driveway, and she taught us how to transplant them with the roots. They grew and started to bloom until…somebody paid us a visit.

They tore up our little house, overturned our cakes and pies, ripped the curtains off the window, killed all the flowers, and threw dirt and mud everywhere. We knew exactly who did that dirty deed!

Shortly after the vandalism of our playhouse, Dad took an axe to it and tore it down. His reason was, the roof was wobbly and it might cave in. The real reason was instead of raising more chickens, he wanted to grow a big garden, and our playhouse was in his way. Well, it was fun while it lasted!

Another time we were going to the garden where my father had rented some land from an old lady named Mother Ray who lived on Vine Street. It was about one and a half acres of very fertile land. Dad worked hard in the garden and Mom would work in it, as well. One evening when the sun wasn't as hot, Mom took us to pick veggies in the garden. Dad grew string beans, tomatoes, okra, black-eyed peas, lima beans, peanuts, beets, cantaloupes, and lots of watermelons. Mom taught him how to grow this stuff, because she was the one who had the green thumb.

Mom told us to put on long sleeves and hats or scarves. The garden was about a quarter mile away.

We saw this same kid who wrecked our playhouse, riding his bike; we knew him.

Mom said, "Don't talk or pay any attention to him."

So we didn't.

He asked us, "Where yawl gone, to the cotton fields? Yawl a bunch of cotton pickers? Ha-ha-ha!"

We kept walking, carrying our garden hoe, rakes, baskets, and water jug. Ready to work!

He watched us from afar, then sped off.

The next day Dad came home from work and said, "Someone went into our garden and tore it up! They threw watermelons in the street and busted them open. Tomatoes were thrown everywhere. Even the green ones. I wish I could catch the rotten skunk who did it."

We had a pretty good idea who had done it. But we would have had to catch him in the act.

CHAPTER 50

Ice Cream on Clayton Avenue

One lazy afternoon, a pickup truck hauling all kinds of ice cream came to our neighborhood. The driver had to get rid of a whole freezer full of ice cream from the A&P in Glassboro, NJ. The freezer broke down and they had to get rid of everything ASAP.

Someone told them about our neighborhood and the man came to deliver it.

I happened to be outside playing that day and heard and saw a lot of commotion down the street. People were running, yelling, and laughing. Some were carrying big pots and clothes baskets filled with something that I couldn't really see.

Someone saw me and yelled, "Kat, you'll better come and get some of this ice cream. It's free so hurry up before it melts! And bring something to carry it in."

Well, I took off running to our front door and told Mom and the rest of my family.

"Hey ya'll, there's a man down the street with a truck full of free ice cream. Get the clothes basket. Hurry," I said.

Well, we didn't get as much as everyone else, but we had plenty. Even the dogs were liking half gallons of ice cream.

There were novelties like ice cream sandwiches, cones, Dixie cups, Eskimo Pies, Twin Pops, orange cream cycles, and half gallons, pints, and quarts of every kind of flavor. We were so blessed to get whatever we could get.

Mister Softee would come around to our neighborhood but we were never allowed to buy anything. No money!

This ice cream giveaway was like a dream come true!

CHAPTER 51

Mom and Pop Stores

In our town, there were many mom and pop stores that carried different items, and you knew which store to get whatever you needed. Lots of men and women would visit our neighborhood to sell their wares long before the Acme was built. A big bus selling fresh fish came every Tuesday afternoon, at around four o'clock. He always had the same kind of fish—porgies, whiting's, butters—and sometimes fruits and vegetables. If he cleaned your fish, he would charge extra.

Dad always said, "No, we'll clean it." He taught me how to scale, gut, and clean the fish and I was good at it. My sisters would always rupture the fish's gull bladder, which would bitter the taste of the entire fish. Then somebody would fry the fish. Every Tuesday was fish night. We had fried potatoes, cornbread, fish, and a vegetable. I was about twelve years old when I started to learn to cook well.

The first time I peeled potatoes, at about nine years old, no one showed me how. I cut so much potato off on the peelings that there was hardly enough potato left. My dad fixed that problem right away. Somebody ratted on me and showed him my wasteful workmanship, and he yelled and threw the skins in my face. Well, I learned quickly after he made me cut the thick parts off the peelings.

Dad loved my pancakes because I made them from scratch, and they were huge. When our stepmom was with us, she made him salt mackerel fish nearly every Sunday morning. This was very bad for him, because he suffered from hypertension, and this fish was loaded with salt. Maybe this is why he yelled so much! His pressure was so high!

Getting back to the neighborhood vendors, there was the milkman, the egg man, the bread lady, the soda man, the junk man, the Avon lady, the watermelon man, the coal man, and insurance man, the fuller brush person, and the ragman, and oh yeah, Dad would sometimes get pastries and other freebies from whoever or wherever he could find them. He was a scavenger by trade!

One time he got free fish from a fish market in Glassboro. They were so small that you couldn't hold them to clean them. They just fell all apart. Other times, he got tough chicken, horse corn that you could hardly eat, and hundreds of cracked eggs. He managed to bring home huge snapper turtles that he found by the railroad tracks. He raised them for a few months, then butchered the poor things to make turtle soup for his compadres at work. Just fifteen cents a cup. He gave us the turtle eggs to take to school and sell them for five cents each. Or we'd bounce them like balls for pleasure.

CHAPTER 52

Daddy's Little Helper

I had many chores at nine years old. Our dad loved cars; in fact, he would get another car almost every two years so that people would think he had money. NOT!

He always made me clean out his car every Sunday morning, inside and outside, before church. He didn't want to see a speck of dust on it. He showed me how to do it one time, and that was all. It seems like I was raised to do all the outside work. His work!

If he worked in the garden, he called me to help. He taught me how to recognize each tiny vegetable plant from the weeds. And every day I had to water the plants, when it got hot, and no rainfall. He never wanted any of the others working in the garden because they would pull up the weeds with the plants. When the harvest was ready, they could pick. It seemed like everything got ripe at once. I still have some of his gardening tools.

Later on in life, I wrote a children's book called *Pa Pa's Working Tools*. It's all about my father and his many useful tools. In my story, my father has many jobs and tools. He was a gardener, worked on the railroad, a barber, a preacher, a handyman, and a doctor (unlicensed). All of which he had tools for. Every project he worked on, I was there watching and learning from him.

CHAPTER 53

Burning trash

When I was nine years old my father was working in the garden and I was outside burning trash in the incinerator. Dad always told me to never put glass or tin cans in the incinerator. Well, I accidently let a jar with a lid slip into the burning fire. After the fire got good and hot, a loud *POW* went off, sounding like a gun. Daddy ducked down with fear and started looking all around.

Staring at Dad I said, "I'm sorry, Dad. I think it was glass."

He looked at me with an evil sort of look and replied, "Girl, you're too dumb to live!"

I was crushed! Why would my father say such a wicked thing? I'm not dumb, and why did he say I shouldn't live just because I'm dumb? In my mind I asked him, *Dad, please don't call me dumb. It was just a mistake and it won't happen again.*

Needless to say, I began to feel dumb and that my life meant nothing to anybody, until years later, when I met the boy I would marry.

The strangest thing was, whatever he was doing he always wanted me to work beside him. He seemed to trust me and wanted to teach me to fix things. I wrote a children's story about my father, and how I would have wanted him to be. Loving, caring, gentle, peaceful, patient, affectionate, and generous; to show integrity and be physically strong. Well, one out of eight was what he was. He would have to work on the rest, but he was still my dad.

CHAPTER 54

Daddy, Get Your Gun!

Our father had a very bad temper, but sometimes his bark could do more harm than his bite. When my sister Elnora was a teenager, she made a bad choice by getting into a car with a few other kids, with one boy who was old enough to drive. It was dark outside and the car was parked in front of our house. Although Elly knew better, Dad hadn't made that a rule yet. Dad came home and noticed the parked car. He went to investigate and found his oldest daughter in the car, sitting and listening to music. Dad told her to get out of the car and get in the house.

The driver got smart with Dad and said, "Go in the house and mind you own business."

That's when Dad got mad, went in the house, and got his gun! Loaded! "Boy! You mess with me and I'll blow your head off! You better get away from my house!" had told him.

And with those words, the car, loaded with teenagers, sped off like a bat out of you know where!

We were afraid that Dad would fire at them, because he was that angry.

Elly came in the house crying, mainly because Dad embarrassed her. Little did she know that her father was protecting her.

CHAPTER 55

Linda Palmer

There was a little interracial girl who lived on Clayton Avenue, closer to town. Her name was Linda Palmer. She was a cute little curly head, with brown skin and brown eyes. She had a white family. She was sired by a black man in our neighborhood. My sister Loretta brought her home one day when she was coming home from downtown. Her mother let her go home with a total stranger. This little girl stayed all evening playing with us. We wondered when or if someone was coming to get her, but they didn't, so Loretta took her back home.

The very next day, early in the morning, she came back, all by herself. She was only four or possibly five years old, but her mom let her roam freely.

She had three elder brothers and a sister, but no one seemed concerned about her welfare. Her white father, or stepfather, was a quiet man who kept Linda around as a constant reminder to his wife, for her infidelity. But he was good to her.

Having a dysfunctional family, my father wanted my sister Elnora (who was married) to adopt Linda and take her away from some of these disturbed people she lived with.

We all loved her and was always willing to give her love and attention that she wasn't receiving at home. Billy and Anna were closer to her age than I was and they played a lot together. Her mom had monkeys as pets. It seemed as if the monkeys got more attention than Linda. I hated those stinking things. Linda's mother would bring the monkey to see us. One day she brought a big bag of marshmallows with her so that the monkey could hand them out to us. That was not cute! We were throwing them away as fast as that nasty monkey was handing them out. This monkey had diarrhea and pooped all over our curtains and sofa as it swung all over our living and dining room areas. Our mom was furious!

Many people said that Linda and I looked like we could be sisters. And it might be a possibility that Linda was our half-sister. But we didn't have the same mothers and I look nothing like my dad, but more like my mom. So for many years no one came forth until Linda's real father died.

Our stepmother would have several confrontations with her mom, and accuse Dad of having an affair with her.

People can be so cruel and heartless! They all went to their graves, while Linda was left in the dark, not knowing who her biological father really was.

Until a visitor came to reveal to her the highly guarded secret.

Linda's father, who lived right around the corner from us, was a member of this visitor's family. This poor little girl probably passed him on the street many times, not knowing he was her father. How sad!

Recently, I made contact with our childhood friend and we talked and reminisced about the past. I was shocked when she told me, but happy that her father wasn't my dad. Because he would have committed adultery. But she'll always be my sister in the Lord.

I love this girl, because she overcame so much heartache in her life and she is still standing.

GOD IS SO GOOD!

CHAPTER 56

Stolen Bag of Goodies

I was blessed with the ability to know when something was not quite right, to feel something was going to happen. My dreams were always coming true and sometimes they were my worst fears. It's like, I was thinking of someone and the phone would ring and it's the person I was just thinking of, calling me. Was this a gift?

We loved to go trick-or-treating. Dad didn't seem to mind as long as he could nibble on a few candy bars here and there. He was never home on Halloween night, anyway. We never had treats for other trick-or-treaters, either. As soon as it got dark, us kids were on the prowl all over Clayton. Bert, Ida, and I would hit the streets, gathering all kinds of goodies. Sometimes we had so much we would run home, empty our bags, and go out again. It didn't matter if you went to the same houses twice.

One year we were just about done and it was almost ten o'clock, which was curfew for trick-or-treaters.

"Let's take the shortcut home," Ida said.

We had to pass by the cemetery and I had a strange feeling that something was about to happen. It weighed on me heavily. "No, Ida,"

I begged. "I don't want to. Because something will happen. Please, Ida, don't make me go," I kept begging her.

She said, "Are you afraid to go by Mom's grave? Because you shouldn't be scared."

"No, I'm not scared of Mom's grave! I just don't feel right," I insisted.

"Oh, come on!" she said and grabbed my hand.

We were almost halfway past the cemetery when three or four white teenage boys came running toward us, screaming their heads off. "Boo! Boo! Get 'em! Get their bags!"

Well, Ida and Bert took off running like lightning. I couldn't keep up with them because my too-big hand-me-down shoes were coming off, so I had to slow down. Under the streetlight, I could see the face of a pimple-faced white boy, who ran up to me and snatched my bag, then they all ran back into the cemetery to feast on my Halloween treats.

I was crying so hard when Bert and Ida ran back to get me. "They got my bag, Ida. I told you something bad was gonna happen!" That was my first premonition.

No chocolate candy that Halloween!

I did get some penny Taffy's from my sisters, who didn't want them, anyway. And Linda Palmer's older brother Arnold gave me some of his. Yikes! Scary dude!

CHAPTER 57

Oh No! My Face Is Spotty!

For nearly three years, I suffered from skin discolorations on my face. Every summer leading into fall, I anticipated its return. It started with a small white spot that turned into a blotchy mess over my entire face, turning my pretty brown complexion into the face of horrors. And some people were afraid to come near me. I should have screamed, "Unclean! Unclean! Stay away! Unclean!"

I felt ugly and contaminated! And of course everyone noticed. How could they not?

Some adults who were very insensitive toward my feelings would call me names, like Spotty, or said I had leprosy. My father said I ate too many sweets and took my sweet tooth away from me. "I better not catch you eating anything sweet!" he'd say.

I began to stay away from my playmates because they stared a lot. If I went to the store, the white folks would stare in disbelief and move away from me. I was without a doubt the ugliest girl in the world, and it seemed like no one cared. Dad never took me to the doctors. That would be unheard of to spend a dime on a rash.

·

Mom thought she had a good remedy. She put a copper penny in a cup of vinegar and let it set for a few days. Then I would rub it on my face three times a day.

It didn't work!

Then tiny bumps started showing up on my face, which formed a perfect circle with a soft center. Mom said it was ringworms, and that I would have this, as well, for several years.

"Oh, my gosh! What will I get next?" I said to her.

"Oh, Chile', you be all right," she told me.

After three years of this continuous torture, I thought that I would start praying to God. He would help me. I knew it and believed it. And He did! My face cleared up and the white spots and ringworm rashes never returned. I was twelve years old.

Thank you, Heavenly Father, for making me clean again!

CHAPTER 58

Janet Harris, My BFF

The first time I saw my best friend Janet Lynn Harris, she and her brother were on their way to school. We were in the fifth grade but different classrooms. I knew they were new kids because I had never seen them before. After lunch, I looked for them on the playground and found her. I introduced myself and we became friends immediately.

She told me where she lived; I was overjoyed to learn that they lived right around the corner from me. Through the fifth and sixth grades, we would walk to school together and share our most-guarded childhood secrets. In the seventh grade, we became partners in crime. Nothing bad, just silliness. Some of the pranks we pulled were so crazy, like drawing pictures on the blackboard of the students, just to make people laugh. Or asking the one teacher, Mr. B, a stupid question, just to get a rise out of him. He thought we were nuts.

Back in the day, slang books were popular and just about every student had one. A slang book was a composition book with names of the students in your class. You signed your name on the first page. If you signed your name by the number seven, then your page was page 7. It was sort of like your own page on today's Facebook page. Then everyone would sign something nice about you on your page. We'll, it got nasty. Some kids would curse, lie, and slander each other. The teachers started confiscating these books and some kids got detentions for having them in their possessions. This was not for us! And we didn't have time for that kind of foolishness. We had other devious antics up our sleeves.

It was a trend to call students by your parents' names. The girls by their father's name and the boys by their mother's name. Lord have mercy! When the kids found out that my father's name was Wiggy, there was no stopping them. My name went from Kathleen Williams to Wiggy Williams immediately.

I knew who told them. It was Beaky Buzzard, a nasty-mouth white boy with big, frog-looking eyes and a long beak for a nose. He used to play with us when we were little and my uncle Dave gave him that nickname many years ago, and I was the only one in my class who knew it. Plus, he was one of the nasty boys who chased me home from the grocery store. It's payback time, Buddy! I fixed him really good! Need I say more?

I don't think they ever found out about Janet's dad's name. I didn't even know it. Ha-ha-ha!

Janet and I were inseparable. We did everything together for a long time, until I met David, and now it was time for me to act like a young, mature lady.

The first time I had a glimpse of this kid named David, it was at Janet's fourteenth birthday party. He and his homeboys had come to crash the party. They were asked to leave because Janet's mom, Miss Henrietta, said they were too old to be there, and of course they weren't invited. He never noticed me because I was at the party with another fella.

Janet was dating David's brother William, who was at the party, dancing on his toes, like James Brown.

That summer I would see him again while working in the blueberry field.

In 1963, Janet and I joined the Glee Club. I don't think she wanted to join. It was only half credit per year. But it was added to your senior final grade, as an extracurricular, to boost your credits.

Poor Janet, my friend, my best bud, I didn't realize she had missed me so much. And I missed her, as well. Years later we reunited, talking and laughing over every conversation of crazy things we did during our youth. She came to my fiftieth birthday party, and that's when our lives were rekindled. I always tell people who lose contact with friends, "Once you have found them, never let them go."

We are best friends forever!

CHAPTER 59

The Birds Are Coming!

There were times when food was scares and the cupboards were nearly bare. Our stepmom, or Mob, as we started calling her, had the perfect solution. Someone came up with the nickname Mob. It was short for Moby Dick, the big, white whale. She never knew we called her that because we never called her that to her face.

Anyway, we had metal crab cages that were the perfect traps for black birds and squirrels. She would rig up several cages with bread inside, and when the birds went in, bam! Got cha!

She caught birds all day long with her sidekick Ida, who wasn't afraid of anything. After a while, Ida caught three or four birds at a time. She would bring them in the house and Mob would have a pot of boiling water on the stove waiting. She would wring their little necks and drop them in the pot to loosen the feathers. She would spread newspaper on the kitchen table and pluck off their feathers, burn off the little hairs, gut and clean them, season them, and throw them in a pot to cook.

I hated seeing those tiny birds being tortured and cooked, and I was determined not to eat any.

That night when we were at the dinner table, Dad asked what was for dinner. Mob put a big bowl of fluffy white rice on the table and another pot filled with little carcasses floating around in white gravy.

"What's that?" Daddy grunted with his nostrils flaring.

"Dem birds, Wiggy," she blurted.

"What do you mean by 'birds'?" he asked her.

"The kind that fly outside," she said and laughed.

"You must be a crazy woman!" he yelled, and pushed his plate away. He was like a wild man who couldn't believe he had married such an ignorant woman.

Mob laughed at him and continued to suck on those itty-bitty bones.

That night I ate rice and margarine for dinner!

The next day Phyllis brought home a dead pigeon that was full of lice and other bugs. Mom left that bird alone.

This lady was fearless! We had a truant officer who lived practically in our backyard. And when his car wasn't home, Mom went bird catching. Sometime later, Mom found out about the government surplus food program, or relief, as most folks called it. She found out through the neighbors that all you had to do was sign up and you could get lots of food to feed your family. One night she and Miss Stitch, our neighbor, went to the Borough Hall to collect.

She came back with government cheese, peanut butter, Spam, powdered milk, butter, canned chicken and beef, lard, powdered eggs, canned fruits and vegetables, oatmeal, and sometimes juice was given out to the poor people to supplement their income.

Mom had struck it rich and she was proud of her accomplishment. We were eating like kings, or should I say queens and a little prince. Mom made so many different dishes that we loved.

Dad found out about this free food and he put his foot down. He wasn't taking any charity from anybody. He told her that if she went again, she would be sorry!

My stepmom was so hurt. She couldn't do anything right in his eyes, even if it was for the best for his children.

Mom said, "I'm tired of this nonsense. I'm getting a job!" That's exactly what she did. She got four or five jobs, cleaning houses for the white folks. They loved her and would often ask her to cook and serve at their parties. She was always coming home with great stuff to share with her kids. She was the "Help."

She started to bond with me more, and after about three years the beatings finally stopped! I was around ten years old, and I might add that the beatings haunted me for years. Why? When Mom became independent, she stopped caring about what Dad thought. She saved her money and got a bank account. She wanted her driver's license badly and she worked hard on getting them. She contacted a driving school, took the oral and road test, and before long, "Heavens to Murgatroyd," as Snagglepuss on the Yogi Bear cartoon would say, she got her license. "Exit! Stage right! Let's go, Kids!"

We went everywhere with her. To the "Main Line," in Pennsylvania, where her sister lived. She chauffeured us to Cow Town, shopping, swimming, skating, school, and any place she knew how to get to.

One summer day, Mom took us to Franklinville Lake to swim. Phyllis went too far out into the water and was sinking. She didn't know how to swim. None of us did. We could all see her but didn't know exactly what to do. Mom screamed from the bank of the lake for me, Bert, and Ida to go out and get her. Ida told us to form a chain and go out and get her. We did and Ida caught hold of Phil while Bert and I pulled them in. Phyllis was full of water, but nothing in her lungs.

"Phyllis," Mom said, "I told you not to go out to the danger spots where they have it roped off. You didn't listen to me with your hardheaded self. You was lucky this time, so let this be a lesson to you."

Thanks to Ida, we saved Phyllis's life.

Before we left, our stepmother warned us not to tell Dad about what happened. "Your daddy won't let me take you kids anywhere anymore."

So we all promised not to tell him.

She saved her money and purchased a car all by herself. She wasn't going to let Wiggy Williams dictate to her about when, where, and how to drive her car. Her little two-tone Chevy that jerked us around when she let off the clutch too soon. We would laugh at her and she would get mad and say, "Shut up, you Degu's!" Mom was independent and she didn't need any man to take care of her. No, siree!

Before they got married she bought beds for the two back bedrooms. She cleaned our house beyond recognition and purchased all new curtains for every room. Plastic flowered curtains were on parade!

She taught us to always display our best manners, and how to act like young ladies. She continued what our real mom had started.

Our stepmom began to clean up the awful mess Miss Em had left behind. Rats, roaches, and anything that could invade our home. It felt good living in a nice, clean house again.

She woke up all the bed-wetter's every night at around 11:30 until we kicked the habit and learned to get up by ourselves. After all that she had done for us, my father never bought so much as a dress for her. I don't recall him giving her anything that was personal.

CHAPTER 60

My Teacher, My Friend

When I was in the fifth grade I would come home for lunch. I had to run all the way because I only had an hour. The school was about two miles away. By the time I got home it was time to head back. I gobbled down my hot soup and homemade roll and Mom would give me a few sugar cookies to eat on the way back. This went on for a few weeks—and I was so tired.

My teacher Mrs. Frye asked me where I lived; when I told her, she said it was much too far for me to go home each day for lunch. She got me a job in the cafeteria, drying dishes, and I got a free lunch. She made sure I didn't miss any lessons, and I only worked for a half hour.

When my stepmom started working, she got a job working for my teacher. My teacher had no idea that I was her daughter until she asked Mom about her last name, which was the same as mine, and a few other Williams's girls she had taught. Mrs. Frye somehow put it all together and asked if she had a daughter named Kathleen.

Mom said, "Oh, she my daughter. She in the fifth grade."

With all this information, Mrs. Frye and I began to bond right away. I loved her.

On the second or third day of school, Mrs. Frye was trying to put her reading groups together. There were the red birds, blue birds, yellow birds, and black birds. I remember the four reading groups because I was with the black birds. This group was for the extremely slow readers.

One day, we gathered in our reading circle and our teacher called on each child to read. I knew this book because my sisters would bring it home from year to year. There was a poem that I loved, so when the time came, I raised my hand to volunteer to read.

"Okay, Kathleen, do you want to give it a try?" she asked me.

With that, I began reading.

"THE CAT IN THE YARD"

The cat in the yard is out sleeping
The duck has gone down for a swim
My pony comes strutting right up to the gate,
He knows I have carrots for him.

I read this poem with emotion and feeling, because I knew it by heart. My teacher looked at me, jumped up, and ran out into the hallway to talk to some teachers. Two of them were peeking in the window and appeared to be pointing in my direction and staring at me.

Mrs. Frye came back in to the classroom and asked me to continue reading the next page. I froze! I couldn't read!

Question, how do you continue to promote a child to the next grade knowing that they have a reading or learning problem? How did I get to the fifth grade?

That's the way it was!

Mrs. Frye talked to me after school. She said, "Kathleen, you are going to learn how to read. We will work together about twenty minutes a day, during recess."

Every day, after I ate my lunch, I would go back to the classroom and she would teach me. In just a few months, I was promoted to another reading group! This was our secret!

I had another problem, this time with math. I didn't know all of my math tables. So Mrs. Frye sent me across the hall to the fourth-grade class to learn. I got to sit with my best friend who lived in our neighborhood, Terry Jackson. We sat together and she made me feel really special. Sometimes we walked home from school together and recited the hard tables.

I learned very fast and was rambling off those math tables like I never had a problem.

Whenever we had a class trip or parties, my teacher paid for me to go. She purchased all of my school supplies, and of course, this helped me to build up myself esteem. From time to time, she talked to my mother about my progress; no one ever knew that my mom worked for my teacher.

CHAPTER 61

Sixth Grade

My mom would take me to school every day before she went to work. There were a bunch of my classmates lined up by the fence, waiting for our teacher to come out and escort us to class. Several white boys saw me kiss mom good-bye, get out of the car, and wave back to her. They asked me who she was and I replied, "She's my mom."

Well, those boys laughed so hard. "Kathleen has a white mother," they kept saying.

Before long, most of the kids were taunting me. I didn't tell my teacher because I knew they would keep doing it when she wasn't around. When I got home, I told Mom about it. She was as proud as a peacock, hearing that the kids thought she was a white lady.

"Dat ain't nothing, Chile'. Everybody think I'm white," she said, laughing.

The next day, the mischievous boys were waiting for me and my "white mother." I didn't kiss her good-bye this time, because I didn't want to be teased again. That didn't matter to them because they found a soft-hearted cry baby—I always wore my heart on my sleeve. Naturally!

That afternoon when I got home from school, my mom asked me, "Why didn't you kiss me good-bye today?"

I wanted to tell a lie (or fib, as we called it) and say I forgot, but she knew why.

"Are you ashamed of me?" she asked.

"No, Mom," I said. "They just keep laughing at me and saying you're a white lady. And it hurts my feelings because my skin is darker than yours."

She hugged me and said, "Kafrin (that's how she pronounced my name), they just jealous, Honey! You keep kissing me good-bye and they will stop."

And sure enough, they stopped.

Yes, bullies existed back in those days, too.

CHAPTER 62

The Big-Game Hunter

D ad thought he was a great hunter! Sometimes he'd come home with little, pitiful squirrels with pellets embedded in their bodies. After they were skinned and cleaned, you could count the holes. He never shot anything larger than a squirrel. He claimed to be a small-game hunter.

One night as I was sleeping on my now tiny fold-up cot, an animal made its way into our bedroom. Ida went into the bathroom, spied the critter, and ran frantically out of the room.

I slept undisturbed. After Ida told Dad what she was very adamant about, Dad went to get his riffle! Finally, he would get some big game! And right in his own house!

"Are you sure it wasn't a rabbit or a raccoon?" he asked again.

"No, Daddy! I saw it and it was black with a white tail. It looked at me and walked under the bed!"

Well, I happened to be sleeping on that bed.

He cocked the double-barrel shotgun and opened fired right under my bed, while I was sleeping. He didn't know if he hit it or not, but out came the big black-and-white critter, bleeding with its tail up and spraying right in my direction. Oh, my Lord!

The stench was everywhere! All over the house! In every crack and crevice. This horrible odor would stay on me for a couple of days. The scary part of it was, Dad didn't know I was in bed asleep. Until someone screamed, "Kat's in there!" He just opened fired! *Boom!*

Mom said, "Wiggy, you should have let the skunk leave the same way he came in."

Then to top it off, he made poor Ida pick up the bloody skunk and take it out to be buried it in the morning. Dad was a real coward! Somebody said Mom would have been a better shot than Dad, but that's another story. So much for that big-game hunter!

Mom lit sulfur candles all over the house. She washed my hair in tomato juice, washed my bedcovers, scrubbed the floor with pine oil soap, but nothing could take away that horrible smell.

The next day when I went to school, embarrassed, afraid, and nauseous, the kids turned up their noises and moved their desks far away from me.

"She stinks!"

"Ooh, she smells like a skunk!"

I was so ashamed. I wanted to hide my face and cry, and I did.

My sixth-grade teacher had to agree with them. I did stink!

She asked me what happened and I told her the whole story, how my dad shot a skunk under my bed where I was sleeping, and that it sprayed me.

"YOUR FATHER DID WHAT? OH, MY LORD!" she blurted; she put up her hand and covered her mouth.

Some of the kids started laughing.

I often wondered what she really thought but couldn't say about the situation. But I'll say it. "That was stupid!"

Because I was so close to the skunk, I think it damaged my sense of smell, which affected my taste buds, as well. But after a couple of days, I was back to normal.

They use skunk musk in perfumes? That sounds comforting!

CHAPTER 63

Stepmom's Parents

O ur stepmom was a descendant of President William Henry Harrison, the ninth president of the United States, who was interracial. His father sired a son with a slave woman. Probably a mulatto. Although he looked white, he had Negro blood flowing in his veins.

Our mother would tell us all the time that President Harrison did not die from pneumonia during his inauguration, but was hung in the back of the White House, because he was of Negro descent.

Her family never wanted to expose what they knew for fear of getting into trouble, or disappearing, and not on their own accord. They often talked about the documents that were shared for many years under private family secrets, and they took all this information to their graves.

The first time I met our step-grandfather, I was in the second grade. I came home from school one day and saw an old white man sitting on our porch. I looked at him and then ran in the house to tell Mom.

She laughed and said, "That's my father, Chile'! She took me outside and introduced me to him. "Pop, this is Kat, another granddaughter. She go to school in the afternoon. She the last one for you to meet, 'cause you met all the rest."

I corrected her and said, "My real name is Kathleen."

The old man smiled and patted me on the head. "Kathleen," he said. "That's a pretty name."

That was the first and last time I would see her father, Walker Johnson.

Mom told us stories about how this man tarred and feathered his stepson Charlie for stealing a piece of leftover fly infested cornbread. And how her mother said or did nothing while this mad man performed this crazy act of violence. That was his punishment. Horrible!

This man just didn't look like he had a mean bone in his body, but in his younger years he was brutal. Mom said he was strict on his kids and beat them for everything. His family was from South Carolina, and just after the Civil War they all became sharecroppers in Virginia. Mom grew up in Virginia, and later, at the age of nineteen, she gave birth to a son named Donald Johnson. Mom moved from Virginia to Avondale, PA, where she met and married Nathan Brown, who died around the same time our mother did.

Mom's mother came to live with us for a while after her husband died. She was so scary! She was a little, hunched-over woman and looked exactly like a witch with long, white hair that she could sit on. She ate like a pig and would stay at the dinner table until every morsel of food was gone. She slept in the room with our granny and they got along well, until Grandma Johnson started calling up spirits every night. She kept Granny awake, talking in her sleep, passing gas, and spitting in her Clabber Girl Baking Powder can.

That was really nasty! Yuck!

Granny would say, "Woman, go to sleep and stop all that foolish talking. I done had enough of your mouth!"

She loved black jelly beans and that's about the only candy she would eat. Bags and bags of black sugar babies or black jelly beans. Licorice!

Her stories were really spooky! She always talked about her four-year-old daughter who told her one day, "Two white horses was coming down from Heaven today and take me away."

That same day her little girl fell down the well and drowned. They looked for her and found her in the well, head first with her dress floating on top. They got her out and laid her on the cooling board (a cooling board or slab of cement to lay the dead on) until they could bury her.

After a couple of months, she went to live with her other daughter Annie in PA. That was Grandma Johnson! One scary old woman!

CHAPTER 64

Fish in the Street?

It was the summer of 1961. My stepmother and sisters were working in the blueberry field and had to catch the work bus to Hammonton, NJ (the blueberry capital of the world). They left early in the morning and would return at around 5:30 p.m. This day they came back home within a half hour to get containers.

"FISH ARE IN THE STREET!"

They kept saying little fish were flopping around in the street! They brought some home in their thermoses and got water from a house nearby. We put them in tap water and they lived. All day long we sold them for five cents each to all the neighbors. My sisters said they must have come from the clouds in the sky, but I think a minnow fish tank was on a truck and spilled over.

However, it was the craziest thing you could ever see—fish flopping around in the wet street.

CHAPTER 65

It's My Bike!

When I was in the sixth grade, I walked home by myself because my sisters got out of school at around 2:30, and I at 3:15. One day, I took a different route by the football field. I spied a bicycle lying in the bushes by the side of the road. I looked at it and it appeared to be in good condition. The bike was close to a house where I knew the son and some of the family but never met them formally.

Every day I would pass by this bike to see if it was still there. Finally, after a several days passed, I got up enough courage to go to the house and see who this bike belonged to. I knocked on the side door and a cute little girl named Rita and her friend came and opened it.

"Hello," I said. "Is your mom home?

She didn't say anything, but ran to get her mother. I stood there listening.

"Mommy, somebody wants you!" she said in a playful voice.

After a couple of minutes or so, her mother came to the door and asked me if I was waiting long.

"No, not long," I said. But I really was.

Then she asked me, "What can I do for you?"

I told her about the bike near her property and if it belonged to her son.

She and I walked down the long driveway to see it.

"No, that's not my son's," she said.

Then I brought up the big question. "Can I have it?"

She thought for a moment and replied, "Let me find out if it belongs to anyone first. You come back in a few days, and if no one claims it, then it's yours."

I walked by this bike two more days, praying it would still be there. On the third day, I went back to see Mrs. Doughty. She told me that I could have it because nobody had claimed it. I was so happy, I almost cried. I finally had my own bike to ride two miles to the old elementary school. I shall never forget that kind lady, Mrs. Marie Doughty.

CHAPTER 66

Little Brother Gets Hurt!

When our little brother was about nine years old, he had a bad accident while playing. He fell on some broken glass on someone's property and lost his sight in one eye. Some of our neighbors took Billy to the doctor. When the doctor took off the bandage, Billy's eye almost fell out. It was hanging by threads. All the doctor could say was, "Rush him to Elmer Hospital." They did.

When we got home from shopping for school clothes, we got the news and Dad took off running to the hospital.

Our father could have sued the pants off that junk man for leaving glass everywhere. But he didn't. Dad said Billy had no business being there. Billy was just a little boy wanting to have fun. Dad just didn't think like that! And most black people didn't know the laws.

He stayed in the hospital for a week or so but the doctors could not save his eye. We were all saddened by this unfortunate accident. It seemed like our brother was always getting hurt.

Little did we know that later in life, he would become a famous artist, despite his disability.

CHAPTER 67

The March on Washington

There have been many events in my life that I choose to remember. Most of these events made a great impact in the future of mankind.

August 28, 1963 was truly a day I will always remember. The civil rights movement march on Washington. Over 250,000 African-Americans and white sympathizers marched in D.C.

The purpose of the march was to advocate for the civil and economic rights and the freedom of African-Americans. At the march, Dr. Martin Luther King Jr. gave his historical speech, "I Have a Dream," as he stood in front of the Lincoln Memorial. This march was to end racism.

My sisters and I were in the vegetable garden, picking string beans and tomatoes. I put on the radio in the kitchen and cranked up the volume, so we could hear Dr. King's speech.

It was powerful! I still get the chills when I hear it some fifty years later. That man had a way with words, whether he was giving speeches or preaching. You could just feel his plea for freedom for our people.

When the speech was over, the radio began to static and wouldn't stop. *Oh no*, I thought, *why now?* So I ran back to the house to fix the problem. I happened to be the technical person in the family. Every station I turned to, I didn't hear that STATIC sound! Except this one!

After about three minutes, I gave up and left the radio alone to fix itself, only to find out that all that static was the sound of the marchers clapping after King's speech.

In my heart I knew he was a powerful man. I would have loved to meet him face-to-face. Although we joined the NAACP, we couldn't attend the meetings, for lack of transportation. I wanted to know more about civil rights; I would have devoured it.

Being a big advocate for the cause, I sold NAACP newspapers to the many blacks who lived in Clayton. I recall the papers costing twenty-five cents each. I never could sell one to my dad. He didn't have time to read it, anyway.

Once a month, I filled up my sack (that I had made) with newspapers and rode my bike to sell them. After a weekend of selling papers, my sister's boyfriend, Joey Brooks, would come to collect the money. I was very proud of myself. This was not a job but a privilege.

I have lived through twelve presidents, from Truman to President Obama. Madalyn O'Hara, an atheist who played a devastating role in one of two 1960s Supreme Court decisions banning mandatory prayer and Bible reading in public schools.

November 22, 1963, President John F. Kennedy was assassinated. I was in the seventh grade, and on a class field trip to Gettysburg, PA. When our class returned back to the school, the American flag was flying half-mast. We knew that something had happened. It was truly a sad day.

On July 20, 1969, Neil Armstrong became the first man to walk on the moon.

Dr. Martin Luther King Jr. was assassinated on April 4, 1968.

Robert Kennedy was assassinated on June 5, 1968.

The Vietnam War lasted over eighteen years.

September 11, 2001 (also known as 9/11) was when Islamic terrorists attacked the twin towers of the World Trade Center in NY, killing 2,995 people.

Barrack Obama became the first African-American to be elected as president of United States.

These are just a few events that changed our country and impacted my life completely.

CHAPTER 68

Goofing with the Bees

Kat, Billy , and Anna – 1960

After Ret retired from hiking and got married, I took over with Billy and Anna. Those two little guys rarely went anywhere, so I was their trailblazer.

One summer afternoon we went to get peaches from the orchard down the street. We brought three big pots to carry the fruit in. After walking a short distance, I stopped because I saw something huge in a small bushy tree. It was big, round, and grayish. I decided to take my walking stick and poke it a couple of times. Suddenly a swarm of hornets came at us! We started running and they were hot on our trail.

"Cover your heads, Kids, and run as fast as you can," I shouted. We ran a few country blocks before the bees stopped chasing us. Those pots really came in handy! And no one was stung! Thank goodness!

Continuing down the dusty road, we went to ask the orchard keeper for peaches and he allowed us to pick them off the ground. Mom would use these for fruit preserves.

This scary adventure taught me a lesson: never mess with anything that looks peculiar enough to poke at.

LEAVE IT BEE!

CHAPTER 69

Stealing Is a No-No!

A couple of days before I got the near-death whipping, I was hungry. My dad had eaten a cantaloupe and left the seeds and rind in the kitchen sink. Now, I loved pumpkin seeds but never tried cantaloupe seeds. After scraping and eating the melon rind down to the green, I started eating the seeds. Humm… Not bad! Within an hour or so, my stomach started aching. I was so sick! I wouldn't tell anyone. I drank lots of baking soda and warm water, and the pain gradually went away.

I was about twelve years old when this happened, and it shouldn't have happened. I stole a candy bar from the store because I was hungry. My little brother was with me so he took one, as well. I knew better! We'll Dad found out through my sister and he didn't ask us why we did it. He was the type of father who beat first and ask questions later.

He grabbed Billy and beat him really badly, and threw him in the chair. Then he looked at me and said, "You're gonna get it worse because you know better!" He beat me long and hard and it hurt so badly! I went hopping around in circles as he lashed his leather cat-o'-nine-tails across my butt and back. I didn't think he would ever stop beating me!

"I'll beat the blood out of you, Girl! If you do it again, I'll bust you wide open!" And with that he threw me across the room and into another chair, and as always he would yell, "Shut up or I'll give you some more!"

I vowed never to do that again. I don't care how hungry I get!

Question: How do kids learn this behavior?

Answer: by seeing others do it!

CHAPTER 70

Teenage Years with Our Stepmom

As time went by we grew, and some were in those difficult teenage years. Then after seven years of marital problems, our stepmom left Dad, leaving us children to fend for ourselves. As the old song goes, we were "alone again, naturally." I didn't understand why she left us so quickly. I knew she loved us all, some of the time, but I also knew Dad wasn't the best husband he could have been to her. This was painful for some of us. I would go through my best years of growing and maturing with no mother to share those precious years with. But life goes on. I was twelve years old when she left us for good.

I remember Mom in her younger days, dancing with us in the kitchen to her favorite songs and teaching us how to do the Charleston, crossing her hands over her knees. She loved the Connie Francis song "Everybody's Somebody's Fool," and "Sugartime." When she was happy, she could be so much fun. But when she was angry, look out, everybody!

Whenever she took us to Cowtown, there were lots of smelly cows on the way, or in Westville, where you smelled the famer's stinky pigs. We girls would say, "Pee yew! What a horrible odor!"

Then Mom would say, "Close your legs, Girls," and we would die laughing.

Mom would take a few of us to a farm for fresh milk. Straight from the cows but pasteurized. This milk was loaded with fat, and when it sat for any length of time the cream would rise. It was so good!

We took large metal cans to carry the milk and store it outside on the back porch during the winter.

She made the richest ice cream, usually vanilla or peach. We started to put on a little weight, especially in our cheeks. Both sets! Ha-ha-ha!

CHAPTER 71

Get Your Spoons Ready!

M ineral oil, castor oil, or cod liver oil were a must!
"You chill-ren needs a good cleaning out." A *physic*, she called it.
Mom knew it would keep us healthier. Whenever we were feeling sick,
she would ask, "How is your bowels?" If you said that you were consti-
pated, on today's menu would be castor oil for you! Yuck!

We hated this stuff and would cover our mouths when the spoon met
our lips. One day Bert and Ida ran around the block to escape their portion of this awful-tasting oily stuff.

I took mine like a champ! And I got a teaspoon of molasses for a
chaser.

When they got back, Mom had two spoons ready for them, and with
no chasers. After their dosage, Ida ran to the sink and drank gobs of water
with her hands under the faucet. Bert kept saying how much she liked its
flavor and didn't need a chaser. RIGHT! Then why did she run around
the block?

CHAPTER 72

Wash Day

M om worked hard at everything she did, except wash days. I think she hated wash day because it was a bit hectic. So she would get angry with us and stay in her bedroom all day long until the washing was done.

All hands on deck! Get out your dirty clothes. It's a sunny day and its wash day! Many times I prayed for rain but that would be even harder. More clothes to wash later. Wash day in the winter was brutal! You wash the clothes and hang them out to dry and they would freeze and be stiff as a board. Then you had to bring them in before dark and hang them all over the house to dry. Why couldn't we have a washer and dryer like most people? "Because it is a waste and will use too much water and electricity," Dad would say.

When our mom was living we had a new dryer that someone gave us, but Dad wouldn't have it installed. "It will use too much gas," he said.

Poor Mom didn't have a voice. "Ok, Wiggy, whatever you say," was always here reply.

Then he sold it.

My job was to get the water for the old Maytag Wringer Washer and two rinse tubs. Nine buckets for each tubs and twelve for the washer. This was done manually and took lots of time, strength, and muscle.

I was a curious and inventive girl who would try different ways to make my jobs easier. One wash day, I came up with a great idea! I found an old water hose and hooked it to the faucet.

BINGO! IT WORKED!

The hose was long enough to reach the washer and the two rinse tubes. "Hurray!" I shouted.

My sister, whose name I won't mentioned, saw my invention and put a halt to it. "No," she said. "You do it by hand. Lazy thing! You think you're so smart! Trying to be slick."

What she didn't realize was we could have finished the wash earlier using the hose.

Oh well, I'll use my inventions for my own pleasure. And I did.

Finally, in 1963, Dad promoted us to the next level. The Laundromat. Twenty-five cents for the washers and ten cents for the dryer! Hallelujah!

CHAPTER 73

Pee Yew! Chitterlings

One time only! Dad got a big tub of fresh chitterlings (pig intestines) from a butcher. And I do mean they were fresh! And we had to clean them. Poop was everywhere and the smell was so bad that you wanted to barf! This was gross!

Our stepmom was used to this stuff! She was raised on it. Living as a sharecropper's daughter, this was all they did, if they wanted to eat. This woman cut off a section of the chitterlings and put it to her mouth and blew hard into it. The poop shot out everywhere, even on us. I might add that she found a few worms that were moving.

Mom said, "Next time we'll do this outside with the water hose."

I said, "No, thanks!"

Dad said, "It isn't worth the trouble."

But everyone knew he had a weak stomach.

Until this day, I don't eat that mess!

Dad would bring home pig testicles, pig feet, hog maws, ears, and tails. No wonder he had such high blood pressure. My sister Loretta took after Dad in that respect. She once got a big hog head and cooked it and grinded it up for scrapple and souse. Nasty!

I like scrapple but I didn't need to know how it was made.

CHAPTER 74

Canning Day!

C anning day was fun! Mom had us wash all the mason jars, and she would sterilize them. During the summer, we took baskets and a wheelbarrow and went to the peach orchard down on Clayton Avenue. The farmer would give us the softer peaches, or let us have the ones that fell from the trees to the ground.

In the fall, we gathered apples off the ground for apple sauce or fried apples.

Mom taught us how to skin the peaches in hot water. "Just like tomatoes," she'd say.

Then came the processing. Pack the jars with peaches and pour hot sugar water over them. Take a knife and stick it down in the inside of the jar to release the bubbles.

Place the lids and rings on and put them in a hot water bath for half an hour.

I loved to hear the *pop* sound of the lids sealing. It was cool to hear all the cans pop at almost the same time. I will always remember how to can, and use the same technique as Mom did.

Usually, when the canning was done for the day, she would reward us with a peach cobbler, or something sweet made from apples.

Sweet potato turnovers were my absolute favorite! She put sweet potato filling in a small circle of piecrust, then seal the edges and fry them in hot oil. When they were cooked and cooled, she would coat them in cinnamon and sugar. Yummy!

CHAPTER 75

Baking Day!

Baking cookies was like being in a candy store with unlimited selections of anything you wanted. Mom made dozens of sugar cookies with multiple toppings—peanuts, almonds, raisins, coconut, and anything we could garnish the tops with. Our reward was cookies for lunch, and desserts.

Her donuts were awesome! After frying them in hot oil, she'd let them cool off, then let us powder them with confection sugar or cinnamon and sugar.

Making hot rolls every Sunday morning was the norm. She would prepare the dough in the morning, and when we came home from church, she would let us punch them down. Then she'd shape them into little balls, to let them rise again. I always asked her if she was going to make cinnamon rolls, as well. When they started baking, you could smell the yeast all around the inside and outside of our house, which usually drew a small crowd of kids. Victor asked her if she could sell him a pan of rolls. Out of pure generosity, she gave him a few hot buttered rolls and he was happy. He knew that it was hot roll Sunday.

HOT ROLLS OR COOKIES!

Our house smelled like a bakery!

All these domestic things and good morals that she taught me, like cooking, cleaning, saving for a rainy day, taking care of my household, treating people the way you would want to be treated, holding my head up high, and being best of whatever you are, I put them to good use. And one of her famous quotes was "be kind to the people going up the ladder, 'cause you gonna meet the same people coming back down."

I raised our children with these same values, and to always reach higher to better themselves.

CHAPTER 76

Giblets and Gravy

At the age of ten, I had many jobs to do. I was always afraid that I would forget to do them and get into trouble. So I tried my best to stay on top of my chores.

Every Saturday, I had to clean the bathroom and utility room. My weekly chores were to dry the dishes, sweep the dining room, clear the dinner table, feed Billy's dog and Loretta's rabbit (after she left home), empty Granny's slop bucket, get the water on wash days, and most importantly, take out the trash.

One Sunday night, after an All Day Meeting at church and we came home, as soon as I hit the door, I ran to empty the garbage. I didn't need anyone to remind me; I was being responsible. Mom had left a whole pot of giblet gravy on the back of the stove, because she forgot to take it to church to serve with the two turkeys she had roasted. Not knowing the details, I quickly emptied the big pot of garbage. Mom always kept the garbage on the stove. This pot was a bit heavy and it smelled like savory garbage, so I ran outside to empty it in the garbage pail. Then I brought the pot back in and placed it in the sink to be washed.

"That's done," I said to myself.

Mom came in the kitchen and discovered the empty pot that once held her giblet gravy.

"Oh Lord! The chile' done threw out my giblet gravy!" she said.

My mouth flew open. *Oh no. What have I done?*

Mom knew that I had made a terrible mistake and told me not to worry. "You didn't go to do it!" Translation: "You didn't mean to do it!"

When Dad found out about the gravy, it was a different story. He wanted to holler, but Mom said, "She was only doing her chores and didn't know it was gravy."

Then Dad backed off but he mumbled sarcastically, "I ought to break your neck, Girl." He paused, then he said jokingly, "Well, I guess the maggots ate well tonight."

Poor Dad, he sure loved himself some good giblets and gravy!

CHAPTER 77

The Great Egg-Travaganza!

One summer day I decided to take Billy and Anna hiking again. As we hiked, we sang songs and absorbed nature that was all around us. This particular day, we packed a lunch. Warm Kool-Aide and peanut butter and crackers.

We hadn't got far when I spied a small chicken coop on some vacant property. Peeping in the coop's window, our eyes were fixed on one lonely egg sitting in the middle of the hay-covered floor.

"Wow! That might be a baby chick in that egg, just waiting to hatch. Wanna get it!"

"You guys stay here and I'll go in and get it." I opened the door, ran in, snatched up the egg, and scrabbled out. The egg was extra-large and appeared to be warm from the sunshine that peered through the window. We were so excited to possibly have a pet chicken, I just had to see what was inside.

I tapped it lightly and BAM! That egg exploded right in my hand and all over me. "Stand back, Kids!" I told them. Then I forced them back with my slime-covered, stinky hands. This rotten egg smelled so bad, it almost made us puke. All the way home we held our noses, and I teased and chased them home with my stinky hands.

The moral of this story is to never trust a sitting egg!

CHAPTER 78

Coal Gas Nearly Killed Us!

Our stepmom left Dad when I was in the sixth grade. After she left, Dad needed someone to keep the furnace going while he was at work. There was no one else he could trust but Ida. She was the strongest of all the sisters, so Dad gave her the job of tending the fire that heated the house. She kindled, banked, and put coal in the furnace three or four times a day. After sifting the ashes every day, she would take them outside and dump them in the garden or on the ash pile. It was hard work for such a young girl!

Ida was strong and knew just how to keep that fire going. We happened to be the only family on our block that still used coal because coal was on its way out of circulation.

Before Mom left Dad, whenever they went out for several hours, we would get overcome by carbon monoxide or coal gas. It was the worst chemical sickness anyone could experience. Several times, someone forgot to close the damper and the gas would escape into the house instead of up the chimney.

Dad always blamed her and put too much on her.

We would get sick as dogs! It would always happen when we went to bed. The gas would seep into the house and overtake us. If no one woke up, we would all have died in our sleep. This was an undetectable smell that caused you to feel woozy and fall asleep. When you woke up, the house would be filled and ready to explode, if a spark or match was lit. I remember someone waking up one night screaming, "Coal gas! Wake up! Wake up, everybody!"

Granny never got sick. In fact it gave her a buzz! She always slept with the window partially open.

As soon as you opened your eyes, you were overpowered by an excruciating headache. Then you had to get out of the house quickly. As soon as you hit the fresh air, your head would start pounding and your heart rate would go sky high. This lasted for about two hours. When the headache started to wear off then you'd throw up profusely until your stomach was empty.

Ida always said, "I closed that damper, Dad! Please believe me!"

I believed her. She often took me in the cellar to let me watch her at work.

We were near death numerous times, and we dealt with this for about three or four years until Dad switched over to natural gas.

Through the waking of a sister,

GOD WAS REALLY OUR WAKE-UP CALL!

When I was in the ninth grade, I told my science teacher what happened to us. He was appalled. In full detail, he told the students just how serious this gas was. "Kathy and her family could have been killed." After class he thanked me for sharing my experience. We went through a lot as kids. Today a person would be hospitalized for several days. Times have really changed.

CHAPTER 79

The Smokey Mosquito Truck

The coal gas was a terrible experience, but that didn't stop us wild kids from running behind the mosquito truck every summer. A cloud of thick, billowing smoke containing killing fumes for insects. We thought this was fun. "Let's do it again!" The driver never told us not to do this. He didn't care! He laughed at us!

There was hardly any supervision after our stepmom left. We were just poor, raggedy, motherless, wild kids.

Our brother Billy said, "That's what's wrong with us today. We're crazy from all that coal gas and mosquito fumes!"

Huh! There might be some truth to that!

CHAPTER 80

Dad Divorces Mom

D ad divorced his second wife on the grounds of mental cruelty on her part, not his. What a joke! He tried all kinds of ways he could put her away, through legal grounds for divorce. He asked me once, "Where did you sleep when you went with your mother to Pennsylvania to visit her sister, Aunt Lee?"

"I slept with Mom and Aunt Lee," I told him.

"Where in the bed did you sleep?" he asked, as if he were fishing for information to use against her, to incriminate her.

"I slept on one end and Aunt Lee slept on the other. Mom slept in the middle of the bed," I replied.

Then he asked me if I felt any movement between them in the bed, and I said, "No, Dad."

He looked disappointed in me. Dad always taught us to tell the truth, and that's exactly what I did.

Later, when I was old enough to realize what he was implying, I was appalled.

He tried to use a few of my sisters to be witnesses on his behalf when they went to court.

One of my sisters didn't want to swear on the Holy Bible, so Dad told her to say, "I affirm."

After two years, the divorce was final and Dad went around bragging and saying that he was "TIRED AND DISGUSTED, SINGLE AND CAN'T BE TRUSTED!"

What a clown! I thought to myself.

CHAPTER 81

Going Fishing for What?

In the summer of 1962, Dad was on the prowl again, looking for another woman. One Saturday afternoon, he put on a clean, short-sleeve cotton shirt and dress pants. He announced to us that he was going fishing. I looked him up and down, wondering why he looked so polished and dapper. Usually Dad wore a dirty, green work cap and railroad work clothes when he went fishing.

Every time he went fishing, he usually caught a few measly minnows and a big ego.

If anyone asked him, "What did you catch, Daddy?" he would snap your head off, thinking you were poking fun of his fishy failures. So we knew to keep our mouths shut!

"Can I go with you, Dad?" my little brother asked him."

"No, Boy, not this time, 'cause I got some business I gotta take care of, when I'm done fishing. Ok?" he said, and rubbed Billy on the head, like he was giving him a reward for disappointing him. Dad paused for a few seconds, mumbled something to himself, and repeated, "Yep, I got business to take care of today."

Dad always parked his car in the driveway, but this time he parked it on the street in front of our house. He proudly jumped into his spit-shined, squeaky clean car that I had toiled over for hours. I guess you can say that he wanted to make a clean getaway.

Several hours later, he returned. I just knew we were going to have a guppy-fry, because now Dad was in a pretty good mood. Humm... *Where's the fish?* I wondered.

After waiting patiently to hear about his super-fish-cial story, he finally 'fessed up and told us that he didn't have time to go fishing. Then I remembered that he didn't take his fishing pole and tackle box, and no worms for bait.

With a sheepish grin on his face, he proceeded to tell us about a lady he met.

"I knew her for many years, even before I met your mother," he said with a grin, showing his one and only gold tooth.

"What's her name?" someone asked.

"Ellen... Ellen Bass," he replied with a little hesitation.

Well, using her last name, we kids made up a cute little phrase that went like this: "Dad went fishing and caught himself a Bass.

A few weeks later, when Dad brought her to the house to meet us, the phrase changed: "Dad went fishing and caught himself a Big Mouth Black Bass."

I think my little sister Anna started that.

His new girlfriend was very dark complexioned, but her skin was smooth and powdery, and her hair was tinted blue. She seemed to be an elegant woman—and motherly, as well. But she had a particular way about her that you just couldn't put your finger on. She sure could talk, though.

CHAPTER 82

The Birds and the Bees

A fter about a year or so, Dad trusted Ellen to talk to us about the do's and don'ts of dating, or better known as the birds and the bees.

"Phyllis, Ida, Bert, and Kat, come here. Ellen would like to talk to you girls about something," Dad said.

Little Anna was only about ten, so she wasn't involved in the conversation.

Immediately we began to whisper among ourselves.

"What does she want?"

"Maybe she's gonna take us shopping again," Ida said.

"Nah, I doubt it."

I could use a new bra. I'm tired of washing this one and only bra, and it's starting to fall apart. I thought.

She finally entered the back bedroom where we were waiting, anticipating what she was going to say to us. Bert and I laid across our beds and Ida and Phil stood. Miss Ellen began her speech. "Girls, you know that I love you like you was my own girls, and your father asked me to talk to you about dating boys. Keep your dress down and don't let those boys get into your panties, and keep your legs closed!"

Those were her only and final words on that subject. We all looked dumbfounded at each other. Was that all? Now, this conversation took less than one minute, if that. She got right to the point.

I could always tell when Phyllis disapproved of something, and this one-way conversation was eating at her. Her nostrils flared uncontrollably as she took a few deep breaths. Then Ellen proceeded to walk out of the bedroom, thinking that she had earned the respect and approval of the Williams girls, and that she had won our hearts as their soon-to-be stepmother. How could Dad believe that she knew what she was talking about, or how she would present this serious subject to his daughters? Or was that what he told her to say? Dad was a gullible man. He had jumped out of the frying pan and into the fire. His daughters knew more about this subject than he thought. And Ellen knew very little.

I had just turned fourteen and it was time to go on our once-a-year church outing. This time it would be at an amusement park called River View Beach Park in Pennsville, NJ. We didn't go to many places, but this was something we looked forward to. These were our happy times!

In Sunday school we would give our pennies and Phil would save it, and when she had enough change, she would approach Daddy about a trip somewhere for the kids who came to church. Dad would agree to bring it before the church meeting and then the planning would begin. It seemed like we always had to go in the afternoons because some adults had things to do, so we would have to wait for them. They would always say 10:00 a.m. but show up at 2:00 or 3:00 p.m. They always knew about the trips a month in advance. We call it CPT: Colored People Time. Then they'd bring extra kids who never came to church but would take advantage of the church's generosity, and as a result we had to limit our rides to maybe two rides per child. But we had fun, anyway.

We would pack a big lunch and make a jug of Kool-Aide; we also brought cupcakes or cookies, and chips.

The kids who showed up unannounced always had money for ice cream, popcorn, cotton candy, and other goodies, but never shared. Yet we were just glad to be out and about.

I recall the first hit record of The Isley Brothers, "Twist and Shout." Our dad wasn't too keen on this worldly music, so he slipped away and didn't pick us up until late that evening. He could have given his children money for ice cream.

CHAPTER 83

Dancing at the Police Station

It was the summer of 1963. I never knew how it started, but our town's police station let the community kids have dances at the old Clayton Police Station. It was a big hit! It started at around 7:00 p.m. and the kids would dance until maybe 10:00 p.m. Clayton was pretty small back then, but they still had a crowd of kids from other towns. We weren't allowed to go but what Dad didn't know; he would never find out. He was always out late with his lady friend, anyway. After all, we were teenage girls and we were almost normal. Ha-ha-ha.

Ida always led the way. "Hey, ya'll, you wanna go to the police station tonight?"

"Sure, Ida, let's go!" Bert and I would say.

We never had money to get in the police station parking lot, where the kids would dance. And they always had a rope around the entrance, so you couldn't sneak in. It might had been only twenty-five cents to get in. You paid for your own hot dogs and sodas. But like I said, we had no money, anyway.

The kids would bring their records and the officers would play them over the loudspeaker. This was the time when kids respected policemen and did what they were asked to do. Most of the time.

When the music began to play, the kids started kicking up their heels and freaking out. It was so funny watching them doing all those crazy dances, like the fly, pony, slop, the "Hully Gully," monkey, the swim, mashed potatoes, and the jerk. And some kids were still doing the bop from the fifties.

Most black kids didn't dance to the white music, and vice versa. But everybody got their feet moving to Chubby Checker's "The Twist" and "Pony Time"!

"Get Up! Boogety, boogety, boogety, boogety, shoo."

The Marvelettes were very popular back then, and everyone was "Dancing in the Street!"

My friend Janet was always there, dancing and trying to teach the kids her style. She and her brother Larry could really cut the rug!

One time somebody paid Ida's way in and we watched her dancing with her boyfriend George. She was so shy. Those guys could really bop, though! George always used one hand to hold up one pant leg. I guess that was the thing to do back then. Funny!

A vocal group called The Shirelles had just made their debut. Their hit song was "Will You Still Love Me Tomorrow?" My friend Janet loved this song and taught it to me. Walking home from school each day, we would sing it until I had the lyrics down pat. We were a duet! Sha-da-lat-dat! Sha-da-lat-dat!

CHAPTER 84

Boys Chase Me

O ne night, I was the only one allocated to go to the store before it closed at 9:00 sharp. And my sisters always waited until the last minute to have someone run to the store for lunch meat and bread. Usually Ida and I would go, but I guess she was too busy that night. So I had to go by myself.

When I came out of the house, I noticed three boys across the street. Hoping they weren't watching me, I tried to slip by them unseen.

When I reached the streetlight at the corner, I crossed over to the store. Inside were a few shoppers being waited on. I got a loaf of Wonder Bread and waited in line for bologna and cheese. It was finally my turn to check out and I asked for a pound of each.

I started to feel uneasy about walking home. I just felt like something bad would go down. I've had these same feelings many times and they appeared to be warning signs.

The store owner walked me to the door and locked it behind me. Then the store's front light went out. It was too quiet so I walked up a little ways, thinking I would cross over and go around the block, and cut through someone's backyard to get home.

All of a sudden I heard one of them say, "Get her. There she is. She's running. Hurry up, hurry up!" They were hiding on the side of the store, lurking like lions in hunt for prey. I knew they would be because I felt uneasy. I had to act quickly!

I ran a little ways up the street, and when they got closer, I took off like a bat out of you know where! I crossed the street and ran past them. One of them grabbed the back of my jacket. I heard him say, "I got her!" But I snatched it away and kept going.

It felt like the Lord had put wings on my feet. I was moving fast and never dropped the bread, bologna, or cheese. When I reached our driveway the boys took off in another direction. I was so frightened because these boys had issues with girls, and they didn't care about consequences.

I took a few deep breaths and opened the door. No one but Ida knew the hell I had just gone through. And I didn't tell her right away. I never said a word for fear that my Dad would think I had prompted it.

I never went by myself again. Ida went with me. Or better yet, I went with Ida.

CHAPTER 85

The Fur Stole

In 1963, my sister Phyllis was nominated queen of her senior class. "Madam Butterfly" was her class theme for the Halloween parade. She looked beautiful, dressed in a gown and a real mink stole that Dad had purchased for this special occasion. Her float won first place that year. We were so proud because she was the first black girl to be nominated in the history of Clayton.

When Dad purchased this fur stole for Phyllis to wear in the parade, he said we could all use it, and that it would be kept in our family.

Ellen came over one day and said that Dad told her she could have it. She came in our bedroom, went in the clothes closet, and took it. We were devastated! How dare he take our only prized possession away and give it to his girlfriend? And she could have said no. But out of greed, she took it. We never saw it again.

I think I lost some respect for my dad that day. He was a coward, a deceiver, and a conniver.

How could he do this to his daughters? How do I trust his integrity again?

Before the fur coat incident, Ellen had taken us shopping for new outfits. White lace trimmed blouses and black skirts to wear when we had singing engagements.

Hmm… I smell a rat!

CHAPTER 86

The Williams Sisters

The Williams Sisters 1962

We were a group of popular gospel singers and we sang from our hearts to the Lord. From 1962 to 1966, Phyllis, Ida, Bertha, and I, Kathleen, entertained people with the gift that God gave to us. Our voices.

We always dressed alike. We had about five different outfits that we would wear. Blue wool pleated dresses with a wide black belt. White blouses and black skirts. White wraparound skirts with blue blouses that Phyllis made us, and the prettiest was the lacey, lined summer dresses.

These same dresses would be worn at my wedding.

Sometimes we would mix and match our outfits.

Oh yes, I can't forget the little cross earrings with a pearl in the center was given to us by Phil.

Some folks said we should audition for the Ted Mack show, which was a TV talent show that could help you get to the top. The Linen Sisters would have had some competition with us. We were invited to sing at the World's Fair in Trenton, NJ. But we had no one to take us.

Well, I guess we weren't ready for the big time yet and we had no connections to help us get there.

God had a plan for us later on in life.

"Somebody Bigger than You and I" was a favorite song of mine. When we sang it some folks would be in tears, because it soothed their soul. One time, we were asked to sing it twice.

"Walk in Jerusalem Just like John" was the much-loved song by our audience.

They would stand up and applaud when we sang that song, and ask for an encore.

Miss Ida sure could get down with her bass. Other groups were so amazed that she had the ability to get down so low. I tried singing bass, but it was messing with my vocal cords. I just couldn't cut it. So Ida took over and I became alto. Thank goodness! Usually we sang three to four songs at each engagement. "Remember Me" by The Caravans was our theme song, and also our warm-up song.

One Sunday we had an All Day Meeting at our church. Dad called us up to sing and I fell apart with tears. I couldn't stop myself from crying. Then Bert and Ida started crying. Phil kept her composure. We didn't know why we were so emotional. Dad said it was the Holy Spirit. But I was thinking about leaving my sisters in a few weeks to get married, and David being drafted and going to Vietnam. After it was over Phil said, "Ida's girdle was too tight. And Bert started crying when you did." Regardless of what really happened, we were in perfect harmony until the last verses, when Phil started quoting the lyrics and we were humming in the background. The song we sang was from the famous Staple Singers called "Be Careful of Stones That You Throw."

Our father was very proud of his girls, and this boosted his ego big time. Once in a while someone would write a note, while sitting in the audience. The note would work its way up front to the MC. A request for the Williams sisters to sing another song with their father.

Now, who do you think wrote that note? I'll give you one guess! Being the oldest, we would look at Phyllis for a decision. Yes, we sing— or, no, we don't. Dad did not like the word no. One time Phyllis said no, because we hadn't practiced with him this one particular song, Daddy got mad as a hornet and blasted Phyllis all the way home. Because he was embarrassed.

Then he came up with another strategy: just go up front and call his girls to assist him in a song.

"Oh no!"

"What nerve! How dare he put us on the spot!?"

He knew we hardly knew some of these songs. But that didn't matter to him. He would get Ellen to write a request, and his other cronies, as well. I think he wanted to relive his younger years, when he sang with the Silver Tones quartet. Our dad loved to shine.

He would tell us, "If you're singing for the Lord, He don't care how you sound."

I guess it didn't matter that our sweet voices were drowned out by his harsh, ten-octaves-lower bass-sounding voice. We sounded like kitty cats purring with a roaring lion, in an imperfect harmony. Hah!

Our dad wanted to be in the spotlight in the worst way! His girls, or as he would say, his "bloody hussies," were now his pride and joy. As we got older he eliminated these degrading words from his vocabulary. Thank goodness!

CHAPTER 87

My Baptism

A t the age of fourteen, I decided to give my life to Christ. I knew that I was a sinner, and now I was at the age of accountability. And I was now responsible for my own sins. In other words, "I knew better." It was time to make that change, turn from my foolish ways, and follow Christ!

My father would ask me from time to time, "How old are you? When are you going to get baptized? Because if you die, you will be lost. Don't make hell your eternity."

Well, I certainly didn't want to die and go to hell. I had to get serious! One Sunday morning, He mentioned this to me again, and I was ready. He took my confession in the kitchen.

Upon making the confession, this is what he asked me, "Do you believe that Jesus Christ is the Son of God?"

I replied, "Yes, I do!"

We had to travel to Chester, PA, for my baptism, because this particular Church of Christ had their own baptistery. You could either go to Chester or go to the nearest lake. Burr...

Usually Dad would take two or three kids every six months or so to be baptized and be saved. This church was once a small house that was gutted and turned into a sanctuary. The baptismal pool was under a trap door, in the middle of the floor of the sanctuary. When they opened the trap door, there was the cold water. All the congregation gathered around the perimeter of the pool and Dad and I went down into the water. All the saints began to sing.

"Yes, we'll gather at the river, the beautiful, beautiful river.
Gather with the saints at the river that flows by the throne
of God."

And that's when I started to cry. I don't know if I was nervous or happy, but the tears were flowing.

Dad took my confession again, so all could witness it. "Okay," he whispered in my ear, "just bend your knees, hold your breath, and I'll do the rest." Then he raised his hand and said, "Upon your confession, I baptize you in the name of the Father, the Son, and the Holy Spirit." And backward I went. *Splash!*

When I emerged from the water, I immediately became a part of God's family. I was the daughter of the King, a child of God. I was born again; I became a Christian that day. I made a commitment to follow Christ and live by his teachings until the day I die.

My sister Ida's boyfriend George Rowe and a friend named Richie Gibbs were baptized on that day, as well.

HALLELUJAH! AMEN! AND AGAIN I SAY AMEN!

My dad was very proud of his kids on becoming Christians. When his girls started dating or got serious about marrying, he would warn us to always marry someone in the Lord.

"Don't be unequally yoked. In other words, be of the same faith or you will have many problems. And don't marry anyone who doesn't love the Lord," he said.

Dad was absolutely right. Never marry an unbeliever!

CHAPTER 88

Oh My, What Is That? My What!?

I was now fourteen years old, and one day I was feeling not myself. I went to the bathroom and noticed a brown discharge but wasn't too alarmed. Several hours later I felt wet and feeling lousier then I did earlier, so I went to the bathroom again. "Oh my Lord, what is that?" I said aloud.

I was afraid! Was I dying? Was I sick? Did I hurt myself inside? I have to tell someone quick before I keeled over. I couldn't tell Granny; this would upset her. I went to talk to my sister Phil and explained that I was in some kind of trouble.

She looked at me and said, "Do you have any money?"

"Yes," I said, "about $1.50 that I was saving for a pair of Earth Shoes."

Then she said, "I'll make a list of what you will need. A box of Kotex and a sanitary napkin belt. You're not sick, Kat. All girls your age have it. It's just your monthly period, Kat."

And that was all she told me! Then I remembered several girls at school saying, "I got my period."

They seemed happy and bubbly. Why? I was feeling awful.

I never had cramps so that was a blessing, but I wondered, would this go on for the rest of my life? I guess I should have paid more attention in health class. I couldn't wait to ask my friend Janet what I should do. Maybe she had hers, too. After the third month, I adjusted to my new way of life. Blah!

CHAPTER 89

Dad's Working Girls

D ad and Mom had only one boy and seven girls. We were all work-horses. We had jobs by the time we were fourteen. My first job was cleaning house every Saturday and working in the fields during the summer, picking blueberries, tomatoes, and string beans. It was hard work and you didn't make a lot of money. The farmers paid six cents a pint for blueberries, or seventy-two cents a crate. A mere twenty-two cents a basket for tomatoes, and sixty cents a basket for string beans. This was slave labor! By the end of the week, I proudly brought home my pay, which was usually $35 to $42 dollars a week, and gave it to Dad. He would look at me up and down and hand me just a couple of dollars for my troubles. Then he would add a comment like, "Be glad you got that!" And he never would say thank you. We were his money-making machines. Dad could clear at least $80 to $100 a week from his girls. It felt like all I was getting out of this was a deep, dark suntan from working in the fields. I was charcoal black!

After a while, my sister Loretta refused to give him a dime and would sit in church in front of him, eating candy, cracking nuts with her teeth, and chewing bubblegum and blowing big bubbles. Dad never said a word, because of her condition.

After two years of working the hot fields, I decided to get a real job: babysitting. I watched three little boys all summer long and gave every cent to dad. Again he would give me a couple of dollars and I was grateful for that. At the age of fourteen, I had personal needs. I had to buy my own Kotex, deodorant, hair grease, stockings, and other previsions. I save all summer to buy a pair of $6.00 Earth Shoes, which I hated because they collected mud and were hard to keep clean. Sometimes I would envy some of the girls at school who would brag about getting allowances and not having to buy any of their personal needs, including their lunches.

Before she left us, our stepmother Lavinia started teaching us to save. When she got a job, she purchased little brown glass piggy banks from the five-and-ten cent store, and put our names on the bottom with scotch tape. Every week she would give us a dime, nickel, or quarter and we put it in our banks. We couldn't spend it. No... no... "Don't let money burn a hole in your pocket," she always told us. In other words, don't be too anxious to spend all that you have. Save some!

I saved a lot.

One night my big sister wanted to go skating but had no money. She asked me to help her, and I did. Mom asked me if I was sure that I wanted to do it, and I said, "Yes, she can borrow it."

Well, that was the end of my savings. I received "no deposits and no returns"!

CHAPTER 90

Baggie Pants and Bad Bones

In our neighborhood there were many junk men. One in particular, who looked to be about sixty-eight, had a great grandson. Although this man looked like a poor individual, everyone knew he had quite a bit of cash stashed away for safekeeping. He dealt mostly in selling junk, cast-off clothing (better known as rags), and old newspapers. I guess you could say he was introducing folks to the world of recycling. Occasionally he would go to the dump and find stale Italian pastries that he tried to pawn off on us. One day, out of generosity, he gave us a big box of pastries. They looked so good until the ants came pouring out of the bottom of the box. Yikes! No thanks!

Now, young boys these days think that they discovered the style of wearing pants under the butt. Nope! It goes back farther than the 90s. Our neighbor wore his pants the same way. And sometimes without a belt. He was an old, broken-down bachelor who would walked by our house daily with a pot of something, or perhaps nothing in it, for his lady friends. I wasn't too fond of getting too close to him because you could see his butt hanging out. How disgusting! If you said, "Hello, Mr. #@+*," he would look at you and grunt—unless there was an adult present; then he would speak. He would always tell my dad, "You got the money and I got the time." I could never understand what that was all about. Perhaps it was just a junk man's joke.

He had a grandson who lived in the city but left there to come and live with his grandfather. It was said that his parents couldn't deal with him any longer, so off to the country they sent him. Oh boy!

This boy was bad to the bone! He was a nasty little skinny, bee-tle-headed black boy who loved to cuss, steal, smoke, and vandalize your property. He had a face full of acne and a receding hairline, and four rows of thick, yellow teeth. We nicknamed him 52 Teeth, but never called him that to his face. We knew all about his wrath!

What the neighborhood boys didn't know about gangster life, this kid would teach them soon enough. He enjoyed getting suspended from school, so he could stay home and conjure up more criminal activity. He happened to be one of the boys who chased me home from the store one night. Fact was, I wouldn't trust him with my doll baby, if I had had one.

When he rode on his nasty rusted bicycle that had no seat or brakes, or when he was running on foot, his tongue would hang out of his mouth like a dog, drooling. His hands were always ashy and his face was always shinny and greasy. Keep in mind that I am not making fun of him but describing his physical appearance that matched his personality. Pitiful!

Living on our street and being a young teenage girl could be somewhat scary. There were many dysfunctional boys, including the out--of-towners, whom you had to be aware of. I know of several girls who were raped or sexually mauled by these delinquents. But as long as I had breath in my body, I wasn't going to be one of them.

This kid stayed in Clayton for almost a year, then he disappeared. No one knew when or why he left so quickly. But we all agreed, good riddance!

There was another old man in our neighborhood who would ask you to go to the store for him. Then he would lure you into his house and offer you a nickel to let him kiss or touch you inappropriately. We were not allowed to go near him unless his wife was present.

Our father kept us off the streets for a good reason: to keep us out of harm's way. A girl's not safe in a neighborhood of delinquent boys and dirty old men. Bad bones! And for this, I thank my father for keeping us safe, and letting us know that "there is always safety in numbers."

CHAPTER 91

Black Equality Comes to Town

There were times when I would strike back to get even and this was perfect timing. My sister Bert used to always play practical jokes on me. She loved to tease!

One night our uncle David came to visit us and his mother, Granny. As usual, he was stinking drunk. He lived in Harrisburg, PA, and would come to town usually twice a year. This time he brought his city slicker friend who was drunk, as well. His friend looked very dapper in a fine suit and a long chain hanging from his pocket. He wore blue suede shoes, which were long out of date, but he was sharp. He wasn't a handsome man at all, but Uncle Dave said, "This man is a genius!" All he talked about was "black equality," which we didn't understand. He kept repeating this same phrase, "Do you believe in black equality?"

This little man was looking for a date, somebody to go out with him. A light went on in my head! It's payback time for Miss Bertha! I really had to think this set-up blind date through. And I only had a few minutes to do it.

Bert happened to be taking her Saturday night bubble bath, and I wanted to surprise her with a date. I talked to this simple-minded man and assured him that she would be delighted to meet him. I told him how beautiful she was and fed him all kinds of foolishness. He waited a good half hour in the kitchen for Bert to come out of the bathroom. When she did, he was so excited and told her he would take her out and show her a really good time.

"Oh, Lady, you so fine like a fox! I take you back to Harrisburg with me and show you to my friends." He meant it! He was serious! And I was in trouble!

Bert took one look at me and said, "WHAT DID YOU DO? YOU HUSSY! What did you tell this man about me?"

I started laughing so hard I nearly wet my pants.

Bert got in his face and told the man, "Get out of our house, you Drunken Bum!"

Uncle Dave got mad because his friend was humiliated and wanted to leave. He was scared of Bert. "You kids are disrespectful to my friend, and I'm gonna tell your father on you!"

Billy, who was about eleven at the time, said, "Yeah, go ahead and tell Dad. We'll tell Dad that you and your friend came here drunk as skunks. And you'll be in trouble."

And with that Uncle Dave and his city slicker friend stormed out of the house just a fussing. Billy, who was wearing his steel-toe shoes, kicked the man in the butt as he walked out of the front door and said, "Get out and stay out!"

Our uncle could be brutal when drunk. One night he came to say good-bye to his mother, our granny, before he left for Harrisburg. Dad happened to be home and they got into a big argument. Uncle David had stayed with us some time ago, after he got out of jail, and he promised to pay Dad for food and board. Once he got on his feet he refused to pay, and Dad was angry. He brought our four cousins, Uncle Johnny's boys who were in their late twenties, with him. His plan was to have Dad's own nephews beat him up. While the confrontation was going on, Uncle David started mocking Dad about how much money he was making as compared to Dad's income. He said he made $150 a week and Dad only made $75.

"You ain't got no job, Man! That peanuts!" he said. Then he told the boys, "Get him, Boys!" Beat his ***!""

The nephews stood there and laughed at their uncle. Needless to say, they would never ever touch our dad, because they respected him. They all jumped in the car and took off. Dad would not see his brother for a while, until Uncle David got sick from drinking and needed a place to crash. Again!

CHAPTER 92

My First Apron

As a young teenager in the seventh grade, my first project was to make a simple half apron. My sewing teacher gave our class a ditto with handwritten directions. No pattern, just measurements and directions.

Since I knew the anatomy of an apron, I was sure to get an A+. Well, it took me the entire semester to complete that apron. I tried every way to jazz up the apron's style by using lace, buttons, fancy pockets with bows, I even tried scalloped edging. But my teacher wanted everyone to follow her directions. Precisely!

After going back to the fabric store again and again, I knew it was time for me to be serious and get busy. When my apron was finished, my teacher was very generous with her grading and honored me with a B+ for my continuous efforts.

When I was younger, there were many aprons in our household. Seven girls, one brother, a dear grandmother, and stepmother. All loved to cook and wear aprons. My Dad loved to cook, as well, and always tucked a tea towel around his waist. It worked for him and protected his masculinity.

For hours I watched my stepmother sew on the old Singer sewing machine. Little did I know that my curiosity was preparing me for future sewing projects.

Guiding the fabric through the machine, I listened to the hum of the machine's motor. This was more fun than watching my favorite TV shows. At the age of seven, I asked her, "Mom, what makes the machine work?"

She replied, "When I say go, it will sew and when I say stop, it stops."

Well, I tried it and nothing happened. Huh! Did those magic words work only at her command?

One day while picking up some scraps that were scattered on the floor, I accidently touched something that started the machine running. Eureka! I found it! Mom was using this metal thing to make the machine go.

Mom loved to sew but I don't recall her making any aprons. Most of the aprons were purchased at rummage sales or given to her when she worked as a housekeeper for rich folks. Some were really fancy, too. Many years later, I would write a children's book called *Miss Mattie's Aprons*, about my husband's grandmother who loved to wear aprons. I designed an apron pattern from my book and made aprons to purchase separately. My friend Lorraine Haddock helped me with all that sewing. Piggy aprons were everywhere.

By the time I was in the tenth grade, I became somewhat of a fine seamstress. I made dresses, shorts, skirts, and tops, and could follow most patterns. I made clothes that I actually wore. Some of my dresses even had matching headbands.

By the tenth grade, my boyfriend David purchased a brand-new Singer sewing machine for me, and sometimes helped me with my fabric purchases.

My typing teacher complimented me one day on how I looked and asked me if I would be interested in sewing for her. That really built up my self-esteem. I felt so special and took pride in every garment I completed. I never knew that twenty years later, I would be designing prom gowns for my daughter and wedding gowns for my future daughters-in-law.

CHAPTER 93

I Love Quilting!

Herbs of The Bible - 2013

In 1973, I visited a friend named Lauren. She was my son's den mother for Cub Scouts. She had taken a course in quilt-making. The beauty of the color in the fabrics and tiny stitches overwhelmed me with delight. I wanted very much to learn this skill, but we were raising four children and sometimes there wasn't enough money for recreation or hobbies. Knowing my situation, Lauren began teaching me everything she had learned in her quilting classes. I was extremely grateful!

Once a week, in her cozy kitchen, we pieced and appliqued squares, creating our first handmade quilt. I enjoyed quilting so much, it became my daily pleasure, and I gave up watching soaps on TV.

Moving forward and many quilts later, my life changed when our second son Darrell was killed by a drunk driver. I needed something to ease my pain from this tragic loss. One month later, while lying in bed thinking of him, a calmness came over me and the Holy Spirit spoke to me. "Make a quilt in your son's memory!" I began that very day, picking out scraps, cutting, pinning, and piecing together squares.

One year later, on Thanksgiving Day 1989, I finished the quilt. God had given me this gift of quilting as a comfort to me. I gave the quilt to my husband as a gift of love, and he uses it every day.

There was another quilt I made for Darrell when he turned seventeen years old. He always wanted a quilt for his bunk bed, but I made it larger to fit a full-size bed. When he went into the service, he left it home and I took care of it for him. Two years later, I would bury him with his quilt. I washed it and pressed it for him. As I pressed it, my tears began to flow. I could hear the sizzle of the iron as it pressed on every tear. Within his quilt are his mother's tears.

When I studied the history of slavery, I found out that most slaves were buried with their own quilts. This motivated me to continue doing research on quilts and sparked my interest in writing a play.

I began to name my quilts and giving meaningful stories behind them. The quilt I gave to my husband is called "God's Children are Gathering Home." It depicts little black children with happy and sad faces. Happy to be in the Kingdom of Heaven but sorry to leave their loved ones behind.

My two small children and I along with the quilt and the story were featured in the *Good Housekeeping* magazine in 1994.

Two years later, I started teaching the art of quilting to adults and children, and taught for ten years. I never knew that this gift that God gave me would take me so far. My stepmom always told me that I was good with my hands. And until this day her words continue to motivate me, and now I am quilting through my golden years.

I've entered my quilts in shows and won many blue ribbons for First Place, Best in Show, Best in Applique, and People's Choice Awards. My next endeavor is to have them photographed and published for quilters and those who appreciate the art of quilting.

CHAPTER 94

The Dating Game!

W hen I was fourteen years old and almost very mature, I met this very nice kid who came to our house for a birthday party for my stepbrother Wayne. We started liking each other right away.

He soon got up enough courage to ask my father if he could keep company with me. My dad told him yes, but I wasn't allowed to go out on dates yet, because I was so young. Dad was very strict about the dating age, and sixteen, he felt, was a proper age. This young man happened to be the nephew of Dad's girlfriend Ellen. So this kid had a free pass, and Dad had made an exception this time. But I better obey his rules. House visits only!

He was a nice kid and we had lots of fun together. We saw each other for about a year and a half.

I had to work in the blueberry fields for two years, and I made up my mind that this would not be the life for me. It was stinking hot, riding in the back of a covered truck in the blazing summer heat. The second year, I went to a different overseer, named Al, who had an old broken-down bus. It was just as bad riding in that, too.

I saw this older kid who was picking about two rows from where I was. Now, I wasn't a flirt, but I loved to play jokes on people my age.

There was another boy working with him I knew, but I wouldn't dare mess with him, or I just might get cursed out.

It was time to quit for the day and the overseer called, "Quitting time! Top off your blueberry crates and cash in." I needed about four pints of blueberries to cover the tops of my crate, so I marched over to this kid's row and snatched about four pints from him. I topped my crate off and threw the empty boxes back, near his row. He saw me and just laughed. Little did I know that he would be going to Clayton High School in the fall, and that's when we officially met. I was a freshman and he was a senior. He was on the football team and was very popular. He had come from Williamstown to Glassboro High School and did not want to come to Clayton High.

When he went to Glassboro High, they found out that he lived on the Clayton side of the railroad tracks and must go to Clayton. Well, he went kicking and screaming.

"There's nothing in Clayton for me," he said. "Their football team stinks and they didn't have as many extracurricular activities that I was used to." But he had to go; it was the county law!

I saw him every now and then changing classes, but never said anything to him. Until his brother William asked me, "Did you meet my brother David?" He told me the year before that he had an older brother who was a square. But I never made the connection, because they looked nothing alike.

I was still dating the other guy and I wanted to be true to him, and with that, my sister Bert had some tricks up her sleeve.

David was visiting the boy across the street from us and Bertha called him over. She started screaming out the front door, "Hey, David Lindsey! My sister Kat wants to talk to you."

Well, with that friendly invitation, who could resist? He came running!

I was getting ready to do my homework, my hair was all over my head, wearing skimpy, short shorts and flip-flops. He came in smiling, showing all of his dimples, and I said, "Hi."

Bert started talking about how I was interested in him, and that I had another boyfriend I was going to dump, which she made up. She could be a real stinker at times, but I always managed to pay her back one way or another.

About a week later, our school had our first pep rally. The football players were sitting on chairs in the center of the gym. When they called his name, "Meet David Lindsey from Williamstown High School," he stood up, and while the entire gym clapped and screamed, he turned his head and winked at me. Oh, my goodness! Everybody knew that David was in love! Many of my classmates said, "He's winking at you. He likes you, Kat."

But I'm just a freshman nobody, and he's a senior, I thought.

What's a girl to do? The following Monday, he sent me a love letter. It said:

"From the first time I met you, I was in love with you."

What a jive turkey he was! Love? He often told me that he loved me, about a thousand times, and called me "sugar pie honey bunch." David loved music lyrics and used them to impress me all the time.

There was a great deal of competition between those two guys. Both would show up at the house at the same time. Not good! And neither boy would leave.

There I was, sitting between two guys who refused to walk away, and I didn't know what to do. My sisters thought it was funny. I didn't know how to weasel my way out of this situation like my sisters could. They were good at playing this game. Example: one sister might tell her boyfriend, "Oh, I'm too sick to go out tonight," but then turn around and go to the movies with another guy. Or cover for each other when talking on the telephone. They could imitate one another's voices. And they were good at it, too. That was deceitful! Especially when a question came up that they couldn't answer.

Suddenly the front door opened. It was Dad coming home from his date. He looked at me and, with his bulging eyes, gave me the stare from hell. He went in the kitchen for a drink of water and in a few minutes came out and went to bed. He said nothing!

For some time, I watched the clock that hung over the entrance to the dining room. I was relieved when 11:00 came. That was another rule of the house. All boys had to be out of the house by 11:00 p.m.

Dad had already gone to bed, so I figured I was safe from his wrath. Not!

The next day he cornered me in the kitchen and let me have it with both barrels.

"Kat!" he yelled. "Who do you think you are, dating two boys at the same time!?"

I tried to explain that I didn't want this to happen, but he wouldn't let me get in a word edgewise. He didn't even try to hear me out. "But, Dad! Dad! Yes, Dad! No, Dad! I didn't, Dad!"

Oh boy, here comes the tears!

Well, my dad ripped me up one side and down the other. And threatened to make me wait until I was sixteen to start dating. A whole year!

Then he said the unthinkable! "Girl, you look like a 'whore' sitting there with two jackasses! You better choose one or the other, or I will choose for you."

Everybody knew that Dad's bark was worse than his bite. But this time he was roaring like a lion. And I was afraid that he would attack.

The next day when he got home from the barbershop, where he worked part time, he called me again.

"Kat, come here," he said in a much calmer voice. "You know, if you continue to date this other kid, that I let come see you, and you decide to marry him someday, you would be committing incest. Because I'm planning to marry his aunt one day. I'm gonna make it easy for you... Stop seeing him right now!"

I obeyed.

Funny thing! He never approached my other sisters who were dating sometimes three boys at a time. What's up with that? I had only two boyfriends and married the second one.

At the age of fifteen, I was too young to even be thinking about marrying anybody, and I certainly didn't know what incest was, let alone the other word. But I knew it had to be something awful.

CHAPTER 95

David's Baptism

As I mentioned before, our father always preached to us girls about dating and marrying someone who was an unbeliever or showed no interest in seeking the Lord.

After dating David for about ten months, I began talking to him about how much I love going to church. We sang songs on the front porch. I wasn't pushing him, but was trying to get a feel for how much he knew about the Lord. No pressure. He informed me that he attended St. Matthews, when he lived in Williamstown. But when his family moved to Glassboro, he had no way of getting there. He even sang in their choir. Hum......

After we finished that conversation, I wanted to impress him by singing some songs I learned in glee club. He thought they were funny. Then I sang him a love song by Johnny Mathis called "The Twelfth of Never."

He looked at me, smiled, and said, "That was nice."

I was so impressed with this guy, and couldn't wait to tell Dad the good news.

"Dad, he used to go to church!" I said.

"That don't mean nothing!" he replied. "Did you invite him to church yet?"

"Yes, I did, Dad, and he's coming."

The following Sunday as I sat in church, I thought to myself, *He's not coming*. Moments later, the church doors opened and in walked my "knight in shining armor," dressed in a suit and tie, grinning from ear to ear and showing his deep dimples. He sat down beside me and we shyly held hands. Little did we know that one year later, we would be joined together, holding hands, at the altar.

God had a plan.

After a couple of months David felt he wanted to be baptized again, because he was too young when he was baptized the first time, which was under his mother's (won't take no for an answer) persuasion.

In 1965, he was immersed into baptism. He didn't even tell his mother, because he knew what her reaction would be. It was one happy day for both of us. I said to him, "You are now my brother in Christ.

CHAPTER 96

My Last Whipping

When I was sixteen, I got my last and final beating. One night, several of my sisters were cutting up and teasing Granny. When Daddy came home, he asked Granny, "Why are you so upset?" She told Dad that I was teasing her, but it wasn't me. It was another sister, and Granny was mixed up.

Well Dad never asked questions. He just whipped off his belt and started beating me. I tried to tell him that it wasn't me, but he wouldn't listen. After he finished with me, he threw me in the chair.

Then Granny said, "No, Wiggy! It wasn't Kat. It was HER."

Daddy turned and looked at me, and said, "You needed a beating, anyway."

I was humiliated and hurt. My sister Ida's boyfriend George was there and witnessed the whole thing, and I knew he would tell David everything that happened. And he did.

David was so angry that he wanted to hurt my dad. But I calmed him down.

My father could have apologized to me but he was too prideful, or was he seeking to have an altercation with David? He never showed any remorse.

Our family was becoming very dysfunctional!

CHAPTER 97

Meeting David's Mom

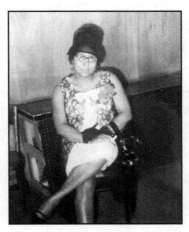

Laura Ann, my mother-in-law 1972

Mother's Day 1965, David came to church and asked me to come to his house for dinner.

My father said it was okay, but to be at home by 6:00 that evening. I was very nervous about meeting her, but I managed to hold my composure. After church, we walked around the block where he lived. When he opened the door, several of his siblings came running in the living room to greet me. Allen, Alease, John, and Jennie. William, another brother, was still asleep from a hangover from the night before.

Miss Lindsey was in her bedroom with her boyfriend.

After talking with the kids for about an hour, David took me back into the living room and went to get his mother. He knocked on her bedroom door and stuck his head in, then he went in. He wanted her to come out and meet his girlfriend, his first girlfriend. Sometime later, she came out and David introduced her to me. She said a simple hello.

I wished her a Happy Mother's Day and she thanked me.

I guess she wasn't ready to meet anyone today, because it was her day, Mother's Day. She didn't hold any conversation with me after that and I felt that I was imposing. She told her daughter Alease to warm up the leftover turkey that they had the day before, when her mother, Grand mom Mattie, came on Saturday for an early Mother's Day dinner.

Sad to say, there was hardly anything left. But that was okay; she wasn't expecting company.

Later, she came in the kitchen and started cooking a chicken dinner for her boyfriend.

Now, I'm not one who wants the "red carpet treatment," but all I got was the silent treatment. I was relieved when David asked me if I wanted to go home. He spoke to his mom in private. I assume he asked her for bus fare.

On the way to the bus stop he asked me, "What do you think of my mom?"

I told him, "I'm not sure, because she didn't talk at all to me.

He replied, "It takes time for her to warm up to people."

Then I understood.

Over the years, she and I would have a few confrontations, but I always handled myself with dignity and always respected her. Through time, I would grow to love her, because she was my husband's mom and the grandmother of our children.

CHAPTER 98

The Junior-Senior Prom

The Junior/Senior Prom 1965

I t was prom time, May 1965. David asked me to go with him. I was so excited that I wanted to jump for joy! But I would have to ask my dad first, because I wasn't sixteen yet. I felt he might say no.

I waited a few days to catch him in a good mood. And when I asked him, he said, "Yes, you can go. But I don't have any money for anything. Be home as soon as everything is over."

What was I to do? I needed money and I needed it fast.

My sister Phil worked at the Elmer Hospital, and mentioned to her coworker that her little sister needed a gown to go to the prom. Her friend provided me with a bell-shaped pink gown with spaghetti straps. It fit me perfectly! I sent it out to the dry cleaners right away.

I needed shoes and Aunt Rose gave me a pair, and hooked me up with a swinging hairdo. That woman could set in some waves! I went to the florist to get David a boutonniere for his lapel. The owner gave it to me and told me to have a good time. I used the fur stole that the sisters used at one time or another. And Bert fixed my makeup and shaped my eyebrows. When I got the gown back, I noticed that the straps were missing. We called the cleaners and they had lost them. NOW WHAT? I had to go strapless. Boy, I had to take precaution not to make any sudden moves or that gown would drop down too far. Bert stuffed my bra with toilet tissue.

When David arrived, he put my flowers on my wrist and we were off to the prom.

Phyllis volunteered to chauffer us to and from the prom. When we got home at 6:00 a.m., we could hear the morning song birds chirping. David said, "Listen, they are singing our song."

Phyllis dropped me off first, then took David home.

Oh, I wish Dad could have seen me. I know he would have been proud. I looked and felt pretty special.

This was the first formal event of my life that I will cherish.

David once told me that when he was much younger, he would sit under a big tree, where he lived in Virginia, and dream of a beautiful girl he would meet one day and marry.

He often talked about seeing a flying saucer among the trees, when he was a young boy. One night he went outside to get some firewood for heating the stove, and lo and behold, there it was, a UFO! It was round with lights, and a puff of smoke came from behind it.

It stood still hovering over the trees and then took off, never making a sound. He ran in the house to get someone to see it, but when they went outside it was gone. Later, it was seen by many others in that area of Gordonville, Virginia. Wow!

Today, I tease him when he does something that's so remarkable. I tell him that the aliens took him up in the spaceship and reprogramed his brain. And when I get angry at him, I say the aliens switched his brain with a bird's brain and the bird flew backward. Bird brain! Ha-ha-ha!

CHAPTER 99

Meeting David's Grandmother

Apron gift from Grand mom Mattie   Grand mom Mattie Lewis - 1973

M attie Lewis was the matriarch of David's family. She was born in 1887. The first time I met grand mom Mattie, David had taken me to Philadelphia to meet her. She came to the door with a smile. "Come on in. Well, I be dog foot, it's David!"

He gave her a big hug and kiss and introduced us.

She said, "I didn't know you had a girlfriend. Boy, you been busy!"

We walked in the polar and talked a while, then Aunt Lillian, her daughter, came home from the YMCA. We had a nice visit with them and they told us to come back again. I noticed that grand mom was wearing a white apron. One pocket contained red and white mints, and the other pocket a lacy handkerchief.

In 1966, when Dave and I were married, grand mom Mattie gave me a beautiful patchwork apron. As a young bride, I became very domestic and enjoyed puttering around the kitchen—anybody's kitchen.

Fifty-two years later, I would write a children's story called *Miss Mattie's Aprons*.

Whenever I visited grand mom Mattie, she would look through her kitchen drawer, choose one of her prettiest aprons, and gather it around my waist, always taking her time to tie it carefully. I always got a warm, fuzzy feeling around my heart when she tied those aprons. It must have been her way of saying, "I love you." On many occasions she would visit our home and I would make sure my special patchwork apron was washed and ironed just for her to see. She knew that I appreciated her special gift.

Many years have gone by and I don't use my delicate apron anymore, but it hangs neatly in my kitchen, on the hutch door, as a constant reminder of that precious lady who loved to wear aprons.

When my husband was born, his grandmother saved his life by keeping him for several months, because his mother's husband wanted to kill him. David was not his biological son. This explains why he didn't look like his siblings. Grand mom told me this story many times, along with many other stories about her life. She died at the age of ninety-two.

CHAPTER 100

Laura Ann's Creepy Little Boyfriend

In the fall of 1965, David had just started working for DuPont. I had a visitor one afternoon. It was Mrs. Lindsey's boyfriend, a Puerto Rican guy named Richard. I didn't know exactly what he wanted, but he asked to speak to me in private. So we went to the side of the yard, where I knew Mrs. Sadler would be watching me. He started talking, and then suddenly put his arm around me.

That's when Mrs. Sadler came out running, yelling, "Take your hands off of her or I'll call the cops!"

I said, "Mrs. Sadler, I know him."

"Well, I don't, so he better get out of here right now! Go! Get out of here! Chile', he means you no good, and I know rotten when I see it!"

He started speaking Spanish and I could tell he was disrespecting her with foul language by the expressions on his face and his hand gestures. And that's when I smelled the liquor on his breath. I pointed for him to leave!

He had come to try to break us up! Someone had sent him! Who? He didn't know where I lived and somebody had dropped him off near my house. I was so naïve to think he meant well.

I told David about the incident and he told his mom what her boyfriend did. He told her that it better not happen again.

Yes, our neighbor was protecting me against a possible molestation. Thank you, Mrs. Sadler.

IT DOES TAKE A WHOLE VILLAGE TO RAISE AND
PROTECT A CHILD!

CHAPTER 101

Approached by a Stranger

I was walking home from school after tryouts for the Clipperettes drill team. I felt that I hadn't made the squad. So I went home. I was about to turn the corner of the football stadium, on Academy Street, when a man pulled his car over to ask for directions. He said he wanted to get a cup of coffee and asked if I could show him where a store was.

I turned and pointed down the street toward the traffic light. "The store is across the street from the traffic light."

"Well, could you show me? Then I'll take you home. Come on, get in."

When he said that, I took off running and didn't stop until I got home.

You see, I remember when my sister Loretta was almost abducted by two men. After they were caught, Dad took her to the police station to identify them. They were being held with a possibility of arrest. The wife of one of the guys cried so hard, saying that they had two little children, so Dad didn't press charges. Loretta was lucky!

I remembered my granny's words: "Always be careful out there."

Lord only knows what that man had on his mind and what he could have done to me.

Oh yeah, I found out a few days later that my name was called to be in the finals for the drill team, but I had gone home. Oh well, maybe next year! The following year I tried out for the majorettes and was chosen.

CHAPTER 102

David Pops the Question!

I was sixteen years old and a sophomore in high school. It was a cold football night in October, and being a majorette, I wore a skimpy uniform. Burrr! It was so cold; I was shaking like a leaf.

At halftime, David took me to his car so that I could get warm. He sat in the back and I in the front. He turned on the heat and it was blasting. We only had about ten minutes before the second half started, and I had already performed with the Clayton Clippers Marching Band.

He started up a conversation, but he seemed to be very nervous getting his words together. He said, "You know I love you very much and I was hoping that someday we will get married, do you?"

I replied, "Maybe someday, when I finish high school. I only have two years and seven months to go."

He said, "Do you love me?"

"Of course I do."

"Then, we'll get married now!" He smiled.

"NOW!? But I'm too young to get married now." I laughed.

Suddenly, he reached into his pocket and pulled out a little black box. He said, "Close your eyes and give me your right hand."

I extended my hand and he put the ring on my trembling, frozen finger. Oh my, this can't be! It was a diamond ring in a silver setting with little diamonds on each side. It was beautiful!

"Will you marry me?" he said, with a pitiful, pleading look on his face.

"I… I… I would love to marry you, Dave, but we have to ask my father and I want to finish school first. And I'm too young."

"School! I'll teach you everything you will need to know. I have it all figured out," he said.

Hum… I thought.

We got out of the car and he walked me back to the stadium. I could hardly breathe!

I couldn't take my eyes off the ring, and my heart was beating so fast, I forgot about how cold I was.

My sister Bert was head majorette. She was sitting on the bleachers, waiting for me to return. I didn't tell her yet, and she didn't notice the ring. I told my best friend Janet Harris, who was also a majorette, and she was speechless for a bit.

Then she blurted out, "Engaged! Kat, you're too young to get married!"

"No, not yet. I didn't say yes to him. He wants me to wear the ring and think about saying yes," I told her.

This was a lot of pressure on me, and I was going to have to deal with you know who. How and what do I tell my dad!?

A few days later, David came to visit me. He knew what he had to do but wondered how he would ask my father for my hand in marriage. He went into my father's bedroom and asked him, and without hesitation, my dad said, "Yes, but under one stipulation. If you feel like you want to hit her or put your hands on her, bring her back home."

Dah!

He didn't say anything about me finishing school or where we would live, or for that matter, when we wanted to get married.

David came out of Dad's bedroom with a big smile on his face. "Your father said yes!"

That was a load off my shoulders!

The very next day, Dad approached me. Dum-dee-dum-dum!

"When are you two planning on getting married?" he asked me.

I told him, "We are thinking about a June wedding, after school lets out."

"No," he said, "that's too long for an engagement period. Anything can happen. Take off that ring right now, give it back to him, and get engaged in December. I don't believe in long engagements."

Why? I wondered.

Dad had gone to see my older sister Elnora and told her what his plan was. "I want them to get engaged in December because if she gets pregnant, she won't show that much."

Dad once told me, "If you get pregnant, I'll put you in a home and put the baby up for adoption."

All I could do was shake my head. Why doesn't he trust me?

Sometimes he would say, "Girls bring home their problems, boys don't!"

No, Dad, boys cause the problems, I thought to myself. Maybe Dad should have had all boys! Then he would see things differently.

I left school after the tenth grade to marry David. I knew that I was too young, but in my heart, I knew I would be happier. More about this subject later.

In September of 1965, I wanted to continue my education at Paulsboro High School. David lived with my sister and her husband in Paulsboro, and he was saving his money to get his own apartment. His family had moved to Detroit, Michigan, in January 1966 and David refused to go with them. He was a man now and it was time for his mom to cut the apron strings.

He got a job right out of high school, working for DuPont in Deepwater, NJ. He would work there for forty-four years until retirement. Hallelujah!

Well, we officially got engaged on December 31, 1965 in Atlantic City, just before the New Year of 1966 came in. Oh, my curfew was still eleven o'clock. Dave and I had to leave AC before the New Year came in.

We began making plans for our wedding almost immediately. I used to do house cleaning on Saturdays and usually made $1.50 an hour cleaning an entire house. I would bring my money home and Dad always had his hand out. One Saturday, he told me if I gave all my money to him, he would save it for my wedding and I would have a nice wedding. I believed it! So he would give me $2.00 or $3.00 dollars for working all day. Sometimes I'd work after school, as well.

David bought most of my clothes, coat, and school supplies for my sophomore year, and my father was not happy with this.

"Pretty soon he'll be asking you for favors," he said.

"No, Dad, he's not like that. He just wants me to have everything I need. He purchased a typewriter because I had typing in school and a Singer sewing machine because I liked to sew. I never asked him for anything and neither did he ask me. He's a real nice person."

David would leave the house by 11:00 and double back with a big banana split just for me, from the Twin Kiss.

After fifty-two years, he still treats me at the TK.

CHAPTER 103

Christmas Gifts

T he holiday season was upon us, and us kids where used to not getting gifts or celebrating the *good tidings of comfort and joy*. It just wasn't happing on Dad's watch. But this year would be a big turnaround for us.

Our sister Phyllis did the unthinkable! She brought a little cheer in our lives with gifts galore! She bought a little each time she got paid and hid those presents in her car, the church, anywhere, and completely out of sight. As I mentioned earlier, Phil always had entertainment for us after we did our chores. But this time we didn't have to work for it. She had been buying stuff for us for about a year and no one knew about it. Not a soul!

She was always good at keeping secrets.

It was Christmas Eve 1965, and I was sitting in the living room, watching Christmas specials on TV with David. Every once in a while, he would strike up a conversation about how much fun Christmas was for people who celebrated, but I wasn't interested.

"David, how can anyone understand something that you never had?" We never had Christmas with all the trimmings.

Then he told me he was coming back tomorrow to bring me something for Christmas. That made me feel so special.

Ida's boyfriend George was there, as well. They had plans to get married in January.

George and David usually came to see Ida and me, and those guys were very close. They both lived closer to the Glassboro side of town but had to go to school in Clayton. It depended on what side of the railroad tracks you lived on. Many times those two guys would walk the tracks together to come see us. And sometimes they would hitchhike. They didn't mind, because we were always worth the trip.

This night was different! Phil got the guys to lock us up in Dad's bedroom, which was the only room besides the bathroom that had a lock. At first we refused to go, but Phil said it would only be for a few minutes and we would be surprised.

The guys herded us kids together and we walked willingly, but we were a little apprehensive in the room. Ida, Bert, Billy, Anna, and I were wondering what was up with Phil.

After about twenty minutes, they let us come out.

"Close your eyes, and don't peek," Phyllis said. When they led us in the dining room, she said, "Okay, open your eyes!"

OH MY GOODNESS! WHAT A SIGHT TO BEHOLD! "IDA, THERE IS A SANTA! AND HE IS A SHE, OUR SISTER PHYLLIS!"

Gifts were everywhere! They covered the table, floor, and dining chairs. Our dining room was covered with presents for us, Daddy, and Granny.

We had to be the happiest kids alive. In my entire sixteen years of life, I never would have imagined ever getting so many gifts at once. We didn't have a tree or decorations, but Phil was taking it one step at a time with Dad.

The next morning, Dad came home, and when he saw what she did, the only thing he said was, "I better not see no Christmas tree back there."

Then he took his gifts and went into his room. Dress shirts, socks, cologne, and a few other items. I never heard him say thank you to Phil.

The next day David came to visit me and gave me more gifts. A blue mohair sweater, a bottle of perfume, and a necklace. How sweet!

After Christmas was over, I bought him a pair of gloves and knitted him a scarf.

CHAPTER 104

Me, Go to France? Notta!

It was almost spring break and Phil had been writing to Loretta, who lived in France, where her husband was stationed in the Army. She said that Loretta wanted me to come and visit her for a few weeks. I didn't want to go because anything could happen and I wouldn't see David again. Her husband went to his credit union and took out enough money for my ticket. I talked to David about the matter and assured him I wasn't going and that was that! He was my best friend and I would never leave him.

About a year later, I found out, through my sister Loretta who was living with us at the time, that it was a one-way ticket for me to come to France to live with them. Rudolf, her husband, went to the credit union and borrowed money to purchase my ticket. The reason was, some of my family members felt that I was too young to get married and wanted to ship me off so I would forget about David.

I'm glad I stood my ground! I also knew Loretta would have turned on me sooner or later. Because that's the way she was.

In April, our lives took a turn. David was drafted into the Army. He didn't want to go and leave me, because we wanted to get married first.

He worked at DuPont with Mayor Gene Costill of Clayton. Mr. Costill wrote a letter to the Selective Service Board, and they gave David a Postponement of Induction. He needed one more month to work in order to keep his job at DuPont, when and if he should return from active duty.

Hallelujah! God came through again! They gave him another date for September.

CHAPTER 105

Dad Marries Ellen

Wedding bells were ringing again for Dad, for the third time. The night before he got married he was attacked by his now ex-girlfriend, named Marion. Dad came home all beat up by this woman who was angry at him because he was marrying Ellen.

Dave and I were at the house, making plans for our wedding, when Dad came home, looking all shook up.

"Kat and David, can you do me a favor?" he asked. "Can you take these records to this lady on North Street? They belong to her and she wants them back tonight."

Well, I thought, *why don't you do it, Dad?*

We didn't ask him, but Dad felt he needed to explain to us why he couldn't go. He said, "She attacked me! She's crazy! She's jealous because I'm getting married." Then he added, "I'll give you directions."

"I know where she lives, Dad. I used to deliver newspapers to her parent's house," I told him.

"Okay, good, that's good!" He sounded relieved that I knew it.

Dave and I went to her house and knocked on the door. She opened the door, looked us up and down, and snatched the records from my hands, saying nothing. This woman was mad as a hornet! I think that's why Dad was so nervous about someone speaking up and not holding their peace at his wedding. Ha-ha-ha!

When we got back home, he asked, "What did she say to you?"

"Nothing, Dad. She was rude to us!"

No comment from Dad! No thanks from Dad! We had covered his you know what!

I was the fourth daughter to marry at the age of seventeen, just twenty-five days after my father got married, for the third time. I never shared one day in my father's house with his new wife. She had a small house built about three miles from where we lived. Dad would come home every day for early morning breakfast and a packed lunch, get his laundry cleaned, pay some bills, and give Phyllis a few dollars to buy groceries. At this time El, Ret, and Ida were already married.

My sisters and I worked our fingers to the bone trying to arrange a nice reception for them. They went to Canada for their honeymoon and never told us, until they came back with pictures. How can you leave a house full of kids and your mother with no instructions in case something happened? But then, we were always alone to fend for ourselves. It was just a way of life for us. I guess he trusted that we could hold down the fort. And I'm sure the newlyweds enjoyed themselves.

Somehow I never felt like a daughter to Miss Ellen. I liked her a lot but I never got a chance to bond with her. She had three children of her own—Betty, Alvin, and Wayne, and that's who she focused on, because she was their mother. She always gave my children and all the grandkids $1.00 for their birthdays and came to nearly all of their school functions and graduations. She was close to my little brother and sister when she moved in my father's house, and for that, I was very pleased. I never spent one day under her tutelage. By the time she moved in, I was out of there!

One month before we got married, Dave and I had to go to Woodbury to pick up our wedding invitations. Dad told me to be home by 6:00 p.m. David was off that day but I had to work until 3:00 p.m. That left us only three hours. We had all intentions of getting back on time but there was traffic and finding exactly what we wanted.

Dad had something up his sleeve and I could smell it.

We got back home at 6:08. When Daddy got home he asked my sister what time I got home. She told him after six—and he started hollering at me!

"As long as you are under my roof, you will do as I say. I said 6:00, and I meant it."

My father wanted me to remember that he was still head honcho in his house and that my being engaged meant nothing to him.

My curfew was always 11:00 p.m. What's he up to? At that moment I wanted to leave home. I was angry and bitter. I wanted to scream at Dad. But I didn't. Dave was ready to take me away. "Just pack your bags and go with me." But he could have gotten into a lot of trouble because I was underage, and I didn't believe in shacking up.

I think this was Dad's last chance to provoke a confrontation and to put David out of my life, but it didn't work. All I had to do was leave home and that would have been his excuse to terminate our marriage plans and not sign for me. Good thing he didn't raise his hand to hit me again. We had twenty-five days before our wedding day and I would become Mrs. David Lindsey. So I persevered!

COLOSSIANS 3:23
Fathers do not embitter your children, or they will become discouraged. (NIV)

CHAPTER 106

A Wedding Shower for Kat

I had a few good friends in junior high school. When I announced that I was getting married in June, one of my friends, Joyce Staples, said she wanted to give me a shower. It was supposed to be a surprise but someone had a loose lip. I had visited her home on several occasions and her mom was always receptive toward me. When we were in the sixth grade, we had a group photo of our class taken. I was wearing a dress she had given me. I was most grateful for it. I didn't have much back then because our mother had left our dad for good. We were only allowed to get two outfits a year. Clothes became very scarce and there was almost nothing that could be handed done that wasn't rotted or raggedy. Sometimes I looked like a total rag picker. And at this age I was taller than most of my sisters. Sometimes you could let out the hem on an already faded dress. I was starting to fill out and get taller. When I met David everything changed for the better.

Joyce invited about twelve girls to the shower and we had a blast. Someone gave me a small jar of Vaseline and said that I would definitely need it on my wedding night. I was so naïve. It went right over my head. I told them, "Oh, what for? I don't think we need that!" That's when they all started laughing to tears and carrying on, giggling and acting crazy like most schoolgirls do.

"I'll use it in my hair for hair grease," I said. I wish I could have had pictures taken. We had so much fun that night, and once again, I felt very special.

When Dave came to pick me up, we loaded up his car with gifts. I told him about the shower. He asked, "How much did you tell them about me?"

I looked at him and said, "What I told them, I could repeat to you with no problem."

CHAPTER 107

Who Will Cosign?

We had another dilemma! Dave's Mom refused to sign for him to get married. David was only eighteen and had to have a cosigner. His Aunt Nancy and Aunt Jennie came from Philly to sign for him. When Dave took them to the notary public, they said, "No. Your mother, being alive, has to sign for you."

David was not of age to sign for himself, and neither was I.

He called his mother in Detroit and asked her to sign the papers and send them back. He promised to send her money for a ticket to come to our wedding, but that never happened. He figured she might try to stop the wedding as she had promised him before she moved to Detroit.

Through all the obstacles we had to face, this was one of the most challenging ones, with our parents. They were not fond of each other and didn't want their children to be united because of their differences.

I don't think Dave's mom ever forgave her son, but he had to do what was necessary.

CHAPTER 108

It's Time to Jump the Broom!

Our Wedding Day- June 25, 1966

On June 25, 1966, David and I were united in holy matrimony. Just twelve days after my seventeenth birthday. Our wedding was very small but we were happy. I didn't realize that I would be working so hard to prepare my own wedding feast, but I did the best I could. For about sixty guests, I prepared a large baked ham, string beans, macaroni salad, and punch. Miss Ellen bought the rolls. An elderly couple, Mr. and Mrs. Brooks, bought our wedding cake. This was very helpful for us. David payed for the invitations and flowers.

My father gave me $40 for the food. Huh! He let me order a $25.00 Sears special wedding dress and my big sister Elnora purchased my veil. Cousin Blanch loaned me her pearls. I still had my long, white, hot winter gloves from the prom. I needed a long slip, so I cut the bottom half of one full slip and sewed it to another full slip. Bingo! Long slip!

I washed and curled my own hair and my sister Bert put on my makeup and plucked my eyebrows. Believe it or not, I sat waiting for everyone else to get ready. I went to Granny's bedroom so she could see me dressed. She cried.

"I wish I could go," Granny said. "When you come back, tell me all about it."

"Granny, I'm not coming back. I'll be living with my husband from now on," I explained.

I made a promise that I would come back as often as I could to spend time with her, and I did.

On the way to the church, my sister El, who was my maid of honor, rode with us. Before the wedding march played, Dad took my hand and asked, "How do I look?"

I looked at him and smiled. "You look fine, Dad." Then I turned my head and rolled my eyes from one side to the other. *What a conceited little man*, I thought. *This is your daughter's wedding day, not your first début.* He couldn't even tell me, "You look nice, too." Daddy showed off so much; it was embarrassing!

We invited the mayor of Clayton to our wedding because he was so helpful in getting David a Postponement of Induction from the US Army. My father showed off so bad, yelling, "Mr. Mayor! Hey, Mr. Mayor." Dad was a name-dropper. He wanted everybody to know that the mayor of Clayton came to his daughter's wedding. Good thing I didn't tell Dad that we had invited him.

The wedding march began to play and Dad escorted me down the aisle, grinning like a Cheshire cat! As we repeated our vows to each other, my sister Bert began to cry uncontrollably. I felt sorry for her, but I had to focus on Minister Paul Cantrell and what he was presenting to us during the ceremony. Poor Bert, she felt she was losing her sister, I think.

Dad never broke the bank when I got married. Everybody else chipped in and came through for us. In fact, I thought he purchased the wedding cake until an elderly couple, Mr. and Mrs. Brooks, asked us if we were pleased with what they chose for our wedding gift, the cake. We had no idea! We thanked them and told them that no one had told us. Dad only told me not to worry about it, so I assumed he and his new wife Ellen took care of the cake. My Dad was something else!

Our honeymoon consisted of going to Atlantic City and walking the Boardwalk. We had a few rides, went into the haunted house, and had enough money for a cheap lunch—hamburgers and fries. Oh yeah, we took four black-and-white pictures at the Boardwalk photo booth. For $1.00, David had an artist draw me. I still have that portrait. Ha! Ha! Ha! Needless to say, we only had a total of $20 to spend. But we were happy.

CHAPTER 109

Vietnam, Here He comes!

D avid had two months before he would leave for boot camp. I stayed on my knees, praying to God to please keep him from going into the service. "Lord, I can't go back home. I'm not happy there," I prayed.

David had passed his physical before we got married and he was told that he would definitely go to Vietnam. Yes, he was drafted and America was in the heat of the Vietnam War. September 23, 1966 was his day to leave.

I cried a lot and prayed much.

We took a trip to Detroit, so that he could say good-bye to his family. We stayed for about four days. When visiting his cousin Mattie, everybody was in the basement listening to music and smoking. It was so smoky that I could hardly see, because my eyes were burning. I felt ill and ran upstairs to the bathroom. Cousin Mattie followed me and found me puking up everything I had just eaten. She asked me, "Are you pregnant?" And she touched my stomach. "You pregnant, Girl! When was the last time you seen your period?"

I had to think for a moment and told her it was in June.

"Well, Kat, this is August." She gave me a hug and said, "Don't be scared. You'll be all right."

When I went back downstairs, it seemed like everybody was looking at me and asking me if I was feeling better. I heard Aunt Alease (Mattie's mother) say, "Yeah, David, take that child to the doctor when you get back home."

On the way back to Jersey, David said he thought that I was pregnant but didn't want to build up our hopes. I knew I had missed my monthly for July and August but thought nothing of it. I was stressed about David leaving me and I wasn't concerned with myself.

"For about a week, you seemed very tired and you slept nearly all the way to Detroit, and that was ten and half hours. A couple times you said you felt nauseous. Yep, Kat, I think you are!" David said with excitement.

When we got home, I went to see a doctor and he confirmed that I was about six weeks pregnant. Well, we were ecstatic! David had the doctor write a note for the Selective Service Board, and without delay, they gave a Cancellation of Induction. Not too many young men were excused from this duty. He was a blessed young man because somebody had prayed for him. ME!

And the Good Lord had performed another miracle!

In January of 1967, my dad came to visit me. It was so cold in our apartment because we ran out of heating oil and didn't have money to order more. Dad asked me why it was so cold, and I told him. Then, he reached in his pants pocket, pulled out his wallet and handed me $40 dollars to buy oil, but I gave it back.

"No, thanks," I said. "That's okay, Dad. We'll be all right."

He begged me to take it but I still refused.

Later, Bert told me, "Dad came home and cried like a baby, because his daughter was up there in that apartment almost freezing to death."

I didn't mean to hurt his feelings. But he always told us,

"STAND ON YOUR OWN TWO FEET!

Don't take handouts!"

I don't know how fast the news had traveled, but by evening our brother-in-law Richard Gardenhire stopped by and insisted that we pack a bag and come stay with them for a few days.

My sister Elnora once told me, "If all I have to eat is rice, I will share with you."

She and Richard were such compassionate people. We always had good times together. In 2000, big brother Richard passed away. He is sorely missed.

CHAPTER 110

Our First Baby Boy

I had a very difficult pregnancy. I suffered from high blood pressure and I gained thirty-six pounds. One of my doctors was a bit concerned. The other doctor was a pervert. He took me into his office, yanked me across his lap, pulled down my underwear, and spanked me for gaining too much weight. He was a huge man and I disliked him for what he did to me. He thought it was a joke, and the receptionist said, "Oh, he does that to all of his patients that gain too much weight."

David had a little talk with him. I don't know what he said, but that doctor treated me with respect after that.

I stayed in labor for forty-eight hours. I couldn't have anything but liquids. The doctor tried six times to give me a spinal tap, but it didn't work. They decided to put me to sleep and use forceps to deliver my baby.

At the age of seventeen years old, I gave birth to our first son, David Jr. He was six pounds, nine ounces.

Right after delivery they took me to the recovery room, knowing that I would have a seizure due to my blood pressure being so high. They called it toxemia. I stayed in the recovery room for about four hours and they watched me very closely, then they moved me to my regular room.

I had a young white girl as a roommate and we began talking right away. Suddenly I felt strange and turned over. That's when everything went dark, like I was falling asleep. I don't remember anything else.

That night when I woke up, I felt different. My mouth was bloody and my tongue hurt.

My roommate asked me, "How do you feel?"

I said, "I'm okay, I think."

Then she began to tell me what happened. "We were talking and all of a sudden you turned over. I thought I had said something that offended you. You started shaking and your whole bed was shaking. I knew you were in trouble so I called the nurse, and a lot of them came running in. They had to give you shots and they put that tongue depressor in your mouth, because you were biting your tongue. I was so afraid for you."

I thanked this angel for being there for me, or I could have slipped away.

She said, "No problem."

I never saw her again after she left the hospital, but I'll never forget her.

Our son was born on May 13 and they brought him to me the next day, which was on Mother's Day. He had a pink carnation on his nighty and I asked the nurse what the flower was for.

"It's Mother's Day, and the flower is for you. You're a mommy," she said.

I held him in my arms, kissed him, and whispered in his tiny ear, "Hello, Son. I'm your mommy and you're our precious baby boy."

Today as I write this portion of my story, my husband and I are traveling to Chesapeake, VA, to celebrate our firstborn's fiftieth birthday. Wow! Did those years fly by fast?

CHAPTER 111

Loretta Came to Live with Us

About two months before I had our first baby, my sister Loretta came from France to visit but ended up living with us. Bad idea! She tried to rule us in our own place. She knew we were struggling and barely had enough money to feed ourselves, let alone another mouth. As I mentioned before she was bipolar, but at that time she hadn't been diagnosed yet.

She had left her husband but led us to believe she was just there for a visit. Dad was happy when she said she was going to stay with us. I didn't know anything about this until she was settled in. The first week was okay, until she ran out of pocket change. David bought her cigarettes, beer, and anything else she needed. I was so upset because this brought back some memories of what she was like, when I was younger. Loretta could be a lot of fun, but don't cross her when she was in one of her moods.

When I got home from the hospital with the baby, she tried to take over. I could understand if she was trying to help. But she was making me feel inadequate with my own child. It got worse, until David told her, "You gotta go!" So she went to live with Ida; that didn't last long, either.

It got so bad that David went to see about getting a restraining order on her, because she had threatened him. Loretta should had been on medication a long time ago, but she refused to acknowledge that she had a problem. She once told me that her husband, Rudolph, was a wife beater and was put in jail several times. He was very abusive toward her and Loretta was a troubled soul.

CHAPTER 112

The Can of Field Peas

I was pregnant with our second child when we fell on hard times. It was a couple of days before David got paid and we hardly had any food, but we did have a can of field peas, which I had planned to fix for dinner. Our baby needed milk so we went to the store. Back then, it only cost thirty-seven cents for a can of formula, and that's all we had. We had no idea what a food bank was and no one knew that we were broke.

We drove to the store and David went in to get the formula, while I stayed in the car with the baby. There was a lady in the parking lot who seemed to be having trouble with her car. She seemed to be looking around for help.

When David came back to the car, I told him about what I saw, so he went to see if she needed any assistance. I watched him go to the trunk of her car, then I knew she had a flat tire. He changed her tire and she offered him $6.00 for his service. He didn't want to take it, but she insisted.

Well, we went into the store and came out with two bags of groceries. Fifty years later, I still have that empty can as a constant reminder.

PHILIPPIANS 4:19

And my God will meet all your needs according to his glorious riches in Christ Jesus (NIV).

HEBREWS 13:5

Keep your lives free from the love of money and be content with what you have, because God has said, "Never will I leave you: never will I forsake you" (NIV).

CHAPTER 113

Darrell Lawrence Is Born

I t was the beginning of spring, April 2, 1968. This day was unbearably hot and I was nine months pregnant, due any day. David decided to take the baby and me to Woodbury to see Ida and George, who had recently moved there.

Ida and I walked to the park to see the guys play basketball. And I was dragging my feet, trying to keep up with her. I finally asked David to take me home because my stomach had dropped and I was afraid that my water might break. We drove back to our apartment, ate dinner, and I went to bed.

At around 2:00 am, I awoke having labor pains. "It's time to go, David," I told him. I had packed a small suitcase for the baby, woke him up, changed his diaper, and we were on our way to Underwood Hospital to welcome baby number two. After dropping me off and signing some admission forms, he took the baby to Ida and George's apartment.

I was in labor for four hours, and then Darrell was born. This delivery was much easier than the first one and I was grateful for that. They let me see him for a moment then said that I needed to rest. He was born on April 3.

The very next day, the devastating news spread throughout the hospital. Martin Luther King Jr. had been assassinated! The nurse came in with my baby and she had been crying. "Why do the good die young?" she asked me. I couldn't answer her but showed my compassion and concern. I kept staring at my beautiful baby boy and wondering, *Will you make an impact someday for society?* Twenty years later, he did.

When I got home, I watched the funeral of Dr. King Jr. It was so sad seeing his grieving wife, and his kids, who would grow up without a father. My heart ached for them. If I was able, how could I reach out to help them? There was a song that was sang as a tribute to him, "If I Can Help Somebody" by Mahalia Jackson. I still cry when I hear that song.

CHAPTER 114

A Time to Deliver, Again!

D onald Lloyd was the third son to be born. We had moved out of our tiny apartment in Paulsboro, thank goodness, and I was pregnant again. On August 8, 1968, we purchased a three-bedroom house on Dennis Drive, in Clayton. David had just turned twenty-one and it was time to make the move. The house we purchased was across the street from my sister Phil, and it was perfect for us. We had a large front and backyard with lots of roses and perennial flowers that came up every year. My favorite was the large mimosa tree that grew in the front yard. We mortgaged this house for $9,800.00 and sold it six years later for $29,500.00. Wow!

When my time came for delivery, David and a friend was watching a 76ers and Celtics basketball game on TV. Feeling tired, I retired early. Sometime later, I woke up to use the bathroom and noticed my stomach had dropped so much and that I was having pressure pains. After noticing a discharge, I called out to David. "It's time!"

The basketball game was finally over, his friend had left, and Dave was asleep on the sofa.

I called again. "David, help me get up!"

The volume on the TV was so high, he couldn't hear me. *Okay, Kat, what are going to do next?* I thought. I started banging on the wall, and sure enough, the thumping woke him up. "David, the baby is coming! But the pains aren't steady yet. I can't get off the toilet." He helped me to the bedroom and I changed my clothes quickly. Dave took my suitcase to the car along with the half-asleep babies. We packed the boys in the car and away we went.

He dropped the boys off at Aunt Natalie's, who lived in Woodbury at that time, and we headed for the hospital, which was about two minutes away. When we got there, David told me to stay in the car and he would get a wheelchair.

It was cold and snow was piled high all around the parking lot, along with a sheet of thin ice that cover the walkways.

He was taking too long and I didn't want to have my baby in this cold. So I got out of the car, took my suitcase from the backseat, and started walking. I was extra careful. But I should not have taken the chance, because it was quite a distance to walk to the hospital entrance.

After I got in, I saw my husband with a nurse coming toward me, pushing a wheelchair.

David said, "Kat, you shouldn't have walked in here alone. You could have fallen on the ice."

But I knew in my heart that God would carry me through.

They took me to the labor room to examine me. I was fully dilated and the baby was coming fast. David went to the waiting room.

I had the baby about two hours after I left home, and he was my biggest boy at eight pounds, four ounces.

The doctor asked David if he was trying for a basketball team. Ha-ha-ha.

CHAPTER 115

One Is Enough, Two Is Plenty, Three Is a Crowd, and Four Is so Many!

The 4 Little Indians - Lindsey boys– 1974

On July 12, 1970, Dean La`Mont would be the last child born to us. It was on a Sunday, a very hot day. I didn't make it to church that day because I was physically tired and my due date was the next day. The day before, I had lots of energy, running around getting things ready. Making sure everything was in place for the babysitter. This time my sister Anna was going to watch my three boys. She had come a few days early to get acquainted with the boys, familiarize herself with the surroundings, and gather instructions for meals and such. Anna, the unpaid nanny!

At around 2:00 pm, my sister Elnora called me to see how I was doing. I told her that I had a discharge but nothing else, no water breakage, no pains yet. She said, "You're in labor and that baby is gonna come fast, just like the last one did. I'll call Phil to see if she can take you to the hospital."

Shortly after, Phil called me and said she could take me. I kissed my babies good-bye and headed out the door. Before I left, I called David, who was working that day, and told him I was on my way to the hospital.

We got there by 5:00 p.m. and they prepped me.

The nurse told me, "Don't push down because your doctor isn't here yet. He's golfing."

"Huh! This baby isn't waiting for the doctor!" I told her.

Dean was born at 6:00 p.m.

I was the fourth daughter to get married, just twenty-five days after my father got married again for the third time, and I was only seventeen. I never shared one day in my father's house with his new wife. She had a small house built about three miles from where we lived. Dad would come home for early breakfast, get his laundry cleaned, and pay bills.

Somehow I never felt a close relationship with Miss Ellen. No bonding, no small talk, no recipes to share. She had three children of her own, whom she focused on. She was a kind person and took good care of our father when he became ill.

After being married for a year, I knew I was bound to follow in my mother's footsteps. I was "a fertile myrtle," too. I gave birth to four sons, giving all four the same initials. David Lewis, Darrell Lawrence, Donald

Lloyd, and Dean La` Mont. The first three children were almost eleven months apart. But I waited six months before becoming pregnant with the last baby. My oldest son David Jr. was finally poddy trained, but I still had three babies in diapers and I was only twenty-one. WOW!

I did much climbing the walls and crying, especially when they all came down with little illnesses like stomach viruses, measles, mumps, chicken pox, roseola, and many other little germs they could carry. I had to wash diapers by hand, and every day the clothesline was full of white cloth diapers. Shortly before Dean was born we purchased a new washer and dryer. Thank you, Lord!

Pampers had just made its way on the scene, but we couldn't afford them. I never asked my husband to change or feed the babies unless he volunteered, which he rarely did. When I was pregnant with Dean, he did take on the job of bathing the boys every night. My tummy was so big I couldn't bend over the tub any longer.

At dinnertime, I held the baby with the bottle propped up under my chin, feed two little ones and myself, all at the same time. That was my job! So I thought! His mother never taught him, and no one told me that it should be a joint effort. Oh well. That, too, did pass!

When Dean was about a year old, I took my four little Indians outside to play. I had to tie a rope around Dean's waist, so he couldn't run away from me. I was twenty-two years old with four preschoolers. They needed plenty of exercise to grow and stay healthy. So we took plenty of walks and they played outside when the weather was permissible. Many times I have asked this question:

LORD, MY SOUL LOOKS BACK AND WONDERS,
HOW DID I GET OVER?

CHAPTER 116

Just Me, Myself, and I

O ne warm sunny day in May of 1972, I took our four boys out in the front yard to play. I noticed a car that seem to be stalled at the corner of Costill and Dennis Drive, where we once lived. It started moving again, then slowed down. I was reluctant to look directly at the vehicle. After the car drove off, I gathered the kids and took them in the house. Minutes later, the phone rang. It was my aunt Natalie, who was cracking up laughing so hard she could hardly catch her breath. She had just moved in to the neighborhood a few weeks prior.

"Kat," she said, "were you outside in your front yard a little while ago?"

"Yes, I just came in. What's up?" I asked her.

"Well, your aunt Julia (who was Aunt Natalie's sister-in-law) came to see my new place and she is about to have a heart attack! She said that she just saw a ghost around the corner. It was her sister Mae, walking around as plain as day with some kids. She was so shook up, she asked me for a big glass of water, because it scared her so bad. I told her that wasn't no ghost. That wasn't nobody but Kat, Mae's daughter! If you saw her with four little boys, on the corner, that was her all right." Aunt Natalie couldn't stop laughing. "Just like Mae!"

I hadn't seen Aunt Julia in many years and she didn't recognize me because I was all grown up! Just me, myself, and I.

Mirror, mirror on the wall, I am my mother after all!

CHAPTER 117

Davy Hanging on Swings

It was early spring in 1972, and our four boys were playing outside on the swing set. I was in the kitchen washing some dishes, and every once in a while I would go to the back door to check on them. They were having fun taking turns swinging. A few minutes passed and I thought to check again, but I hesitated, thinking to finish up first. Immediately something stirred in me, and in a stern voice, it said, *Turn around and check the kids! Do it now!*

Suddenly, I ran to the door and saw my oldest son hanging between the swing set and the top bar of the swing. "Oh, my God!" I shouted. He was hanging himself!

He had wound up the swing to the top bar, shimmied his way to the swing, slipped through it, and was almost hanging himself. I could hardly reach him, but I put his legs on my shoulders and told him to push his head out. "Use your hands, Davey," I kept telling him.

Being almost five years old, he was very scared and didn't understand what I was telling him to do. His head was caught and I had to work fast to get him out. I pushed the seat up and he was able to get his head out. I don't know how I lifted him out, but I started pushing his

319

body through. Where did I get the strength to do this? My arms ached as I worked to save my son. I was able to catch him before he hit the ground. God was with both of us.

Those little boys would get into everything, but after that incident, I never took it for granted, not for a moment, that our babies would always play safely. And I would be more attentive in keeping them out of harm's way.

Speaking of harm's way, one day our house was raided by the Clayton police. My husband had just left for work. About two minutes later there came a knock on our front door. I had just changed our infant son's diaper and was getting ready to put him down for a nap. The knock got harder and harder; I felt that no person I knew would knock that hard on our door. This was a pounding sort of knock that stirred me. As I headed toward the front door with my baby in my arms, I heard the back door being broken into. As I opened the front door, in walked an officer with his gun held high. I stepped back and turned around, seeing the second policeman walking into our living room. He, too, had his gun aimed at the ceiling!

I was scared to death!

"What wrong?" I asked them. "Did something happen to my husband?"

"Who is your husband?" they asked me.

"David Lindsey," I replied in my panic-stricken voice.

"Where is he?" they asked.

"He just went to work a few minutes ago."

Then the two men looked at each other and said something I couldn't understand.

"Do you know a man by the name of ******?"

"No, I never heard of him before," I said.

To this day, I don't remember the name of the man they quoted to me.

My two other boys, Davy and Darrell, who were under the age of four, came into the living room and looked up at the officers. David Jr.

put his little foot on top of the officer's highly polished black boot, and that ignorant man kicked my baby's foot away. Why?

My stomach started to boil and I was really getting angry. How dare he?

Again they questioned me, "Ma'am, you said you don't know him but we were given this address by someone on North Street. Do you know anyone on North Street?

"Yes, I babysit for a lady on North Street," I told them.

"Do you know her address?" they asked.

"No," I replied. "I just watch her child."

As they interrogated me, they seemed to be enjoying what they had just done. They had the wrong address! Breaking and entering!

When they both realized they were tricked by someone on North Street, they looked pretty foolish! The real criminal had a good head start in getting away.

They never apologized for upsetting me, scaring me to death, breaking into my house, or possibly shooting the wrong person. No, not one apology!

If my husband had been home, I know they would have shot him. No doubt about it! The description they gave me was that he was black and they were looking for a black man about David's height and size.

What a difference that two minutes had made. He would have been in harm's way! But God was with us.

CHAPTER 118

Dad and the Peculiar Soldier Boy

There was a man whom Dad met at the barbershop where he worked. He was an Army soldier who met Dad that morning and right away he poured out his problems on him. Our father told this man that he was a minister of the gospel and that he had a good listening ear. This man cried and told Dad his long life story about being in the Army, and of his Korean wife dying. He had three kids in Korea and they were coming to the US. They were due to arrive at the overseas terminal in Philadelphia, late that evening.

Dad showed compassion for him, and wanted one of his married girls to take care of the man's kids until he obtained a home for a family of preschoolers.

Dad brought the man to our house and introduced him as a sergeant in the US Army.

My Dad went around visiting all of us girls who were married to see if we could help this man and take care of his little ones.

When I heard the story about his children, it saddened me, but I couldn't take them because we had three kids already. Ida didn't have any at the time, so she agreed to watch them and get an allotment every month to take care of them. The man said it would only be about three to four months. So Ida was more than happy to look after them.

He needed a ride to the Philadelphia airport to pick up his kids, and he would need $200 cash for the kids to go through customs and get their immunization shots. He promised to write Dad a check when he returned with the children, within an hour.

Dad got one of the son-in-law's to drive him to Philly. Then Dad gave the man the money.

"Thank you, Pastor Williams," the man said. "You have given me a new start in life and for my children."

This man, dressed in Army uniform, told Dad to wait in the terminal, because it might take about an hour for processing his kids.

Dad waited and waited and waited! One hour then two, then three, and Dad started to panic. "Where in the world is he?" he said. Finally, he asked several people at the security desk, and they said they wouldn't have given children shots there, and it just didn't work that way. Then they told him, "Sir, you were conned!"

The man walked in one door and went out the other with Dad's money. This thief played the game all day long with Dad, planning and scamming.

The shady thing about it, he never took off his sunglasses!

CHAPTER 119

Losing Our Dad

Daddy's Bible

Dad going to church - 1969

The year was 1974 when my dad passed away. I was twenty-four. He had been very ill for four years with kidney disease. He and Miss Ellen were married for only seven years, as was his second wife Lavinia. What a coincidence! Dad suffered so much. Dialysis was twice a week and he always said he felt like a washrag after his treatment. Everything was wrung out of him. Miss Ellen went to classes to learn how to hook

Dad up to the dialysis machine that purified his blood. She stopped working to come home and take care of him.

My heart went out to my father. He needed a kidney transplant from any of his kids, but my husband said, "We have four children, and if your kidney fails... Well, you know the rest."

My father retired early from the railroad and did very little preaching, and when his illness got worse, he resigned from the pulpit.

Our granny moved in with her daughter Helen, and she died two years after Dad got sick. At her funeral, he stood up in front of her casket and leaned on his walking cane. He looked so old and rundown, I felt he wasn't going to be around too much longer. I loved my dad despite his shortcomings. I learned a lot from him. I learned what and what not to be. But then, no one is perfect. And we all have sinned and fallen short of God's Word.

Our God is an awesome God who loves us, shows us mercy, and gives us grace.

The Bible tells us, "For all have sinned and fall short of the glory of God. And are justified freely by his grace through the redemption that came by Christ Jesus" Romans 3:23–24 (NIV).

He was in and out of the hospital for the next two years. Late one evening, Mrs. Ellen called me and said, "If you want to see your dad, you better come soon. The doctor said he may not last much longer."

That night during my prayer time, I prayed that God would take him home if he couldn't be healed. My dad suffered so much. I hated to see him so sick. I forgave all the hurt and pain I went through and prayed that God would forgive his transgressions because we are all sinners and have fallen short on our spiritual journeys.

The next day a few of us sisters went to the Our Lady of Lords Hospital to see him. He looked terrible! When I walked in his room, he looked up at me and held up four fingers and smiled. I knew what that meant. My four sons. He loved those little guys and used to come to visit, bringing them each a box of Cracker Jacks. As soon as came through the front door, they would frisk him for goodies. Dad called them "a bunch of little Indians."

One day he asked me, "How come you ended up with so many sons?"

"That was God's plan, Dad," I said while laughing.

He thought that was funny, too. He loved all of his grandchildren, and I only wished his kids had had the same type of affection from him.

Due to a water build up throughout his body, Dad's heart gave out. At fifty-six years old, my father passed away. He was married to Ellen for seven years. What a coincidence! He was married to both wives for only seven years each. Our biological mom: fourteen years.

At his funeral, I was filled with grief, but my dad was out of his pain and suffering, and for that, I was grateful. They buried him at Cedar Green Cemetery, but not near our mother. His new wife Ellen didn't want that. So we all respected her wishes.

About a year later, Miss Ellen called us all on the phone and asked us if we wanted anything from Dad's remaining assets. I wasn't there, but she called me and told me what everyone asked for. I went to see her and asked for one of Dad's Bibles. She went to get them and said, "You can't have his new one. I want to keep that for me."

"That's okay, Miss Ellen. I'll take the old one," I told her.

You see, our real mother had given this Bible to Dad when he was ordained. And she wrote in it. And had his name engraved in gold letters on it. Even though it was falling apart at the binding, and the leather had worn down to the brown sued, all of his notes were crammed in this Bible. You could tell which books he studied more. The New Testament.

Someday, I will restore it.

CHAPTER 120

A Family for Nikki

Nikki graduating 8th grade with Miss Ellen,
my 2nd Stepmother, and myself - 1986

When my youngest son Dean was four years old, we adopted a two-year-old baby girl named Natasha, or Nikki, as she preferred to be called. Our little family couldn't be complete without a girl and we were proud of our little love nest. She was as tough as nails and wouldn't take any stuff from the boys. No, siree!

The first day we met her, she chased those boys all over the James Way, which used to be a department store, in Glassboro.

Nikki was given up by her mother when she was an infant. Her mother left her with a friend and disappeared. After three months, the friend called DYFAS, and she was placed in a foster home until she came to live with us two and a half years later.

Nikki had the biggest, most beautiful brown eyes, and a cute little smile to match. I recall a hilarious incident that happened after she was with us for a few weeks. I was fixing dinner and opening up some cans of corned beef hash. She was sitting in her high chair, watching me. After I put the hash into the frying pan, she said, "Ma, you ficking us dog food!" Well, I laughed so hard, because it did look exactly like dog food.

When Nikki was eight years old, we took a vacation to Bush Gardens, in Williamsburg, Virginia. We camped at the campground adjacent to the park. The older boys synchronized their watches and we told them to meet us back at a certain theme park at the appointed time. After begging me, I let Nikki go with them. When the boys returned, Nikki wasn't with them.

"Where's Nikki?" I asked.

"We thought she went back with you and Dad," they all said.

I was frantic! Where could she be? We went to the security desk, described what she was wearing, and they let many of the workers know that a little girl was missing. They couldn't close the park because she was over the age of five. We all split up to look for her, but the park was too big for six people to cover.

We traveled with another family from Clayton, who was camping at the same campground, but they had gone back to the site to have lunch. We could have used their help, as well. But we didn't alert them.

We looked for more than three hours and still no Nikki! Finally, I sat down to get my breath because it was so hot and I was getting dehydrated. When I looked up I could see our friends in a distance, who were coming back from lunch. Walking toward us, guess who was with them?

When we told them what happened, they said, "Nikki told us she got your permission to go with us."

"And we thought she had gone with our boys. She fooled all of us," I said.

I wanted to turn her over on my knee! I was furious with her! And I'm sure our friends felt bad because they hadn't confirmed it with us. They trusted her. And the boys were angry because they lost their fun time looking for someone who wasn't lost. I learned a big lesson that day.

After dinner, we let the boys go back to the park after dark and finish up what they had intended to do. They had fun and they closed the park!

Nikki grew up to be a super athlete! Every sport she went out for, she excelled at it. Basketball, soccer, baseball, softball. She even joined midget cheerleading, which of course, I was the cheering lead coach. She played piano, and clarinet for a while. But that was not her niche. She wasn't the prissy type of kid, but she sure loved sports.

In her junior year, she blew out her knee toward the end of the basketball season, but the following year she was back on the basketball court scoring points. If she were allowed to play football back then, she would have joined that, too. But we were reluctant to let her join. The football coach wanted her to be the punter, but the answer was still no. She was named player of the year for the Basketball Association All Star Game.

On November 10, 2006, she was inducted into the Clayton Sports Hall of Fame. What an honor for her at the age of thirty-three! We were so proud that she was chosen.

Our kids loved all types of sports—football, baseball, basketball, soccer, volleyball, and some did track and field.

Early one morning while camping at Parvin State Park, the boys rolled out their tent, ate breakfast, and geared up for the long ride back to Clayton to attend the first practice day for the football season, August 1. It took them about one and a half hours to get to Clayton, riding their bikes in the scorching heat. Practice started at 10:00 a.m. Our boys were dedicated and didn't depend on their parents to transport them. When they got jobs and wanted expensive sneakers or fashionable clothing, with a little help from us, they purchased their own wardrobe. Three of them were chosen "best dressed" in their senior year. Dean should have gotten it, but they couldn't have four Lindsey's in a row to receive that honor. After completion of high school, three of the boys joined the military.

CHAPTER 121

David's Brother Passes

T he phone rang. It was David's sister Jennie, calling to tell us that their brother William had been shot to death. It was February 22, 1977, the saddest day of my mother-in-law's entire life. Her son was killed by her nephew. How tragic!

The two young men had been arguing over something that blossomed into a full-blown fight, to a loaded gun. Then her son's life ended. William was twenty-four years old and had two young sons.

We went to the funeral in Detroit, Michigan, to bury his brother. David was devastated but tried hard to console his mom and siblings. Grand mom Mattie was there and tried to do the same. It was so hard, but they got through the most difficult part, his funeral. After that was over, Mom and her brother, Uncle Clarence, had to heal and reunite, due to the loss from this horrible tragedy that his son had caused. It took several years, but they finally reconciled.

CHAPTER 122

Milk, Eggs, and Bread, Oh My!

It was time for the collection plate to be passed at church. When it came to me I gave what I had but needed to keep $2.00 for a gallon of milk, for the kids. We were going through hard times, but I felt this would hold me until payday.

I started to go to the Clayton Acme, but I had the urge to go to the one in Glassboro, instead. I got the milk and started to get in line to cash out. My neighbor, who was a dairy manager there, called me. "Hey, Kathy, come here a minute."

I got out of line and walked to the dairy case.

"Can you guys use some eggs, milk, and bread? We over-ordered and we have to throw it out. It's good! It's fresh! But nowhere to keep it."

Without hesitation, I said, "Yes, we'd love some! I came in to get milk, see."

"Yes, I see," he said. "How much can you use?"

"As much as you want to give me," I said with a grateful smile.

"Okay, I'll be right back." In about two minutes, he came out with two shopping carts full of milk, bread, and eggs.

I couldn't believe my eyes! I couldn't stop thanking him. In my heart, I knew this was a blessing from God.

On the way home, I stopped at all my sisters' houses and they took what they could use. I got home and my kids delivered some to the neighbors.

I made egg salad for lunches, breakfast omelets, scrambled, fried, and laid to the side. Lots of bread pudding, French toast, and the kids drank milk until it came out of their ears.

The offering I put in church was $3.00. The Lord blessed me tenfold or more. I received forty dozen eggs, countless loaves of fresh bread, and twenty-seven gallons of milk. Our children needed to see the glorious works of the Lord, and how He blessed us.

Thank you, God, for your many blessings!

CHAPTER 123

Working at Clayton Elementary School And Getting My High School Diploma

I wanted to get a real job to help support the household. I babysat for years for a total of nine children, off and on. But no more than four at a time—plus my own five, and a host of kids who just came to hang out. I started doing volunteer work at the elementary school, helping my sons' teachers with chaperoning field trips, room mother, and achievement testing. My face became very familiar around the school and I was very happy to be of help to many of the teachers.

My sister Phil worked as a teacher's aide and told me that I should put in an application for playground or kitchen aide, and I did.

337

I went to the school to put in an application, and the principal, Mrs. Simmons, said, "There will be an opening very soon for a reading and math aide. If you would like this type of job, work on getting your diploma first. And when the job becomes available, fill out another application."

She did hire me as a lunch and cafeteria aide immediately. My boss told me that I was an excellent worker and put me on full time. Having that extra money helped with the groceries and clothing for the kids. With my first paycheck, we all went out to dinner, on me.

When I was thirty, I started to go to night school, at Glassboro High School, to obtain my diploma. It was hard because when I sat down to study, my kids would need help with their homework assignments, as well. It didn't matter what time it was or where I went to study, these kids used radar to find me. One night, I was so frustrated that I threw all my books and study plans in the trash. My husband dug them out and told me to finish what I had started.

I had to come up with another plan, so instead of studying in the evening, I switched to the early morning hours, after the kids went to school. All I needed was three hours of study a day, and it worked out well for me.

After receiving my diploma, six months later, the new positions were posted and I got the job! Happy days were here again! I got the reading position and loved working with my coworkers. I kept this job for fourteen years. I could have worked a few more years but we adopted two little kids who needed me more. Both were born with special needs and I had to focus on their health and welfare. The school board said they would hold my job for one year, just in case I wanted to come back. But I never returned. God had another plan for me.

CHAPTER 124

Camping / Almost Drowning at Chincoteague Island

We started camping in 1973. The first time we went camping, we had a large tent that we pitched in a gully filled with soft pine needles. It was so soft and comfortable. Extra padding, so to speak.

It started to rain a little but we were dry and comfortable. Suddenly the sky opened up and the torrential rains came pouring in. Soon we were floating on a waterbed. After the gully filled up, the water poured in through the zippers. Darrell had a bad cough so we had to get out of there fast. We all jumped in the car and set out for home. That was just one of the worst camping trips ever. The next day we went back for our camping gear. No more tents for me!

Chincoteague Island, a little island in eastern Virginia, is a place I'll never forget. This was one of our favorite vacation places. We fished and crabbed to our hearts content. One early evening, we all went walking on a secluded beach. Dave and I were walking ahead of the children but keeping a watchful eye on them. It was a little windy that day but warm. The wind started to pick up and blew my straw hat off my head, and out into the ocean.

"Oh no, not my new straw hat," I yelled and ran into the water to retrieve it. The tide was taking it out farther and farther, but I finally got it and put it on my head really tightly and headed back to the shore.

I was waist high in the water, and in an instant my feet left the bottom and I panicked. Every time I went down I took in water; I didn't know which way to turn. I could see my family on the shore cheering me on to swim. They had no idea that I was in danger of drowning. All I could say was, "Lord, help me!"

Then the little voice in my head told me to reach my hands forward, and I did. I felt something hard, like wood. I grabbed it and began to pull myself up. Suddenly I was waist high again.

When I got back to shore, I told my family what I had experienced. David said it must have been an undertow or rip current that dug a hole in the ocean floor that I stepped into.

Thank you, God, for your love that lifted me.

The next day at Tom's Cove Campground, we found out that a man had drowned on that same beach. He was clamming and fell into a rip tide pocket. He had a big, heavy bag of clams tied around his waist, which took him down. He wasn't able to surface.

We started in a tent, but as the years went by and the kids got older, we graduated to pop-up trailers, motor homes, back to a trailer, and now our dream came true, a Class A Motorhome. Through the years we have traveled in many states in the great USA and across Canada.

CHAPTER 125

Gleaning the Fields

The second week of October was harvest time for sweet potatoes. Every year several sisters and myself would find a field that the local farmers had turned over the soil to harvest sweet potatoes. We would ask to glean his fields. After the pickers gathered the best of the crop for the market, we could get as many potatoes as the trunk of our cars could carry. The entire field was at our disposal, and of course the deer and other critters would have their share.

One particular season, when times were tough and the holidays were coming soon, I needed some extra cash for Thanksgiving and Christmas. The sweet potatoes sure came in handy.

I invested a small amount of my babysitting money into buying flour, sugar, eggs, Crisco, and milk. I already had the spices, so I was ready to start my baking. I made so many pies and got orders every day. Some people were buying three to four pieces at a time. I was tired but overwhelmed with gratitude. That year, I was able to help my husband with buying gifts for everybody.

First and foremost, I always thank God for giving me the insight and energy to help make this happen. And those farmers who generously provided the main ingredient: sweet potatoes!

This event inspired me to write my first children's book called *Sweet Potato Pie.*

CHAPTER 126

White Boys Call Me Names!

In 1986, I was humiliated by two white teenage boys who thought it was hilarious to call me names, even though they didn't know me, or my name. I was a mother of five children who loved them dearly and always had special feelings for all children. It didn't matter what color they were.

This particular night my feelings changed. These disrespectful children verbally bullied me with their tarnished tongues. The gutter language that came from their mouths was nothing my ears needed to hear.

There's an old saying: "Sticks and stones may break your bones, but names will never hurt you." These names did hurt me.

Waiting in the car for my sons, Darrell, Donald, and Dean, to finish their shopping for sneakers, I decided to go in to see what was taking them so long. I got out of the car and had a distance to walk from the parking lot. The teenage boys were a few cars away, but they saw me and decided to make a nuisance of themselves.

Although I was an adult, I should have been more tolerant, but this was humiliating. These boys were screaming at the top of their lungs,

"You darkie!" They cursed at me and said things that I could never repeat. Over and over again until I went into the store.

My boys were in line to cash out. My middle son, Donald, looked at me and said, "What's wrong, Mom?"

I said, "Nothing, Don. I'm just tired."

He kept looking at me, trying to read what was on my mind.

Dean said, "Something is wrong, Mom. Are you okay?"

Darrell said nothing, but touched me on my shoulder and motioned that they were done and ready to go. I must have been wearing my heart on my sleeve because they were reading me pretty well. I was hurting!

When we walked toward the car, I looked at the car where the boys were still parked. Don followed my eyes to their car and said, "Mom, did those boys say something to you?"

I didn't want to say yes, they did. And I didn't want to say no, they didn't. That would have been a lie.

My three muscular, weight-lifting sons walked over to their car. "What did you say to our mom? We know you did something to her."

The boys said nothing. They were scared to death!

My son Donald said to them, "Get out the car right now."

That's when I said, "Just leave them alone you, Guys. I'm all right."

Then Dean started in on them, as well. "You guys need to be taught a lesson. We know you said something to our mother."

The boys still wouldn't move or utter a word. They kept looking straight ahead, because they were scared straight! And they had every right to be!

Well, Darrell laughed so hard that he almost cried, watching his younger brothers standing up for what was right. "Mom, go back to the car. We just want to talk to them," he said. "We won't hurt them, I promise."

I trusted them enough to know that no fighting would take place, so I left them. I knew that they had enough sense and respect not to deceive me, and what they said, they meant.

Donald told the boys, "We have a Christian mother! You better consider yourselves lucky. If this had been someone else's mother that you bothered, you would be on the ground and hurting by now. Let this be a lesson to you guys.

I was proud of my boys that night because they stood up for me. And this is what their father taught them to do.

Always protect your mother!

CHAPTER 127

Devil, Don't Steal My Joy!

The Lindsey's 1984

O ur children grew and I continued to nurture them in the Lord. Even though my husband didn't attend church on a regular basis, he insisted that we all go without him. Bad idea! Spiritually, things were getting tough and our marriage was affected in the worst way.

I spent many days and long nights in tears, praying for a change.

You see, for nine years Satan was trying to get a foothold into our marriage and pull us away from God, by using my husband. But I prayed for him and persevered, because I knew he still had the love of God within him. My prayers for him was for me to obtain wisdom, and to understand what he was going through. I prayed to continue to love him and forgive him daily, through sickness and in health. I prayed for patience to handle his toxic, obnoxious moods, because Lord knows, if I had prayed for strength, I would have beaten that man silly. He almost lost his life two times, being admitted to the hospital for pancreatitis. This was when I knew I had to take my burdens to the Lord and leave it there, and not try to fix it myself, because I couldn't. It was too big for me to handle, so it was time to put this burden on God's shoulders. And all these grief and pain had made me stronger. As the old saying goes, "what doesn't kill you will make you stronger."

Amen to that! And again I say Amen!

Because I went through so much pain, I felt broken. My hope had to be restored. I had to wait on the Lord and He showed up just in time. Today my husband is very active in going to church and enjoys the love and fellowship of his brothers and sisters in Christ.

Thank you, Lord, for that powerful blessing!

Another incident in my life was when my child was going through a difficult period in the growing years, as most children do. As serious as it was, I continued to trust that God would prevail.

I always pray for my children when expressing my gratitude, or when times get tough and they become tormented by the things that may befall them. Sometimes I don't have a clue on how to help them, so I trust in my Heavenly Father to reveal to me how I can help them to grow and mature.

I came home from church one Sunday feeling empty and dismayed. I fell down on my knees and began to pray. Crying out loud to Him, I begged, "Lord, I need you right now! Help me to help my child! In the name of Jesus!"

I prayed until I was sweating profusely. I begged and cried some more. Then the Holy Spirit spoke. "Arise, my Child. I am with you."

Immediately, I felt renewed and my soul was revived. He heard my cry, and through all the pain and uncertainty that my child was experiencing, the Good Lord intervened and freed my child from a life of despair.

God, is a mighty good God!

JAMES 1:2–4 (NIV)
Consider it pure joy, my brothers whenever you face trials of many kinds, because you know that the testing of your faith develops perseverance. Perseverance must finish its work so that you may be mature and complete, not lacking anything.

CHAPTER 128

More Days of Grief and Pain

Darrell on USS Guadalcanal

D arrell was my free-spirited child. Before graduating from high school, he went to see the Navy recruiting station and bugged the heck out of the recruiters. He enjoyed the time he had left before going to boot camp. I chaperoned a trip to NYC with the youth group of the Pitman Church of Christ. I vowed never to return to that congested city again, where many people were selling stolen goods and running every time they heard the police sirens. For a country girl, this was scary.

Darrell seemed to take it all in and separated the good from the bad. He spent hours running in and out of novelty stores, buying things that Mom shouldn't know about, like firecrackers!

When it was time to leave the city, we all boarded the bus bound for NJ. I noticed he sat across the back of the bus playing his rap music on his boom box, and hid his many firecrackers under the seats. I was just so happy to see all the kids back on the bus and no one lost that I never noticed all the giggling when I walked back to check on everyone.

Little did I know that Darrell had spent his last paycheck on firecrackers! All types of firecrackers! When we got home and I discovered them, I yelled, "Oh no, you don't! That's illegal! Are you crazy, Boy?"

"Mom, they are legal in NY!" he said.

"Yeah, but not in NJ," I replied.

I was really angry that he would do such a ridiculous thing. I confiscated most of them, but he saved back the best of his stash for his send-off celebration with his homeboys.

Well, what's a mama to do?

The day before he left, my husband asked him to take me to the hospital for pretest hysterectomy surgery. I was terrified with his driving. He was all over the road, but breaking no laws. Driving like a madman and coming to jolting and screeching stops!

After the test, he took me out to lunch at Wendy's, where he worked. He was so proud to show off his mama and introduce me to his coworkers. Our lunch was on the house. I was extremely proud when his boss said Darrell was one of his best workers.

The next morning, I woke up early to see him off. I was sad but tried to look happy for his sake. After all, this was my second son to leave the nest. He gave me that big crocodile smile, threw his arms around me, and kissed me good-bye. I watched the recruiter's car until it was out of sight, then I started bawling like a baby.

A song by the Commodores was playing in the OR, "Three Times a Lady." It was so soothing and relaxing to me. Administering the anesthesia, the doctor told me to count backward from one hundred. I think I got to eighty-something. When I awoke, the first thing I said was, "Did Darrell get to Rhode Island okay?"

"Yes, he did," Dave said. "He called me when I went home."

I stayed in the hospital for four days. We didn't hear from Darrell after that for several weeks, but that's the way boot camps operate. No contact with the outside world.

After graduating from boot camp, he was stationed in Washington, DC, performing his duty as a ceremonial guard in Arlington, VA. He was chosen from thousands of young military men, and once again we were so proud of him.

Darrell became frustrated over these special duties and regulations put before him. He said, "I'm just not cut out for this job." After about three months he was released from his duties and assigned to a ship called USS *Guadalcanal*, which was a minesweeper and aircraft carrier.

He called me from the ship and told me he would be going on a Mediterranean cruise. This would be his first deployment.

Darrell wrote to me every week and I, in turn, would write him back. I prayed for him daily that he would return safe and sound. He often requested snacks like my large chocolate chip cookies. One time David made a huge poster with Darrell's picture on it. I took it to church and everyone signed their name with special messages on it. This poster hung in the ship for all to see and read the funny messages. He would bring this signed poster home. Along with other cards and decorations, the sailors displayed many family pictures with funny captions, for all to admire.

Time for a little fun! Darrell was on the ship for ten months. One of his special adventures was for the ship's crew to cross the equator. It was party time! Lots of shenanigans took place on the ship, along with singing, dancing, and celebration. Many of the men dress up like girls with long hair wigs and big boobs. They laid the rookies side by side, down on the dock of the ship, and greased them with nasty black oil and threw garbage on them. Then they hosed them down with cold water. All day long they played practical jokes on these poor victims. Then a huge feast was served for all and the men settled down for the next day's work. Darrell had so much fun!

Our son was traveling around the world. He visited Africa, rode on elephants, and purchased souvenirs from different countries, which I still have or wear today. While in Africa he learned the word "*Jambo*," which means hello. Darrell, along with several other sailors, was chosen to attend a spiritual enrichment seminar in Bahrain, where he toured many palaces.

Watching the CNN news every day, I heard that war broke out in the Gulf. Every day I couldn't wait to get home from work to see my son's ship still intact and chugging along in dangerous waters. I was so afraid! The enemy activated mines and bombs in the waters to destroy American vessels. Small Iranian boats would circle the ship and shoot at it. The *Guadalcanal* would return fire to warn the gunmen to back off.

One day the ship retrieved them, fixed their wounds, and sent them back. One incident was when my son and another sailor were ordered to carry a wounded prisoner to sick bay, on a stretcher. The Iranian spat on Darrell and the prisoner's hat fell off.

"Okay, Buddy, looks like I have a souvenir." He brought that nasty little hat back home with him. I guess you could say "that's war games." He stayed in the Gulf for ten months.

I continued sending letters of encouragement every week. Sometimes I would fall asleep with my pen in hand. I asked him once, "What if the Iranians attacked with a more powerful weapon?"

This was Darrell's reply. "It would be like waking a sleeping giant. They would not have a chance against us." He always had a way of making you feel safe.

We heard nothing for about a month because the ship was on its way home. We got a letter from the ombudsman, which is a group of individuals that hear complaints and stay in touch with the ship and the crew's families at home. The letter stated that two family members could go to South Carolina to meet the ship and stay the night with their service person. The next day the *Guadalcanal* would dock in Norfolk, VA.

We had two weeks to get Donald and Dean together for this trip to Virginia. They took the Greyhound bus to Virginia and got there safely, spending the night with friends. The next day our boys took the bus to South Carolina to meet the ship, and unite with their brother. Two days later, we arrived in Norfolk to greet the ship and see all three sons together.

On December 18, 1987, Darrell was coming home for Christmas. It was freezing outside and it felt like my fingers and toes would just pop off like pretzel sticks, plus the ship was a few hours late. We had a huge picture of Darrell made, to welcome him home.

Another ship that happened to be docked nearby invited us to come out of the cold and gave us hot coffee and donuts. Thank you, Jesus!

After warming up, this hospitable ship announced that our son's ship was arriving in about fifteen minutes, and about 300 hundred people went out and waited again. It was freezing cold and I couldn't stand it much longer. Suddenly, we saw a little tugboat pulling a huge ship around the bend and into the harbor, and the crowed started cheering. Suddenly, the sun came out and my body instantly warmed up. The ship was home and our son was on it. Or should I say, our sons were on it?

Darrell couldn't wait to get off ship. He threw his hands in the air and waved from the ship's deck. I knew he was yelling, but we couldn't hear him. Don and Dean waved to us, as well. All the sailors stood around the circumference of the huge USS *Guadalcanal*.

Oh, happy day!

When we got back to Jersey, it was a few more days before Christmas. Darrell gave us many gifts that he purchased from many countries. One gift included a picture of him dressed in his white uniform, posing and looking like an angel. I never knew that he would be buried in this same uniform, one year later. I told him, "Darrell, you look like an angel."

His girlfriend came from Virginia to be with him for the holidays. We adored her! Her name is Sonja Rodgers, but we named her "Sweet Pea." They were planning to get married but the relationship didn't work out.

Darrell was unsure of what he wanted in life and she wasn't about any foolishness. We still keep in touch with her and her mother, Miss Fannie. And she still regards us as Mom and Dad. Someday I will meet her two beautiful children.

Darrell was discharged from the Navy in July 1988. Prior to his death, in October, I purchased a life insurance policy for him through the military, and sent in one premium for November; he died the next month.

December 10, 1988, at the tender age of twenty, Darrell was killed by a drunk driver. I felt that my life was over, and these same feelings I had as a child, when Mom died, had come back, but far worse. This affected my heart; it was broken. My pain was unbearable and my husband and I fell into deep depression. But we held on to each other's love. I felt I had no more tears to shed. But God had put them all in a vessel and had counted every one. I prayed for my tear ducts to dry up, and after about two years they did. A few years after that, my tear ducts seemed to open again. No more dry eyes!

Early that morning, at about 3:30 a.m., David and I woke up at the same time and couldn't get back to sleep. We didn't talk; just laid there. Eventually we fell back to sleep.

I woke up again at around 7:30 a.m., feeling strange. I wasn't sick but felt like something had left my body. I didn't feel like I was in my own skin. I felt like I was someone else.

I started to get ready to go to Williamstown to help my sons paint the kitchen in their apartment. I got in the car, put on my seat belt, and tightened it. I didn't tell Dave how I was feeling because he would have advised me to stay home. When I got there David Jr. had gone to work and Don was still asleep. I knocked; he opened the door and let me in.

Then he went back to bed.

After taping the ceiling, I began painting. At around 10:30, the phone rang and I climbed down to answer it.

"Hello," I said, thinking that it wasn't important.

The person on the other line said in a very solemn voice, "Yes, hello, is David there?"

I replied, "No, he's at work."

The man asked, "Who am I talking to?"

I replied, "His mother. Can I take a message?"

"Well, Ma'am, I have some bad news. Is anyone there with you?

"My son Don, but he's asleep. What is it?"

He got really quiet then his voice quivered. "Your son Darrell was killed early this morning."

My heart sank, but I answered him, "Is this some kind of joke? Are you playing a prank on me?"

"No, Ma'am, I'm not! My sister was killed, too."

"Who is this and why are you doing…?" Suddenly I heard someone crying. It was so penetrating that it made my blood run cold. He wasn't playing! This was for real! Our son was gone!

I dropped the phone and paintbrush on the floor and ran to my son's bedroom to wake him. "Don! Don!" I knocked on his door but it was locked. He was in a deep sleep and didn't hear me. I went to the living room, then I lost it. All I could do was scream. I remember hitting my head on the hard floor and my heart felt like it was about to burst out of my chest.

Finally, Don heard me and came running. "Mom, Mom, what's wrong with you?" he shouted. Why are you crying?"

"Your brother Darrell was killed early this morning." I could barely get the words to come out.

He asked me lots of questions, and one thing that I could remember was, he said, "I just saw him yesterday, at the Mall. He stopped by my job just to say hello."

Don ran to get dressed and I had to call my husband. The phone kept ringing and finally Nikki answered it. "Nikki, get your dad," I kept saying. "Nikki!"

"Mom, are you there?" she said. I could hear her but she couldn't hear me that well.

Then I remembered that I had dropped their phone on the floor after talking to the young man.

"Nikki, GET DAD! SOMETHING HAPPENED TO DARRELL!"

She heard me that time and went to get him. He was in the shower and had to dry off, then he called me back. I could hardly talk or think.

David said, "Kat, what's wrong with Darrell? Nikki said something happened to him. What?"

It hurt so bad to break the news to him. Where do I begin, with the phone call or our son Darrell is dead?

"I'm on my way," he said.

Don called his brother David Jr. to come home right away because he knew how to get in touch with the young man who had called me.

Dave and I went back home, which seemed to be 1,000 miles away. We waited for answers as to what had really happened. The accident was on the news that night but I didn't want to see it.

That evening we found out that this young lady had taken Darrell to the Philadelphia airport to apply for a job. They decided to stay in Philly and visit her cousins for a while, then started for home. Stopping for a traffic light, a drunk driver hit them from behind, and drove them 200 or more feet, and the car exploded in flames. The autopsy report showed that the young lady died instantly and Darrell was pronounced dead fifteen minutes after impact. A bus driver saw what happened and tried to get my son out but the flames were too hot. He got a fire extinguisher but it was too late, he couldn't save them. My dream/nightmare had come to reality.

The drunk driver never got a scratch. He worked in a bar and had been drinking all evening on the job, and on his way to a third bar, around 3:00 a.m. Our son and this beautiful young lady friend, who had three little children, were killed. The drunk driver received six years in prison for two counts of first-degree vehicular homicide.

CHAPTER 129

Choosing the Burial Plot

D ave and I went to the Borough Hall to purchase a burial plot. The young man took us to the cemetery to choose Darrell's final resting place. He took us to the back of the cemetery and I thought to myself, *This is the area were Dad was buried.* He stopped at the very section where my dad was laid to rest, and my heart sunk heavily.

"This is a nice spot you might consider," he said. "Coincidentally, this site is right next to my dad's grave."

I looked at the man and said, "My father is buried right here."

He apologized and said he would show us other sites, but I said it was exactly where we want to bury him. Right beside his grandfather.

This plot laid vacant for fifteen years, and at this moment, I felt it was waiting for Darrell.

My sister Elnora called my stepmother Ellen, and she agreed to let us purchase it. After all, $25.00 could have held it for anyone wishing to purchase later. No parent should ever have to bury their child, but this has been going on since the beginning of mankind. It just doesn't seem natural.

CHAPTER 130

Darrell's Funeral

A week before his death I had gone Christmas shopping and couldn't find the right gift for him. The other children, I had no problem choosing what I wanted to buy them. I got Darrell a red hat, and two gift sets of cologne. But I didn't know what to get him for his main Christmas gift. We always gave our children several gifts and one big gift. I had no idea it would be a coffin.

We had to go to the funeral home and choose his casket. Before we left, I pressed his black sailor uniform to bury him in; my tears fell on it and I pressed them in. I took the quilt that I made him for his seventeenth birthday and asked the funeral director to lay it over on top of him after they prepared his body for burial. This was a practice of our enslaved ancestors, to bury the dead with their quilt, if they had one.

Each member of our family had something special to put in the casket. He wore my husband's black sox, as he always loved to do as a teenager. A small bronze unicorn from Dad, a framed family picture and his quilt from me, a small Teddy Bear from Nikki, a Medal of Honor from Dean, and Don gave him a wristwatch that Darrell always liked.

David Jr. wrote a beautiful letter to Darrell; I made a copy for safekeeping.

When we arrived at the funeral parlor to pick out the casket, we looked at several but only one caught my eye. *Darrell would like this one*, I thought to myself. Dave was thinking the same. I stood over it and without thinking I fell across it, sobbing and crying. Grabbing the small pillow that his head would lay on, I couldn't let it go. Holding it close to my heart, I cried in agony.

The funeral was four days after his death, and of course it was closed casket. Our doctor gave David a prescription for valium, but I refused to take them. Before we left for the funeral David and I took half a tablet each, and disposed of the others. No drugs!

The funeral service was so painful. There were so many people and I had to be alert, listening to the kind words spoken by sympathetic and caring people. We were given the cassette tape of the funeral service but we never listened to it. Once was enough!

Whenever I hear the song "Be Not Dismayed What're Betide, God Will Take care of You," I get a lump in my throat. This song was sung and it brings back those painful memories.

David's brother Allen sang a solo called "Millions" by the Winans brothers. Another solo was sung by Marilyn Green, "You're Standing on Holy Ground." She sounded like an angel. It was beautiful! Our minister, Dan Cooper, performed the eulogy and helped Dave and I get through the worst time of our lives. My niece Sharnell, Darrell's cousin and bosom buddy, who is a poet, wrote a beautiful poem for his obituary.

IN MEMORY OF
DARRELL LAWRENCE LINDSEY

A spectrum of color journeys across the skies
I look up at a radiant brightness,
and blink a tear from my eye.
Right now I am a caterpillar wrapped in a soft,
secure cocoon.
This is the first time I realize, I will be a butterfly very soon.

I was ready to grace the world with the newness of my birth.
But it seem to me the cost was high than it's worth.
So I wished the expedition could be put off a little longer.
Until my heart knew what it wanted,
and my wings were a little stronger.
But in a diamond lit sky, the plan is plain to see
The great Almighty God will always have an eye on me.

BY SHARNELL ROWE-LINEN

On the way to the cemetery, our son David asked the funeral director to drive Darrell by our house one more time. He did, and paused there for a moment. I fell apart.

At the cemetery, we all gathered around the casket and the minister prayed and said a few words of comfort. Although he didn't have a ceremonial guard type burial, he was honored with a US flag that was draped over the casket. During the ceremony, two funeral directors folded the flag and placed it in my arms. They said something to me but I don't remember because my mind was somewhere else. My legs felt like they would buckle under me. I couldn't breathe. Oh, how my heart ached to see him, to touch him, and to wake up from this horrific nightmare. I kept thinking, *Please don't bury my son. He should bury me. Why, Lord? Why my son!? Life really isn't fair!*

I visited the cemetery every day after work. During the summer, I walked two miles just to be close to his grave site. One day, I stayed too long lying down or sitting on his grave and talking to him. Someone who lived behind Darrell's grave site noticed me because their dog kept barking, so they called the police. The policeman got out of the patrol car and came over to me.

"Ma'am," he said, "are you all right? Do you need some help? Can I contact someone to come get you? I can take you home if you need me to."

I said nothing.

"I'm sorry for your loss, Ma'am. Was he your son?"

I nodded my head yes. He must have looked at the inscriptions on my son's headstone that read:

BELOVED SON AND BROTHER
DARRELL LAWRENCE LINDSEY
APRIL 3, 1968 ~ DECEMBER 10, 1988
"CHILLY D"

I thanked the officer for his concern and kindness, and he left.

I will share a beautiful letter with my readers. When my son was in the Mediterranean, on the USS *Guadalcanal*, an aircraft carrier/mine-sweeper for ten months, he wrote to me every week, and this poem was in one of his letters. I will always cherish it.

July 8, 1987

Mom, I always wanted to tell you how much I feel about you. It was so hard for me growing up during my growing years and I was certainly a hard child to raise. But what helped me to grow into a mature man was knowing that you would be always there for me. I never will forget the disappointment look in your eyes when I got on your nerves. Especially when I took all your books and lined them around the basement floor to keep the basement from flooding, or how your eyes light up when I caught the biggest fish that came out of Silver Lake, and made you proud of me.

You let me grow and allowed me to explore, even if I made mistakes, you allowed me to be me. Your life reflects mine every day in every way. In the way that I present myself to others and when I hear your words, coming out, when I speak.

It all comes from you, Mom, in many special ways. I love you, Mom, and I'm so grateful for you. God gave me to you. And you were that special gift I was born with.

Love always, and Happy Mother's Day

Your son,

Darrell

P.S. If you have time, Mom, please send me another goody box.

One morning while on the job at Simmons Elementary School, I got a phone call from the producer of *The Joan Rivers Show* in Manhattan, NY. The lady told me that she had read an article in the newspaper about me and our son, and asked if we would be interested in coming to New York and be on the *Joan*'s show. "We want to hear your views and perhaps you can reach out to others with your story."

I accepted the invitation and began making plans to go to Manhattan.

Two weeks later, two stretch limos rolled up to our house to transport us to NY. My family members went with us—also a lady advocate, who was the president of our chapter, came to give us support. I was very nervous and didn't know how or what to say. There was a lawyer from California who was on stage speaking on behalf of drunk drivers, boosting about how he is able to get them off through loopholes. No jail time! I couldn't look at this man. He was despicable! I was in shock when they showed pictures of the crash in which my son was killed. I never wanted to see them.

God had spared me from seeing him this way. He was burned beyond recognition; his friend, as well. The crash happened in Philadelphia, on Roosevelt Blvd. and Streal St.

Only He, my God, could know my pain. I joined M.A.D.D. and met people who felt the same feelings, the same pain. I wasn't going crazy. This was grief. And in my grief, my Heavenly Father was always there with me.

Later, my husband and I were selected to go to Austin Texas for a M.A.D.D. rally. We met so many people who had lost love ones and where grieving just as we were. One man lost his wife and infant baby. His wife was in the backseat of their car, nursing their baby, when the drunk driver hit them. The husband was banged up pretty badly, but he survived. So many stories of precious lives destroyed.

Three years later, Dave and I went out to eat. It was Mother's Day and we decided to go to Seafood Shanty. There were lots of people waiting in line for a table and they told us it would be a thirty-minute wait.

As I glanced around the room, I spied a tall, handsome black man who was waiting with his family, as well. I asked David if he looked familiar to him, but he said, "No, I don't know or ever seen him before."

I kept thinking to myself, *I know this man. I've seen him before. He's someone from my past. But I just couldn't put my finger on it. I know this man!*

As we got closer to getting a table, I walked over to him and politely said, "Excuse me, Sir. I think we've met before, but I can't seem to remember where."

His wife looked at me and I think she felt that I was harmless, so she smiled.

The man said, "You look familiar, too. But…"

Then I asked the million-dollar question, "Where do you work?"

He smiled and said, "Lively Funeral Home in Bridgeton, New Jersey."

Well, you could have knocked me over with a feather. And when I told him who we were, he just kept saying, "It's a small world!" This man came to our house to start the process of funeral arrangements. We talked on the phone and talked at the funeral parlor, when choosing the casket. He was very kind and patient with us and explained thoroughly whatever we didn't quite understand. He had stayed for the repass and visited our family table, making sure David and I were okay.

Then I asked him a very important question. "Did you do everything I asked you to do with the items I gave you to put in my son's casket?"

And he said, "I sure did. The quilt and other tokens are there."

As I said before, we never got to say good-bye to Darrell.

I needed to hear that this favor was carried out. My soul was comforted by a stranger who came into our lives and had disappeared in four days. The Holy Spirit was working that night, in me.

CHAPTER 131

Heart on My Pillow

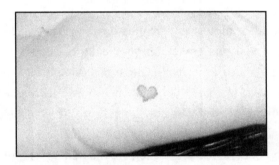

Heart on my pillow February 14, 1989

It was February 14, 1989, Valentine's Day, just sixty-four days after Darrell's death. I had a very hard day at work and cried nearly all day long. When I got home, it was quiet so I went into the patio to stretch out.

It was a clear day; it had not rained in days. The sound of traffic could be heard on Route 55 as usual, and the sound of winter birds could be faintly heard outside my patio window.

As I laid on the sofa sobbing with grief, I heard a bumble bee buzzing above my heard. This bee flew around the room and came very close to my face. I stood still.

Suddenly, it flew somewhere else but it got very quiet. I didn't hear the traffic, the birds, or the bumble bee. Just quiet and stillness. All of a sudden, I heard the sound of two drops of water hit my pillow, on the chair's cushion across the room. The sound of the drops of water was loud enough for me to hear it. I got up and walked over to investigate.

Two drops of murky rainwater had fallen from the ceiling and onto my white cushioned pillow. In falling, it had made a perfect valentine heart. I felt in my heart that God was sending me a message.

"I love you and I am with you always!" This is what the Holy Spirit revealed to me.

I still have this pillow. I've shared my story many times with others who are going through grief. I tell them to watch and listen. "God will send you a comforter. If you only believe!"

Be still, and know that I am God.

It's April 2018, almost thirty years have passed and I still miss our son so much. I visit his grave site on special occasions, like his birthday, anniversary date of his death, Christmas, Memorial Day, Easter, and any time I need to just go. I don't cry nearly as much as I used to. But I reflect on all the good memories. Darrell, my free-spirited child, may your sweet spirit rest in peace. Until we meet again.

God is so good! Three years later, He blessed us with two more children, Sade and Jaquille, who are now thriving at eighteen years old.

On June 13, 1999, I awoke with one thought and told my husband that I wanted to do something different with my life. It was my fiftieth birthday and I was now ready to try to fulfill some of my lifelong dreams. "I want to become a writer. But I don't know what to write about," I said.

My husband looked at me, smiled, and said, "You have so much to write about, just look around you." That's when I noticed our children's pictures embellishing the walls of our slumber room.

"That's it!" I said. "I'll write children's books that tell stories about families."

Three years later, on September 8, 2003, my first picture book called *Sweet Potato Pie* rolled off the presses.

I still remember those Sunday mornings, when Mom would give me a pencil and some ole junk mail to keep me quietly entertained in church. I would pretend to write or scribble down stories about families and read them very fluently to anyone who would listen. I guess this was the beginning of my writing career. Thanks, Mom, for the kick-start!

God has a blessing for everyone, and all you have to do is reach out to receive it.

CHAPTER 132

Let the Marriages Begin!

The Lindsey's 1984   Our two children and six grandchildren - 1999

D ean was called the runt of the litter. He took after the Williams side of the family. He was small as a young kid, but blossomed into a well-built, handsome young man.

He was the first to get married. He met a Portuguese girl named Anabella (Bela for short). They were in the US Navy together and met while driving back to the naval base in Norfolk after the Thanksgiving holiday.

She was a fun person to be around and we got along well. We shared

373

recipes and learned a lot from each other. Some of my favorite recipes were given to me by Miss Bela, like doughboys, or better known as malassadas, rice pudding, morning glory muffins, cold hogs, and numerous other scrumptious dishes.

She loved singing and teaching me silly songs, and was always helpful in my kitchen. She inspired me to write about my ancestors and slavery.

After twenty years of marriage, Dean and Bela divorced. We still regard her as someone we continue to love and respect. And from this union they have two children, Sarah Kathleen and Douglas La` Mont, whom we adore. They are now twenty-one and twenty-seven, respectively.

Today, June 15, 2018, Dean is about to become a corrections officer in a R.I. state prison. He is now forty-eight years old but has the vitality of that of a young, thirty-year-old active man. I am sure he will do well. This was his dream for a long time.

His girlfriend Pam is a special lady who loves him and is beside him 100 percent.

Donald married a local girl named Carla, from Hammonton, NJ. They have three children—Jackie, Donald Jr., and Garrett. And they have one granddaughter, Jordon. In 2006, they all moved to California. Don found a super job that assured him great success.

It's been a long time since we've seen them. Donald works hard at everything, and took the same road as his father did, working with computers. Don is a great dad, devoted husband, and a super grandfather.

David Jr. was the last son to marry. He met a girl from Virginia, who was born in St. Thomas, in the Virgin Islands. Her name is Pat and they have one son, David III. After serving his time in the US Army, he came out, found a job, and started wife hunting. After much searching, he found the girl of his dreams. David and Pat met in Virginia Beach, where he once lived. Pat attended and graduated from Virginia State University. She's is a great person who works hard to fulfill her goals in life.

When David and Pat got married, there was an empty space at the altar. This was not planned, but David always wanted his brother Darrell to be his best man. Coincidence?

I guess you could say he was there in spirit.

David's wife Pat was kind of shy at first, but once she got to know you, you became her friend for life. Whenever we visit them, she always plans for her and me to have our special time together. Whether it be shopping, working in the concession stands selling hot chocolate and hot dogs at football games, or hiding thousands of Easter eggs in the city park for the annual children's extravaganza, we always enjoy one another's company.

She constantly spoils her father-in-law (my husband) with her scrumptious carrot cakes.

When my first book was published, she acted as my agent and arranged for me to perform in many Virginia schools for three straight years. I am so grateful for her kindness.

CHAPTER 133

Adopting Sadie and Jay in 1994

Starting over - 1996

Good Housekeeping Article 1994

O ne night, I was home alone and feeling kind of melancholy. I sat down to eat and the news was on. The newscaster said that a little girl was left in a car while the foster mother went in the store to make a purchase. People passing by heard the infant crying and called the police. The child was taken away and placed in another foster home.

This news made me cry and I couldn't stop. How could somebody do that to a child?

When Dave came home I was still crying. He said that I was still grieving and that story made me upset. But I felt it was more.

When I went to bed that night and prayed that God would give the baby girl a good home with Christian parents who would love and take good care of her, I fell asleep peacefully.

In September of 1993, three years later, my friend Gloria Meyerson came to visit me. She brought her friend Karen Smith with her. Both ladies were into quilting and wanted to see my quilts. Karen had three little children with her and I asked her if she was babysitting.

"No," she said. "I'm a foster parent, but Tianna is mine."

I fell in love with the little boy named Nelson. He was the cutest little guy!

David was working late that day but came home just in time, before my company left. He took a great liking to Nelson, as well.

We talked to her about adopting again and Karen told me to call her husband Bruce, who worked at the adoption agency. We talked with him and he told us how to apply. We didn't get Nelson, but they had a little girl going up for adoption as soon as the parents' rights were terminated. After the paperwork and crime search were completed, the family visits with the little girl started and she was ready to be placed with us. On December 10, 1993, just four years after our son's death, we became parents again.

Funny thing, this happened to be the same baby girl who was on the news and my prayer was answered. The Lord wanted me to see his glory at work, as always. Be still and listen to what the Spirit has to say.

Sade Daleena Lindsey, also known as Squirt, was born crack dependent, but after a year it was out of her system. She suffered from tremors for a year and still has a few side effects due to the drug exposure. Today, at twenty-seven, she is a hard worker and a good mommy. Sade had a very hard road to travel during her teenage years but overcame many obstacles.

She couldn't be raised as an only child. She was hyper and demanded much of our attention. While eating dinner one night, she put a green pea in Dave's ear. Now that was hilarious!

"Stop playing with her while she's eating, Dave!" I said.

We needed to get another child and fast! She needed a playmate because she always lived with other kids. So back to the adoption agency we went.

Three months after getting Sade, they found a little boy named Jaquille, better known as Jay. We had to travel to Reading, PA, and meet him at McDonald's. I was watching out the window when I saw a little, round Mennonite lady running across the street, dragging a little black boy with her. He was wearing pants that were too small, with suspenders and a sweater that crawled up his arms. This was a very cool day in March.

I said to Dave, "Here he comes."

And Dave said, "No, that can't be him. Look how he's dressed."

Entering the MacDonald's, the lady walked toward us and asked, "Are you Mr. and Mrs. Lindsey?"

"Yes, we are," I answered.

"Jaquille, say hello to your mom and dad," she said.

Then the little boy totted over to me, wrapped his arms around my legs, and said, "Hi, Mama."

I fell in love with him at first sight. He was so precious and adorable!

On the way home we talked about the meeting with the little boy and I told David, "We have to take him. He called me, Mama."

Dave said, "Yeah, they teach them all that stuff, you know."

But I knew he felt the same way I did.

We decided to take him after the school year ended for me in June. This way, I could have more time to work with him.

Jay was born with fetal alcohol syndrome and almost died in the delivery room, which was reeking with alcohol. He weighed less than one pound; his weight was measured in grams. He had a list of illnesses that affected him for a long time, due to his mother's alcohol addiction. The doctors thought he would not make it and gave him zero chance of survival. They called him the miracle child. Jay stayed in the hospital for three months, then released to two different families before being placed with us at three and a half years old.

We put him in preschool right away and he adjusted. When he was ready for kindergarten, I went to the school board and asked if he could go full time instead of half day. The board approved this and Jay was able to catch up with his age level, but very slowly. He went on to become a chef and got many honors at Job Core, in Rhode Island.

We are so proud of him and his achievements.

In 1994, I was featured in *Good Housekeeping* magazine with our two little ones, a story about my son Darrell, the quilt I made for my husband, and the adoptions.

Today, at twenty-seven years old, Jay is a hard worker and was promoted to supervisor for a large baking company in RI. He met a fine young lady named Ann, and they plan to marry in 2018. Jaquille is a wonderful young man who overcame many health hardships.

We gave him Darrell's middle name, which was Lawrence. He is often called Jay-Bird.

Sade, who lives in Sicklerville NJ, fifteen minutes away, is our only child who still resides in New Jersey. She has a baby girl named Avah Marie, who is a real sweetie pie and our pride and joy.

CHAPTER 134

Seven Quilts for Seven Sisters

Seven Quilts for Seven Sisters- 1993

To ease my pain and suffering, God gave me another focus. I was doing more quilting and starting to write. As part of my therapy, I wrote a play for my sisters and me. I researched history and visited historical places down South and collected old props for our presentations. Many of my quilts tell stories of historical content, like the "Cake Walk," "Harriet Tubman's Underground Railroad," "Brer Rabbit," "Seven Sisters' Quilt," and much more. Many of my quilts continue to go on tour for historical exhibits.

The year was 1994, the Williams sisters was about to start their new careers, a theatrical play called *Seven Quilts for Seven Sisters Presents, a Stitch in Time.*

This is how it all began. We all went to my sister Phyllis's house to participate in a historical event called the Civil War Reenactment, in a little town called Mullica Hill, NJ. Then there was the quilt show. We didn't have very many, but the people enjoyed the stories we shared with them. We sang old Negro spirituals that dated back to the slave era, and dressed like the women during that time of human bondage in America. We looked the part but we needed authenticity. My daughter-in-law Carla, who majored in theatrical arts at Glassboro State, made a pattern that would fit any size.

We baked all kinds of goodies to sell to the tourist and townspeople.

We carried big baskets of molasses cookies, ginger bread, sweet potato and apple pies, short breads, cakes, and many other historical favorites; they were most welcomed by the hungry Union and Confederate camps.

The following year we added various kinds of homemade soups and cobblers.

A few years later, I made a quilt and wrote a poem of that eventful day and recited it for many years. Later, I added more verses, but I never used them. Two of my sisters, Bert and Phil, displayed a quilt that I designed, called Sweet Potato Pie, while I recited the poem.

It was so funny! We used a real pie for effect. But Bert would get carried away with this. What a mess! Need I say more? Here is the poem I wrote for the quilt.

SWEET POTATO PIE

Pies for sale, pies for sale, the seven sister all declare
Historically dressed in their best, looking pleasantly fare
Anticipating later, a pot of tea to steep
They carried pies to town in very large heaps

We sold them all and oh, what fun
Our baking is work and our works not done
Here, here, try mine my recipes new
I made it last night and I promise you
Not lumpy, but smooth, quite firm, not loose

Add one pound of butter, lots of sugar, eggs and milk
Will make seven yummy pies as smooth as silk
So beat them long, and bake them slow
And just before it's time to go,
Peep into the oven and do not sigh
'Cause there's nothing so delicious as a, *Sweet Potato Pie*

Second verse

Soldiers dressed in uniform, march to the beat in parade
Guide their feet to come and eat, the wonderful pies we've
made
Lovely ladies dressed in lace, carry empty baskets in a haste
Curtsy and chat when they come to buy
Our luscious, homemade, *Sweet Potato Pies*

Laughing children come running to hear
The stories of the quilts we hold so dear
Patchwork and calicos of stories told
Are neatly tucked within their folds
Will the sister come back? Oh indeed we'll try
And bring once again our, *Sweet Potato Pies*

My idea was to take this historical play on the road and do performances. So I started doing research on quilting and slavery. God had given me another focus and this would be part of my healing. As part of my therapy, I began reading about slavery in America and how they used their quilts for sewing therapy, recreation, comfort, warmth, and to bury their loved ones in. I needed to know more about my ancestors, and I felt God wanted me to do something with this information I was obtaining. Through the years the play changed a bit. We embellished it to almost perfection. Instead of sticking to the script, we began to improvise. This made the play really come alive. This was truly a gift from God.

1 PETER 44:10
Each one should use whatever gift he has received to serve others, faithfully administering God's grace in its various forms (NIV).

Our first theatrical show was in 1994, for the Women's Cooperative Extension Program, and that was a big hit! We were given a standing ovation, but I knew we could make it better. We needed music, so we hired my friend Liz, who played the viola. We gathered props and quilts for display and sometimes real foods for folks to sample. We used our daughters to perform when we needed substitutes. Later we purchased a twelve-passenger van and a trailer to carry our speaker system, props, quilts, and luggage. We visited over sixteen states and were invited to come back many times after.

We had lots of fun with the show performing the "Cake Walk" dance, while the viola player played a song called "Cotton-Eyed Joe." Imagine all the sisters dancing up and down the stage with buckets of water on their heads, whirling and twirling and doing high kicks into the air. If they didn't spill any water, the winner was awarded a cake or quilt as their prize. That's the way our ancestors would have done it, and it was fun.

After each performance, we always sang our theme song, called "His Eye Is On the Sparrow," along with displaying a quilt that I designed and titled the same.

All the sisters had their lines and enter acting lines. And they all acted with great zeal.

With the help and support of my husband Dave, who took us to a recording studio in Delaware, we recorded our first CD, called *Down by the Riverside*. We recorded sixteen songs. This CD was dedicated to our sister Loretta.

Steal Away
Swing Low Sweet Chariot
Lay Down My Burden
No Body Knows the Trouble I See
Sometimes I feel Like a Motherless Child
We Are Climbing Jacobs Ladder
I Got Shoes
No Hidden Place Down Here
Sing Because I'm Happy
Mornin' Train
Walk Together Lil' Children
Angels Watching Over Me
It's Me, Oh Lord
Over My Head
I Couldn't Hear Nobody Pray

We had several drivers who took us wherever we needed to go and brought us back safe and sound. The sound person always accompanied us, to set up the system and speakers and such. Everyone had a job to do, setting up and breaking down our props; we did this for sixteen years.

When we performed at outside events like the county fairs or historical sites, I impersonated Harriet Tubman, the famous Underground Railroad conductor who took over 300 slaves to freedom. I recaptured that era, thus taking the sisters to freedom. We went to Cincinnati, Ohio, for four days and preformed twice a day for thousands of people. It was like going back in time, seeing the enormous Tall Stacks riverboats that traveled up and down the mighty Ohio River. The Tall Stacks Festival hosted many impersonators, like Mark Twain, Harriet Tubman, Abe

Lincoln, and famous abolitionists of that era. We got to hear a concert by the famous BB King, who gave a fantastic performance. We all agreed that Mom and Dad would have been so proud of us.

The Entire Williams Siblings in 1998   The six Williams Kids 1963

Memories of Mommy 1998. Quilt was designed by the eight siblings.

CHAPTER 135

Wow! That's a Big Hole!

T ime for a fun vacation! David had to fly to Arizona to attend more classes to update his knowledge in computer technology. He went for two weeks and sent for me and the two little ones to come for his final week. He asked his good friend John Yanzuk to take us to the airport. This was my second time flying, but my first with children. John and David were very good friends and often said they were brothers of different mothers. He and David were always there for each other. After waiting at the airport for an hour before our flight, I told John that we would be fine and he could leave us. He said, "I promised Dave that I would stay with his family until you were on the plane." And that's what he did.

The plane ride was frightening! We went through turbulence several times, yet Sade and Jay thought it was so cool because the airplane was shaking. The flight attendant thought they were the cutest kids and gave them headsets to listen to music. She gave them a huge bag of airplane goodies to take with them. It was a lot of stuff!

When we reached our destination, Arizona, David was waiting patiently for us to come off the plane. He was really getting scared and thought we had missed our flight. Where was his wife and kids? A man came off the ramp and asked him if he was waiting for someone.

"Yes," David said, "my wife and kids should be on this plane, and I see that all the passengers came off." He was afraid that I had missed my flight.

The man said, "Oh, they're in the cockpit talking to the pilots."

When we finally got off the plane, the kids ran to their daddy and told him what they saw and the shaky airplane ride. If they only knew how scared their mommy was!

After we picked up our luggage, we walked through the airport and saw the two airline attendants and the two pilots. They waved and called out, "Good-bye, Sade and Jay!" Our kids must have made a good impression on them. I told one of the flight attendants that we just got them from the adoption agency less than a year ago and that they seemed very happy and content.

We had planned to go to the Grand Canyon on the following Sunday, but we changed our plans to Saturday instead. Good thing we did, because the entire park closed down the next day, that Sunday, due to government funding—or lack thereof. People had come from all over the world to see this spectacular sight that God had created for the world's pleasure. How could our government be so heartless? On the evening news, they interviewed people crying because they had spent so much money to get there. One lady from England said she had saved for years to come to the USA to visit the Grand Canyon, only to be turned away.

Dave and I dreamed for many years of visiting this historical sight, and the Good Lord made it happen. It was something that no man could have created, only God! It was simply breathtaking! The Eighth Wonder of World! Our children kept repeating, "Wow! That's a big hole!"

CHAPTER 136

A Headstone for Mom

In 1998, I had another thought after visiting my son's grave. *Why does our mom still have no gravestone?* This, I felt, was ridiculous! Forty-four years was too long for her children not to have pulled together and got her one. When we were young, our father told us that her gravestone was a heart-shaped marble, only to find out that it was his cousin Mary's. He never got her one. We couldn't read the inscription on it because it had worn away. We didn't know about stone rubbings back then.

After talking to my sisters and my brother, we all agreed that she shall have one, ASAP.

First, I went to the Borough Hall in Clayton to talk to the caretaker of Cedar Green Cemetery. He agreed to meet me there the next day. We found her site, which was covered with grass. From the burial records, it showed exactly where it was. The caretaker plotted it out and staked it, where the gravestone was to be placed.

I contacted the company that did my son's headstone. The lady remembered me and came to my house right away. We all decided on what would be inscribed on her stone and our brother designed her favorite flower, lily-of-the-valley, on each side of the inscription.

The stone was installed on Mother's Day. We miss our mommy, but one day we shall all meet again.

When I was about eight or nine years old, a movie by Walt Disney was shown in the theaters and then on Disney's Sunday night show. Every week they showed an episode from the movie. But I never got to see it in its entirety. I always wanted to see it and inquired about it many times. A friend even called Disney Studious to see if it would be released again.

Some time ago, the NAACP threatened to sue Disney if they didn't take it off the market. This movie was degrading to the black or Negro race because it depicted slavery.

And they truly felt it was racist. The *Tales of Uncle Remus*, who was a fictional slave, written by Joel Chandler Harris. *Song of the South* is a movie I will always cherish. I often told my children the stories of Brer Rabbit, Brer Bear, and Brer Fox. These three characters represented the slave, the overseer, and the master. I gave up, thinking I would never see it again. Only in books!

It was 1998, Christmas Day, after we opened our gifts, my husband told us to come and watch TV. He put in a VHS movie, and on the screen it read, *"Walt Disney Presents..."* The Kids and I started screaming, "We're going to Disney World! Wow!"

Then my husband said, "Nope, just wait a second!"

All of a sudden, I thought my eyes were deceiving me. It read, *"Song of the South."*

You could have knocked me over with a feather! "How did you get this movie?" I asked him.

"Call your son Dean, and he'll tell you," he said.

Well, I called, and he explained how he obtained it.

Dean worked at Circuit City in Rhode Island. A man came to the store and wanted the best dubbing machine his money could buy. Dean showed him one and the man purchased it. Then Dean asked him, "What do you need it for?"

The man said, "I have a rare movie I want to duplicate."

"What's the name of it?"

"Oh, this movie is before your time. I doubt if you would know it."

"Oh, come on, what's the title? I just might know it."

The man said, "*Song of the South.*"

"Oh, my God. My mom used to tell us about that movie! It came out when she was a little girl and she always wanted to see the whole movie in its entirety."

The man said to Dean, "Your mother will see it again! I'll be back when I dubbed it for you."

Then Dean told me, "Several weeks passed and the man didn't show. Then I thought I should have asked for his phone number. Oh well! But about a week before Christmas, the man comes back in the store with a tape for you, and I sent it to Dad right away. I kept thanking him over and over, and all he said was, 'I hope your mom has a Merry Christmas.'"

God knows our wants and our needs.

MATTHEW 7:8

Ask and it shall be given unto you. (NIV)

CHAPTER 137

My Fiftieth Birthday Party at the Holiday Inn

David was busy planning my fiftieth birthday party. This would be my first big party ever! He did everything himself, like inviting the guests, choosing the right venue, (Holiday Inn) and the caterers, and making sure the guests were sending their RSVP on time. Every person he invited came.

My son Donald and his wife Carla decorated the ballroom. It was beautiful!

All of my close friends came and my children and grandchildren showed up, as well. David, who was also the disc jockey, played our teen love song by The Impressions, called "I'm So Proud." We danced alone, then Dave motioned for everyone to join the dance floor.

Our young daughter Sade sang a solo for me, "Close to You" by The Carpenters. This was the most excitement I had had since our wedding day, and our son David Jr. filmed it all.

Our children put together a fund and purchased a gift for me, a wooden glider for the backyard. I still sit and rock myself there, thinking of all the years gone by. Sometimes I can almost envision them playing in the yard as little kids. It makes me happy to know that Dave and I did our best in raising them.

PROVERBS 22:6

"Train a child in the way they should go, and when he is old, he will not turn from it" (NIV).

CHAPTER 138

My First Book

My first children's book - 2003   My first book - 2003

Two days after my party, on June 13, 1999, I awoke with one thought and told my husband that I wanted to do something different with my life. It was my fiftieth birthday and I was now ready to try to fulfill some of my lifelong dreams. "I want to become a writer. But I don't know what to write about," I said.

My husband looked at me, smiled, and said "You have so much to write about, just look around you." That's when I noticed our children's pictures embellishing the walls of our slumber room."

"That's it!" I said. "I'll write children's books that tell stories about families."

Immediately, I began writing my story. In less than one-half hour, I had enough information to build my story premise.

An author named Ferida Wolff came and visited me. She read my script and said, "It's good, but it's got a lot going on. It has to be shorter."

So I worked on it long and hard. And got rid of 400 words but kept my story line. I submitted it to an agent and it sold right away.

Three years later on September 8, 2003, my first picture book, called *Sweet Potato Pie*, rolled off the presses. Thank you, Dear Lord, for giving me the wisdom and knowledge to follow my dreams.

My husband and I had the opportunity to attend the DuPont Theater in Delaware, to see LeVar Burton speak about his fame and success. Before the show was over, he looked directly at me and said, "Never give up on your dreams!"

I only wish that Ret had lived to see my book. She would have enjoyed my story, as she did the sister show.

MATTHEW 7:7
Ask and it shall be given to you; seek and you will find; knock and the door will be opened to you (NIV).

I met another lady named Judy Harch, who is a freelance commentary writer and has published several books. She wrote a column about the "Seven Sister Show." Us three became very close friends and often get together for brunch, and continue to encourage one another.

Sometime later, another lady came into my life, Lorraine Haddock, who came to my book signing. She said she always wanted to write a book, so I shared with her step by step on how to get published. She became an author, as well. Lorraine, who is a doll maker, made two soft toy mascots for two of my children's books and helps me make aprons to sell. Being Italian, she makes the best Italian peach cookies!

Another friend is Miss Thelma Nelson, who came from Jamaica, lived in England for twenty years, and then moved to Clayton, just around the corner from me. She is such a loving, caring person whom

God put into my life. Her wisdom is beyond her years. I enjoy spending time with her and hearing her life experiences, knowledge, and good judgement. I feel so grateful to God for sending these wonderful ladies into my life.

Poster Created by David Sr.
Published by Lee and Low,
New York
Used with permission from
Lee and Low

Kat continues to write stories for Children.

CHAPTER 139

Losing Sister Loretta

We lost our sister Loretta in 2000, and we miss her terribly, but we continue to share our story. She loved the show and always looked forward to saying her lines. I recall one show we did at Cold Springs Village, in Cape May, NJ. It was so hot, and I, being the narrator, was having a hot flash and about to pass out. I was slurring my words and had to stop and adjust my composure. Loretta noticed that I was having a rough time, so she poured me a tin cup of cold water and walked across the platform to give me a drink. I was refreshed. I was revived and I had the vitality to carry on. "Thank you kindly, Miss Retta," I said. She had rescued me.

After the show was over, she wondered if she had made a spectacle out of herself, but I assured her that she had made the show realistic and it felt like part of the script.

"Loretta," I said, "this is what sisters should do. Be in tuned with one other's needs."

I appreciated this so much and I told her that it made the show very special. The audience thought it was part of the script. She smiled and thanked me. I feel that she had found her niche.

We were ten years into the show and still going strong, traveling the country, giving black history presentations. Loretta had another break-down. She stopped taking her meds because our brother-in-law Richard Gardenhire, Elnora's husband, had passed away. She was truly upset. In midwinter, she turned off the heat in her house and went to bed for several days. On the day of Richard's viewing, I was home scrubbing my kitchen floor. The phone rang and it was Phyllis, asking me to go see about Loretta. "I've been calling her, but got no answer."

"Where are you, Phil?" I asked.

"I'm at Richard's viewing with the rest of the family," she said.

This, I knew nothing about. They forgot to call me.

I rushed to Loretta's house as fast as I could. Only to see her through the bedroom window, in bed with lots of covers piled on top of her.

I knocked on the door. "Loretta, please open the door," I called. "Loretta, I want to talk to you."

"Go away!" She screamed.

This went on for about a half hour. Phil came and we tried to talk her out of bed. But she wasn't budging. When the police arrived, they told Phil to keep talking to her, so we kept knocking on the front door while the police broke in through the back door. They had to take her out by force on a gurney.

Phil and I looked at each other as the ambulance drove away. In our hearts, we knew that she wasn't coming back. She stayed in the hospital for a while, still not taking her meds, and one night she had a heart attack and passed away. I miss my big sis, but I know she is in a better place.

CHAPTER 140

The Twin Towers Fell

September 11, 2001 was a warm and sunny day. It was Tuesday, and my sister Anna and I decided to meet at Cowtown and just hang out for the day. We didn't plan to buy anything special, just to walk around and enjoy the day together. I dropped my two little ones off at school and set out to take advantage of the freedom.

We met up and started browsing at rare finds, like antiques, quilts, and anything that sparked our interest. Shortly after arriving, I heard several people talking about an airplane crashing into one of the World Trade Center in New York.

"The plane was flying too low," the man said.

"It doesn't sound right to me. A good pilot knows how high to fly," said another.

"Oh, my God!" I started praying that no one got hurt or worse. But an airplane? The odds would be that many people would parish. Then I prayed that it would be very few casualties. I knew how big those towers were, having seen them just a short while ago on a church outing.

We continued to stick around and listen, to find out more news. My sister and I were talking about what we just heard and before long, we heard more people expressing concerns and listening to the radio that a vendor was playing. I heard one shopper saying, "I bet its terrorists, because airplanes aren't supposed to fly that low." I was starting to feel uneasy about this whole situation. Many were giving their opinions but no one was really sure what was happening.

A vendor who was listening intently, then yelled as loudly as he could, "Another airplane just hit the second tower!"

Oh, my God! The horror on the people's faces was unbelievable. Everyone I looked at had their hand over their mouth looking up, which caused me to think fast. I looked at my watch and it was about 9:15. Immediately, it was announced that all aircrafts had to vacate the skies.

This was no accident! This was for real! I told Anna, "I'm going to pick up my kids from school and go home." I left immediately! When I got in my car, I turned on the news station. The news said it was possible hijackers. On my way home, I drove extra carefully but kept my eye on the road and on the sky. I knew in my heart that this was a terrorist attack on our country.

I went directly to the elementary school to pick up my kids, but all the children were sent home. Where are my kids? Who took them? The few people who were still in the office didn't have a clue. One of the secretaries I knew came into the office and said, "Your neighbor has your kids. We let her take them because you weren't at home. She said she lived across the street from you."

"Yes, she does, and thank you," I said.

I live only a few blocks away so I was able get there quickly, where I found them safe and sound, playing with her children.

After getting the kids, I started worrying about my husband, who was doing volunteer work in Salem, NJ, and our older children.

That night, my dear friend Linda Ewing came over and suggested that our neighborhood have a candlelight vigil. We all met outside on the street with burning candles. We prayed for the victims and their families, for the firefighters, and for the first responders. We hugged, cried, and sang "God Bless America."

It would take years for our country to heal from this terrible, horrible, painful event that changed America—"9/11."

CHAPTER 141

Meeting Miss America

I started giving lots of signings and performances in my new career as an author. It was very rewarding meeting people and seeing the smiling faces on children.

In 2005, I had the privilege to meet Miss America in Atlantic City, on stage. New York Avenue Elementary School invited me to come perform at their school. They invited Miss Erica Dunlap, as well. She was delightful, and when I approached her I took a bow in her honor. She has my first book, *Sweet Potato Pie*, and I autographed it for her.

When Barack Obama became president, I sent his family my book, and that spring, Michelle Obama started a vegetable garden, which was a bountiful harvest. I wonder if she grew sweet potatoes. I am honored to say that today, in 2018, my book is still going strong.

Getting a proclamation from the town of Clayton was quite an honor. I was asked by our mayor, Mrs. Patricia Gannon, to attend a Borough Council Meeting to accept this certificate of appreciation for my outstanding talents and success over the years. David and our two youngest children, Sade and Jay, were there to witness this grand occasion.

After the mayor read my proclamation, the entire audience applauded, giving me a standing ovation.

I wish more of my family had been there, especially my parents. They would have been in awe seeing their daughter receive such an honor and knowing how hard I worked to obtain it.

CHAPTER 142

She's Back! Reminiscing of Years Gone By

Our Stepmother Lavinia

Lavinia in her Golden Years

A fter forty-two years, we have our stepmother back again. She is ninety-one and sharp as a tack. She'll probably outlive us all. She moved in with Ida and George and seemed content with the move. She appeared to be different, but time will tell. This woman looks healthier than any senior citizen I know. Her hair was white as snow but she still walked with her head held high. And doesn't forget a thing. We were all so happy to see her again, and some of us girls had her over for lunch.

I called her one day and asked her over for lunch, and she accepted. After we ate, it was time for small talk. I asked, "Mom, why did I get so many beatings when I was younger? You gave me a licking almost every day. Why? Was I that bad?"

"No, you wasn't bad, but you was the only one that could take it," she said with sincerity. "I would whip you, and the next minute you be up in my arms. If I beat the other kids, they would stay mad at me for a long time."

My first thought was, *This woman hasn't change one bit! As far as I'm concerned, she can stay away for another forty-two years.* Then I began to realize what she went through with Dad and all the problems with raising eight kids along with caring for a feeble mother-in-law. I needed a healing, and that day, I forgave her.

After a while, Mom became very hostile, after Ida became ill. She would say awful things to her like, "You must have done something bad in your life, that's probably why you're sick." She would outlive my dear sister Ida. Before Ida died, our stepmom moved to Delaware, to a convalescent home, where she lived out her days.

CHAPTER 143

Ida Goes to Her Happy Home

I always enjoyed being around Ida; she was not only my sister but also my friend. Ida was humble, a little shy, with a beautiful smile that matched her personality. She was a pillar of strength and the best cook who came out of the Williams family. She always took great pride in her cooking. We often shared recipes, and whenever we found a bargain, we'd jump on the phone to alert one another, then the rest of the sisters would join in. Who, what, where, and why, and how much, she always asked me.

One day, Jamesway put bags of walnuts on clearance for fifteen cents a bag. I purchased about twenty-five bags. When I got home, I called Ida and told her. She and Loretta couldn't get to the store fast enough. They bought the store out, over 150 bags. After cracking all those nuts, she put them in the freezer.

Another time, Eatmores in Vineland was selling frozen turkeys after the holidays. Ida got seven huge turkeys and put them in Ret's freezer. After a while, Ret got mad and told Ida, "Ida, you better come get these stinking turkeys. I'm tired of freezing them for you and their taking up all the space in my freezer. Come and get them now! Or I'll throw them outside."

Poor Ida had nowhere she could house her turkeys, so she kept them outside in the freezing cold and cooked them one at the time. Those two girls were so funny together!

Ida had a great singing voice, and it was bass! Some men couldn't get that low! One of her favorite songs was "Walk in Jerusalem Just like John." When we sang that song, the audience would marvel at Miss Ida's voice. When we started our singing career, I was only thirteen years old. The Williams Sisters was our chosen name because that's who we were. The sisters wanted me to sing bass, but I just couldn't cut it. My voice wasn't fully developed yet. Alto was all I could muster then. As the years went by, in time I could sing soprano, alto, II alto, but still no bass. We always sang four-part harmony.

When singing at funerals, we sang in the front of the casket and the sisters always put me by the deceased's head, which seemed to be still breathing. Talk about scary! It was open casket and I was petrified with fear, but I suffered in silence.

Growing up together, Ida always had a song to sing. She knew every theme song on every TV show, and the commercials, too. At any given moment, she would strike up a tune and we would all join her in song.

One night during practice, our dad introduced us to a new song by Mahalia Jackson. Ida loved this song called "In My Home over There." She led the song and sang it from her heart.

Miss Ida, who was the middle child, closed her eyes on October 12, 2005 and went home to be with the Lord.

Our sister was diagnosed with lupus, and for many years she suffered. This dreadful disease attacked her lungs; she developed many other diseases throughout her body, like scleroderma, which put her on oxygen 24/7. Along with this lung disease, several other diseases invaded her body, like Raynaud's syndrome, rheumatoid arthritis, and lupus.

The night she passed away, Bertha called me to tell me Ida took a turn for the worse and she would not last the night. Bert, her husband

Lawrence, and I went right away to JFK Hospital, where she had been in ICU for two weeks. She passed away shortly before we arrived. I was speechless. I couldn't speak. My sister Elnora began singing this song while we all gathered around her bedside—her husband George, her children, the sisters, and our minister Dan Cooper.

> There's a land that is fairer than day
> and by faith we can see it apart
> For the father waits over the way
> to prepare us a dwelling place there.
> In the sweet by and by, we shall meet on that beautiful shore.
> In the sweet by and by, we shall meet on that beautiful shore.

I couldn't sing. It was like I had no voice. I tried humming, but nothing would come out. My vocal cords seemed to be paralyzed. Grief had hit me hard again!

A few days prior to her passing, I watched her looking up over her head and smiling. My father did the same thing before he passed away. Were they seeing loved ones who proceeded them in death, or angels watching over them and coming to carry them home? I began to sing to her.

ANGELS WATCHING OVER ME

> All day, all night, Angels watching over me, my Lord. All
> day, all night, Angels watching over me. Now I lay me down
> to sleep, Angels watching over me, my Lord. I pray my Lord
> my soul to keep, Angels watching over me. Singing, all day,
> all night, Angels watching over me, my Lord. All Day, all
> night, Angels watching over me.

I miss my sister so much, but I know she is in her "happy home" over there.

411

CHAPTER 144

David's Operations

They say misfortunes come in threes. I guess this has some truth to it. In 2008 and 2009, David had three operations in less than two years. For about a year, he suffered from excruciating pain in his neck. Sometimes he would push down hard on his head to suppress the pain.

After many visits, his doctor sent him to therapy. He got worse!

I kept telling him to get an MRI, but his doctor didn't think it was necessary. Finally, he got the referral and had the testing done. They found four herniated disks in his neck, which was starting to cause numbness down his arms, gradually working down to his hands. He was scheduled for surgery in two weeks. They took out three of the worst disks and replaced them with cadaver bones. His surgery took six hours. The surgeon told me, "In all of my fourteen years of performing this type of surgery, I've never, ever, had one this complicated." David's operation was like working in a car mechanic shop. His body was lifted up like a car and worked on the back of his neck, then he was turned over and worked on the front, where two plates were implanted.

Without this surgery, he would have been in a wheelchair within a year.

After he got out of surgery, it was very hard for him to talk. He whispered very faintly in my ear, but I couldn't understand what he was trying to tell me. He motioned for me to get a pencil and paper, and he wrote, *"No rehab!"* He kept whispering it over and over again. "Please, Kat, don't sign papers."

Then I said, "Okay, David, I understand. I won't let them take you there. I will take care of you. Don't worry!"

Poor David actually had his neck broken temporarily. Everything was out of whack!

No rehab. I will take care of you. In sickness and in health, I will be beside you.

I have to admit it was a little frightening changing his dressings, but I soon got used to it. I gave him a bath every day, shaved him, and put the support collar back on his neck.

I had to come up with nutritious meals that he could swallow. He ate homemade soup for several months, and never the same kind two days in a row. He had trouble swallowing water and juice, or any type of liquid. You had to add a substance called Thick-It, which made the liquid thick, so he could swallow and not strangle.

His visiting nurse came three times a week and said he was healing nicely. She didn't have much to do because I was fulfilling all of his physical needs. I was afraid at first, but I called my sister Elnora, who happened to be a nurse. She told me, "Don't second-guess yourself. You can do this! Take one day at a time." And that's exactly what I did.

While I was in the waiting room for six hours, I prayed for him, and for the doctors to have a steady hand. One slip and his spine could have been severed. I kept thinking of a famous portrait of Jesus standing over doctors and nurses in the operating room, and guiding their hands. Thank you, God, for keeping him safe and giving those doctors a sturdy hand to fix Dave's problem.

After being home for six months on disability, he started back to work half days.

David's second operation was on his thyroid, which had to be removed. This was tedious, and what should have taken forty-five minutes took four hours. The surgeon said that the tissue from the thyroid grew into the plate in his neck and they had to pick it out.

Poor David wasn't able to talk again. But he didn't require any rehab. He recovered nicely and I took good care of him.

David's third surgery was on his rotator cuff, where the tendons were hanging on by threads. They had to go in and repair the tendons. He thinks the therapy was worse than the operation. "No pain, no gain!" He recuperated early again and went back to work.

CHAPTER 145

*David Avoids
an Accident!*

O ne morning while on his way to work, David saw an accident waiting to happen. A pickup truck ran a blinker light and a tractor trailer,
which had the right of way, hit his brakes and jackknifed. The trailer had
swung around toward David at top speed. Dave saw it coming toward
him and, through instinct, stirred his vehicle into someone's yard, almost
hitting a huge landscape rock that was in his path. He drove around it
with ease. To this day, he doesn't know how he escaped from being hit
by that trailer or smashing his car into that rock. But he does know that
our Almighty God was with him. Whenever we pass by that same area,
he points it out to me.

He had one thing on his mind, to retire, but he sure didn't wish to go
out that way.

Dave always said that when our youngest son Jay graduates from
high school in 2009, he would retire. And he did, one month after our
son graduated, and after forty-four years of working for DuPont. He was
finally out of there!

It was 2009 and I was becoming busier than ever before, dealing with
two teenage kids who had something new going on every week in school.

My son Jay was in culinary school at G.C.I.T. and I was taking and picking him up every day until he got a bus pass at school. Then he was picked up right outside our front door. Sade went to Gloucester County Christian School, in Sewell, NJ, and that was a drive to and from. This was taking a toll on me. I was also doing book signings, book presentations for elementary schools, and working with my sisters. I had the job of writing new plays for different events, from the main sister program.

After each school program, I was so tired that I had to take a power nap between morning and afternoon shows. If I had to stay for the entire day, I would go to the car and sleep for a while. Then Dave would come and wake me up. I freshened up and felt much better.

One day, I was feeling awfully dizzy and the room seemed to be spinning. I didn't want to tell David because he would cancel; I didn't want to disappoint the children. So I went in spite of my physical warnings.

We arrived at the library and started unpacking the car. I had to go to the restroom, so David and the two kids started setting up for me. I had a few brief words with the media specialist, then excused myself. Feeling dizzier than before I left home, I tried to hold my composure to press onward. I happened to have my BP meter with me and took a reading. It was 191/93. I came out of the restroom and called my husband two times, then everything went dark. I had fainted!

They called the ambulance, and I could hear what they were saying but couldn't respond. They kept calling my name. At this time my blood presser had spiked again, 198/108.

I was taken to Underwood Hospital and stayed there one week. They could not get my BP down and under control. The doctors concluded that I was dealing with a lot of stress, and they feared that I might have had a slight stroke.

They gave me a test called the Tilt Table Test, and it was brutal! This test helps to find the cause of fainting spells. They lay you down on a bed and strap you down. This electronic bed tilts you straight up in a horizontal position, so that you are upright for a period of time. Then various machines monitor your BP, and measures electrical impulses in your heart and oxygen levels. They inject medication to cause your pressure to rise until you feel like fainting. You can't talk or move and a nurse is holding a barf pan under your chin. You barf! Then the room begins to spin and you feel like passing out! Your heart is beating out of control and your BP is taken again.

This was the worst feeling I ever had, and when it reached its highest point, I was able to say, "Stop!"

I could hear the lab operator say, "I'm taking her down! She's not going out! She's so strong!"

Then they gave me more medication to bring my pressure back down.

The room is called electrophysiology, lab and I never want to see another room like that again. Ever!

Congratulations, Kat. Welcome to the Hypertension Club. EEK!

Today, I try to stay stress free, trying not to worry about things that I can't fix. Sometimes it's difficult to remove myself from certain situations, but now, at fifty-nine years old, I have to take care of me.

CHAPTER 146

Year 2009, the Kids Left the Nest!

Sade and Avah Marie   Jaquille, Sade, and granddaughter,
Avah Marie - September 10, 2017

O ur work is done, the children are gone, and the nest is empty. David said, "It's back to you and me, Kid."

From 1967 to 2009, we raised children for forty-three years. Our two youngest children, Sade and Jaquille, are both twenty-seven and on their own. So bring on the grandkids to visit us, but you better take them home when you leave! Because now, it's just the two of us. Well, maybe they can stay for a day or so. Ha-ha-ha!

May 16, 2014 was another unbelievable day of sadness. My husband's best friend John Yanzuk was involved in a horrible motorcycle accident and lived for several days on life support. His wife Tha Anna is Vietnamese and a very good friend of ours, as well. How will she cope without the love of her life? They met in Vietnam during the war. We met them through our son Dean and their son Johnny, who were in elementary school together. They were best buddies and we became friends immediately. We did lots of touring together, visiting Washington, DC for the Cherry Blossom Festival and sang "God Bless America" at the Lincoln Memorial Reflecting Pool. Sweet memories!

We wanted to be there for her. And it's going to be rough! David went to the hospital to visit him before he died. He was in ICU and the hospital had a policy: no visitors, family only. They asked him if he was a relative of John. And David replied, "We are brothers from different mothers." Then their older son John Jr. informed them that David and his father were inseparable. We were so proud of their three children, who worked together in the planning of their father's funeral.

CHAPTER 147

David's Mom Passes away

November 7, 2015, Laura Ann Lindsey left this world to a place where Jesus has prepared for her soul to rest. We will miss her. I've known my mother-in-aw for fifty-two years.

It's November 12, 2016, and Dave and I were traveling to Chicago, Illinois, for her funeral. He's so quiet. I tried to make conversation but he's not responding. We stopped for breakfast on the turnpike. His eyes wondered sadly. I know this look. They call it grief and pain. He needs a warm hug and a shoulder to lean on. I knew that tomorrow would be difficult for him and his siblings.

I shall, Lord willing, be at his side and do my best to comfort my brothers Allen and John, and sisters JoAnn, Alease, and Jennie. His older sister Nancy did not attend. I pray they will have the strength to get through this.

Today my heart is beating way too fast! It felt anxious! Dave and I dressed and went down to the hotel lobby for a continental breakfast. Just before we left our room, David broke down in tears. He was reading a poem on his computer and he read it to me. Before he could finish the last few words, the tears started to flow. I held him close but said nothing.

Sometimes all a person needs is an affectionate hug to reassure them that they are not alone. I love my husband.

My sister-in-law ordered two limos, one for the siblings and one for the spouses. We were separated. The ride to the cemetery was about forty minutes. Mom was laid to rest in a beautiful, peaceful cemetery, near the shade of a large tree.

As we all gathered under a large family tent, the minister had a few words to say.

He quoted several Bible Scriptures, and as family and friends, together, we quoted the twenty-third Psalm. The minister gave both words of advice and comfort. What I was impressed with was that he told everyone that this was a time to start healing hearts, making amends, and keeping the glue flowing. "Bound yourselves together with this glue, as Laura would want you to."

This is a time to heal!

I pray that her children will unite. Life is too short and none of us are promised another day! After the funeral was over, we rode back to the church for the repass. We talked and rekindled stories of years past. It was uplifting for everyone. We met many of the offspring of Mom's children. She had thirty-three grandchildren, sixty-six great-grandchildren, and ten great-great-grandchildren.

CHAPTER 148

Our Fiftieth Anniversary

Disney World with Jim and Cheryl Coleman
Celebrating our 50th Anniversary, 2016

Kat and Dave clowning
around at Disney 2016.
Happy 50th Anniversary.

June 25, 2016 was our fiftieth anniversary. After much thought, Dave and I agreed that we have earned a two-week vacation to Disney World, in Orlando, Florida. We planned our trip well and made the best of each day. Our good friends Cheryl and Jim Coleman traveled along with us, and this made the trip extra special. Going to Disney made us feel like we were kids again! Seeing all the sights that we couldn't possibly imagine we'd see in our lifetime. We made sure we covered every inch of this magnificent park, and we also visited the Holy Lands. If you ask me which one I was most fond of, I'd have to say *every last one of them*! We arrived at 10:00 each morning and left the park at 10:00 p.m., closing time. Lots of pictures and great memories that we will always cherish.

While we were in Florida, we visited our good friends Iris and Charles Bailey, who used to live in New Jersey. I was the babysitter for their son Charles Jr., who is now in his forties. I found him on Facebook and he immediately contacted his parents. We hadn't seen them in over twenty-five years. What a great reunion! They invited us to their church for Sunday service, which fell on Mother's Day. Then we had dinner at their home.

It was sad to say good-bye, but we plan to go again very soon.

Another good friend, Christine Archer, from Clayton High School had us come to her house for dinner, as well. We had a wonderful time with Christine and Lorrie, her friend. A few days later, Christine and I went to a huge miniature dollhouse store and I went bonkers! We had a great time together. I hadn't seen her in forty-nine years. What a blessing to see her again!

God wanted us to reunite, and He made it happen by blessing us to go to Disney World.

David's sister Joann and her husband Duke have been traveling with us for the past three years. They recently moved from Georgia to Silver Springs, Maryland, which is much closer to us. The first time I met Joann, she was twenty years old and single. Today, she is a great-grandmother and married for fifty-one years. David and his sister Joann have always been close, born two years apart. She and I get along like two peas in a pod. She is a super strong woman who has had many trials, but thank the Lord she made it through. I only wish the others lived closer, but we all keep in touch.

CHAPTER 149

Eagles Win the Super Bowl!

February 4, 2018, we are on our way to Charleston, SC, to watch the Super Bowl with friends, Kevin and Julie Coleman, who is the brother and sister-in-law of Jim and Cheryl Coleman. Each year, they invite us to return for another Super Bowl Festival in their home. For the past three years, we travelled there just to enjoy the game and take great pleasure in their hospitality. This year she cooked a fabulous turkey dinner.

This game was so exciting and different! I cheered until my throat was soar. We sang, "Fly Eagles Fly" by the Dirk Quinn Band after each touchdown. Jamie Coleman, a former Eagles cheerleader, and daughter of Jim and Cheryl, led the living room of cheering fans and kept the excitement at a high.

Even though some were not Eagle fans, they swallowed their pride and cheered, anyway. We, along with most Eagle fans, noticed a change in the team this year. They were united in spirit, prayer, and good sportsmanship. Go, Eagles!

The Eagles beat the Patriots by a score of 41–33.

My cell phone was blowing up with my kids and friends calling me and sending messages about the game.

Philadelphia's first Super Bowl win. David has been an Eagles fan since he was fifteen years old. He was speechless and wanted to both cry and shout for joy!

They finally did it! His dream and their dream had finally come true!

Can't wait until next year!

CHAPTER 150

The Williams/ Barnes Family Reunion

Me and my Aunt Rose (Rosetta) Williams, July 7, 2018 at the Williams/Barnes Family Reunion

David and Kat our senior years of love and devotion

It's July 7, 2018, a great day to remember, filled with excitement of meeting blood relatives whom I have never seen before. God blessed us with an absolutely perfect sunny day with lots of family, food, and fun.

During the family reunion, we honored Aunt Rosetta Williams, better known as Aunt Rose, who is now eighty-two years young, and the only sibling out of fifteen still living. After the death of her son David

Jr. in July of 2017, she desperately wanted to have a family reunion and tried to get everyone together for a happier occasion.

Her health began to fail three weeks prior to the reunion, and she was put on hospice watch. We all began to pray that she would live to see this reunion happen, and she did. She even took my husband's hand and danced a little.

She gave a speech on how families should come together as often as possible and never give up trying, even if it takes years to organize something that will live forever in our hearts.

Our cousin Darnel Williams worked incredibly hard for over ten years on the family's history, which started back in 1788. And Aunt Rose is the only living link of those who are no longer here. I appreciate the work that was put into piecing it all together. Families are forever!

One week later, July 14, 2018, Aunt Rosetta (Aunt Rose), at the age of eighty-three years old, went to be with the Lord. She was ready! And thank God, He allowed her to come together with those she loved before closing her eyes. She was buried along with her son David's ashes, who passed away almost one year ago. Gone, but she will never be forgotten.

I've enjoyed writing my story. Some of it was painful and some hilarious. Sharing my life experiences has made me a stronger person. At sixty-nine years old, I still keep those memories alive and share them with those who appreciate the (sometimes) "good ole days."

I hope that my readers will look to our Almighty God for guidance when they are hurting and filled with the physical or mental despair of life's trials and tribulations. Just reach out to Him, believe in Him, and He will lift you up to higher ground, because you are special and wonderfully made in his sight and He loves us. Forgive those who hurt or physically abused you, as God has forgiven you for your trespasses. Be resilient, and go forward.

CPSIA information can be obtained
at www.ICGtesting.com
Printed in the USA
BVHW010124010319
541532BV00019B/68/P